THE CHRONICLES OF CANADA:
VOLUME IX
THE NATIONAL HIGHWAYS

THE CHRONICLES OF CANADA: VOLUME IX

OUR FIRST NATIONAL HIGHWAYS

EDITED BY

GEORGE M. WRONG

AND H. H. LANGTON

Fireship Press

www.FireshipPress.com

ISBN-13: 978-1-934757-52-9
ISBN-10: 1-934757-52-7

BISAC Subject Headings:

HIS006000 HISTORY / Canada / General
HIS006010 HISTORY / Canada / Pre-Confederation (to 1867)
HIS006020 HISTORY / Canada / Post-Confederation (1867-)

This work is based on the following volumes:

Wood, William *All Afloat: A Chronicle of Craft and Waterways.* Toronto: Glasgow, Brook and Company; 1920.

Skelton, Oscar D. *The Railway Builders: A Chronicle of Overland Highways.* Toronto: Glasgow, Brook and Company; 1935.

Address all correspondence to:

Fireship Press, LLC
P.O. Box 68412
Tucson, AZ 85737

Or visit our website at:
www.FireshipPress.com

1.0

Contents

Part I
All Afloat:
A Chronicle of Craft and Waterways
By William Wood

Part II
The Railway Builders:
A Chronicle of Overland Highways
By Oscar D. Skelton

PART I
ALL AFLOAT: A CHRONICLE OF CRAFT AND WATERWAYS

BY WILLIAM WOOD

CHAPTER ONE
A LAND OF WATERWAYS

Canada is the child of the sea. Her infancy was cradled by her waterways; and the life-blood of her youth was drawn from oceans, lakes, and rivers. No other land of equal area has ever been so intimately bound up with the changing fortunes of all its different waters, coast and inland, salt and fresh.

The St Lawrence basin by itself is a thing to marvel at, for its mere stupendous size alone. Its mouth and estuary are both so vast that their salt waters far exceed those of all other river systems put together. Its tide runs farther in from the Atlantic than any other tide from this or any other ocean. And its 'Great Lakes' are appropriately known by their proud name because they contain more fresh water than all the world beside. Size for size, this one river system is so pre-eminently first in the sum of these three attributes that there is no competing second to be found elsewhere.

It forms a class of its own. And well it may, even for its minor attributes, when the island of Newfoundland at its mouth exceeds the area of Ireland; when the rest of its mouth could contain Great Britain; when an arm of the true deep sea runs from Cabot Strait five hundred miles inland to where the Saguenay river soundings go down beyond an average of a hundred fathoms; and when, three hundred miles farther inland still, on an island in an archipelago at the mouth of the Ottawa, another tributary stream, there stands the city of Montreal, one of the greatest seaports in the world.

But mere size is not the first consideration. The Laurentian waters are much more important for their significance in every stage of national development. They were the highway to the heart of America long before the white man came. They remained the same great highway from Cartier to Confederation—a period of more than three hundred years. It is only half a century since any serious competition by road and rail began. Even now, in spite of this competition, they are one of the greatest of all highways. Nor does their significance stop here. Nature laid out the St Lawrence basin so that it not only led into the heart of the continent, but connected with every other system from the Atlantic to the Pacific and from the Tropics to the Polar sea. Little by little the pioneers found out that they could paddle and portage the same canoe, by inland routes, many thousands of miles to all four points of the compass: eastward to the Atlantic between the Bay of Fundy and New York; westward till, by extraordinary efforts, they passed up the giant Saskatchewan and through the mighty ranges that look on the Pacific; southward to the Mississippi and the Gulf of Mexico; northward to Hudson Bay, or down the Mackenzie to the Arctic ocean.

As settlement went on and Canada developed westwards along this unrivalled waterway man tried to complete for his civilized wants what nature had so well provided for his savage needs. There is a rise of six hundred feet between Lake St Peter and Lake Superior. So canals were begun early in the nineteenth century and gradually built farther and farther west, at a total cost of $125,000,000, till, by the end of the century, with the opening of the Canadian 'Soo,' the last artificial link was finished and direct navigation was established between the western end of Lake Superior at Duluth and the eastern end of the St Lawrence system at Belle Isle, a distance of no less than 2340 miles.

But even the mighty St Lawrence, with the far-reaching network of its connecting systems, is not the whole of Canada's waters. The eastern coast of Nova Scotia is washed by the Atlantic, and the whole length of British Columbia by the Pacific. Then, there are harbours, fiords, lakes, and navigable rivers not directly connected with either of these coasts or with the wonderfully ramified St Lawrence. So, taking every factor of size and significance into consideration, it seems almost impossible to exaggerate the magnitude of the influence which waterways have always exerted, and are still exerting, on the destinies of Canada.

Canada touches only one country by land. She is separated from every other foreign country and joined to every other part of the British Empire by the sea alone. Her land frontier is long and has given cause for much dispute in times of crisis. But her water frontiers—her river, lake, and ocean frontiers—have exercised diplomacy and threatened complications with almost constant persistence from the first. There were conflicting rights, claims, and jurisdictions about the waters long before the Dominion was ever thought of. Discovery, exploration, pioneering, trade, and fisheries, all originated questions which, involving mercantile sea-power, ultimately turned on naval sea-power and were settled by the sword. Each rival was forced to hold his own at sea or give up the contest. Even in time of peace there was incessant friction along the many troubled frontiers of the sea. From the Treaty of Utrecht in 1713 down to the final award at The Hague, nearly two centuries later, the diplomatic war went steadily on. It is true that the fishing grounds of Newfoundland were the chief object of contention. But Canada and Newfoundland are so closely connected by geographical, imperial, and maritime bonds that no just account of craft and waterways can be given if any attempt is made to separate such complementary parts of British North America. They will therefore be treated as one throughout the present book.

But, even apart from Newfoundland, the Canadian interests concerned rather with the water than the land make a most remarkable total. They include questions of international waterways and water-power, salt and fresh water fishing, sealing, whaling, inland navigation, naval armaments on the Great Lakes, canals, drainage, and many more. The British ambassador who left Washington in 1913 declared officially that most of his attention had been devoted to Canadian affairs; and most of these Canadian affairs were connected with the water. Nor was there anything new in this, or in its implication that Canadian waters brought Canada into touch with international questions, whether she wished it or not. The French shore of Newfoundland; the *Alabama* claims; the San Juan boundary; the whole purport of the Treaty of Washington in 1871; the *Trent* affair of ten years earlier; the Panama Canal tolls of today; the War of 1812; the war which others called the Seven Years' War, but which contemporary England called the 'Maritime War'; all the invasions of Canada, all the trade with the Indians, all Spanish, French, Dutch, British, and American complications—everything, in fact, which helped to shape Canadian destinies—were inevitably connected with the sea; and, more often than not, were considered and settled mainly as a part of what those prescient pioneers of overseas dominion, the great Elizabethan statesmen, always used to call 'the sea affair.'

Canada, like other countries, may be looked at from many points of view; but there is none that does not somehow include her oceans, lakes, or rivers. Her waterways, of course, are only one factor in her history. But they are a constant factor, everywhere at work, though sometimes little recognized, and making their influence felt throughout the length and breadth of the land. If any one would see what the water really means to Canada, let him compare her history with Russia's. Russia and Canada are both northern countries and both continental, with many similarities in natural resources. But their extremely different forms of government are not so unlike each other as are their differing relations with the sea. The unlikeness of the two peoples accounts for a good deal; but this only emphasizes the maritime character of Canada. Russia is essentially an empire of the land. Canada is the greatest link between the oceans which unite the Empire of the Sea.

Take any aspect of sea-power, naval or mercantile, and British interest in it is at once apparent. Take the mere statistics of tonnage—tonnage built, tonnage afloat, tonnage armed. The British Navy has over a third of the world's effective naval tonnage; the British Empire has nearly half of the whole world's mercantile marine; and the United Kingdom alone builds more than three-fifths of the world's new tonnage every year.

When all the other elements of sea-power are taken into consideration—the people who are directly dependent on the sea, the values constantly afloat, the credits involved, the enormous advantages enjoyed, and the clinching fact that British naval defeat means disaster and disaster means ruin—when all this is brought into the reckoning, it is safe to say that the combined maritime interests of the British Empire practically equal those of all the rest of the world put together. When it is also remembered that Canada, itself a land of waterways, contains a third of the total area of the Empire, and lies between the Atlantic and Pacific oceans, the significance of these facts is placed beyond a doubt.

Take a very different illustration—the speech of Canada today—and the significance is still the same. We have so many sea terms in our ordinary English speech that we almost forget that they are sea terms at all till we compare them with corresponding idioms in other languages. Then we realize that only the Dutch, the Finns, and the Scandinavians can approach the English-speaking peoples in the common use of sea terms. Other foreigners employ different phrasing altogether. Their landsmen never 'clear the decks for action,' are never 'brought up with a round turn,' or even 'taken aback,' as if by the wind on the wrong side. They never have 'three sheets in the wind,' even when they do get 'half seas over.' They don't 'throw a man overboard,' even when the man is one of those unfortunates who is apt to get 'on his beam ends.' The facetious 'don't speak to the man at the wheel' and the cautious 'you'd better not sail so close to the wind' have no exact equivalents for the Slav or Latin man in the street.

These, and many more, are common expressions which Anglo-Canadians share with the stay-at-home type of Englishman. But the special point is that, like the American, the Canadian is still more nautical than the Englishman in his everyday use of sea terms. 'So long!' in the sense of good-bye is a seaport valediction commoner in Canada than in England. Canadians go 'timber-cruising' when they are looking for merchantable trees; they used to understand what 'prairie schooners' were out West; and even now they always 'board' a train wherever it may be. But even more remarkable are the sea terms universally current among the French Canadians, who come from the seafaring branch of a race of landsmen. Under the French régime the army officers used to say they felt as if they were on board a man-of-war as long as they stayed in Canada. The modern Parisian may think the same today when he is told how to steer his way about the country roads by the points of the compass. The word *lanterne* is unknown, for the nautical *fanal* invariably takes its place. The winter roads are marked out by 'buoys' (*balises*), and if you miss the 'channel' between them you may 'founder' (*caler*) and then become a 'derelict' (completely *dégradé*). You must *embarquer* into a carriage and *débarquer* out of it. A cart is *radou'ée*, as if repaired in a dockyard. Even a well-dressed woman is said to be *bi'n gré-yée*, that is, she is 'fit to go foreign.' Horses are not tied but moored (*amarrés*); enemies are reconciled by being re-moored (*ramarrés*); and the Quebec winter is supposed to begin with a 'broadside' of snow on November 25 (*la bordée de la Sainte-Catherine*).

No wonder Canadian French and English speech is full of sea terms. Even when the Canadians themselves forget, as they are very apt to do, the indispensable naval side of sea-power, they can account for most kinds of nauticality by their economic history, which all depended, directly or indirectly, down to the smallest detail, on the mercantile marine—especially if we give the name of mercantile marine its justifiable extension so as to cover all the craft that ply on inland waterways as well as those that cross the sea. It is calculated at the present day that it is as easy to move a hundred tons by water as ten tons by rail or one ton by road; and this rule, in spite of many local exceptions, is fairly correct in practice, especially as distances increase. Now, Canada is a country of great distances; and by land she once was in nearly every part, and she still is in a few parts, a country of obstructive wilds. What, then, must have been the advantage of water carriage over land carriage when there was neither road nor rail? As even pack-horses were not available in the early days, and good roads were few and only established by very slow degrees, it is well within the mark to say that the sum-total of advantage in favour of water over land carriage, up to a time which old men can remember, must have been at least a thousand to one.

It would be natural to suppose that some knowledge of the sea was widely diffused among the British peoples in general and Canadians in particular. But this is far from being the case. Though there is three times as much sea as land in the world, it is safe to say that there is three hundred times as much knowledge of the land as there is of the sea. The ways of the sea are strange to most people in every country, excepting Norway and Newfoundland. Seamen have always been somewhat of a class apart, though they are less so now. Ignorance of everything to do with the water is exceedingly common, even in England and Canada. The British mercantile marine is one of the biggest commercial enterprises of all time. It is of very great importance to Canada. It is absolutely vital to England. Yet it is less understood among the general public than any other kind of business that is of national concern. Some people even think that the mercantile marine differs from every other kind of business in being under the special care of the government. They are probably misled by the term 'Merchant Service,' which, when spelt with capital letters, has a very official look and reminds them of the two great fighting 'services,' the Army and the Navy. In reality the merchant service is no more a government service than any other kind of trade is.

Ignorance about the Navy is commoner still. Canadian history is full of sea-power, but Canadian histories are not. It was only in 1909, a hundred and fifty years after the Battle of the Plains, that the first attempt was made to introduce the actual naval evidence into the story of the Conquest by publishing a selection from the more than thirty thousand daily entries made in the logs of the men-of-war engaged in the three campaigns of Louisbourg, Quebec, and Montreal. Yet there were twice as many sailors under Saunders as there were soldiers under Wolfe, and the fleet that carried them was the greatest single fleet which, up to that time, had ever appeared in any waters. How many people, even among Canadians born and bred, know that there have already been two local Canadian navies of different kinds and two Canadian branches of Imperial navies overseas; that in 1697 a naval battle was fought in the waters of Hudson Bay, opposite Port Nelson; that seigneurial grants during the French régime made reservations of man-of-war oak for the service of the crown; that while Bougainville, the famous French circumnavigator, was trying to keep Wolfe out of Quebec, Captain Cook, the famous British circumnavigator, was trying to help him in; that there was steamer transport in the War of 1812; that the first steam man-of-war to fire a shot in action was launched on the St Lawrence four years before the first railway in Canada was working; that just before Confederation more than half the citizens of the ancient capital were directly dependent on ship-building and nearly all the rest on shipping; and that the Canadian fisheries of the present day are the most important in the world? As a matter of fact, there are very few Canadians or other students of Canadian history who fully realize what Canada owes to the sea. How many know that her 'sea affairs' may have begun a thousand years ago, if the Norsemen came by way of Greenland; that she has a long and varied naval history, with plenty of local privateering by the way; that the biggest sailing vessel to make a Scottish port in the heyday of the clippers was Canadian-built all through; that Canada built another famous vessel for a ruling prince in India; that most Arctic exploration has been done in what are properly her waters; that she was the pioneer in ocean navigation entirely under steam; and that she is now beginning to revive, with steam and steel, the shipbuilding industry with which she did so much in the days of mast and sail and wooden hulls?

No exhaustive Canadian 'water history' can possibly be attempted here. That would require a series of its own. But at least a first attempt will now be made to give some general idea of what such a history would contain in fuller detail: of the kayaks and canoes the Eskimos and Indians used before the white man came, and use today, in the ever-receding wilds; of the various small craft moved by oar and sail that slowly displaced the craft moved only by the paddle; of the sailing vessels proper, and how they plied along Canadian waterways, and out beyond, on all the Seven Seas; of the steamers, which, in their earlier pioneering days, shed so much forgotten lustre on Canadian enterprise; of those 'Cod-lands of North America' and other teeming fisheries which the far-seeing Lord Bacon rightly thought 'richer treasures than the mines of Mexico and of Peru'; of the Dominion's trade and government relations with the whole class of men who 'have their business in great waters'; and, finally, of that guardian Navy, without whose freely given care the 'water history' of Canada could never have been made at all.

CHAPTER TWO
CANOES

What the camel is to desert tribes, what the horse is to the Arab, what the ship is to the colonizing Briton, what all modern means of locomotion are to the civilized world today, that, and more than that, the canoe was to the Indian who lived beside the innumerable waterways of Canada. The Indian went fishing, hunting, campaigning, and sometimes even whaling, in his bark canoe. Jacques Cartier found Indians fishing in the Gulf of St Lawrence and sleeping under their upturned canoes, as many a white and Indian has slept since that long-past summer of 1534. Every succeeding explorer made use of the Indian canoe, up to the time of Mackenzie,[1] who paddled north to the Arctic in 1789, along the mighty river which bears his name; and who, four years later, closed the age of great discoveries by crossing the Great Divide to the westward-flowing Fraser and reaching the Pacific by way of its tributary, the Blackwater, an Indian trail overland, and the Bella Coola. Mackenzie had found the canoe route; and when he painted the following record on a fiord rock he was bringing centuries of arduous endeavour to a befitting close: 'Alexander Mackenzie, from Canada, by land, the 22nd of July, 1793.' This crowning achievement with paddle and canoe seems very far away from the reader of the twentieth century. Yet François Beaulieu, one of Mackenzie's voyageurs, only died in 1872, and was well known to many old North-Westers who are still alive.

The Indian birch-bark canoe is pre-eminently characteristic of Canada. But it is not the most primitive type of small craft; and it was often

---

[1] For the canoe voyages of Mackenzie, to the Arctic in 1789 and to the Pacific in 1793, see Adventurers of the Far North and Pioneers of the Pacific Coast in this Series.

superseded for various purposes by the more advanced types introduced by the whites. There are three distinct types of small craft all the world over. Like everything else, they have followed the invariable order of evolution, from the simple to the complex. First came the simple log, which served the earliest man to cross some little stretch of water by the aid of pole or paddle. Next came the union of several logs, which formed the clumsy but more stable raft. Then some prehistoric genius found that the more a log was hollowed out the better it would float; and so the dug-out was invented. Log, raft, and dug-out all belong to the first and simplest type, in which there are no artificial parts to fit together. The second type is exemplified by the birch-bark canoe, which has three parts in its frame—gunwale, cross-bars, and ribs—and a fourth part, the skin, to complete it. The third type is distinguished from the second by its keel, as clearly as vertebrate animals are distinguished from invertebrates by their backbone. The common keeled boat, with all its variations, represents this third and, so far, final type. All three types have played their parts in Canada, both jointly and separately, and all three play their parts today. But they are best understood if taken one by one.

First, then, the log, the raft, and the dugout canoe. Any one watching a 'log drive' today can see the shantymen afloat in much the same way, though for a very different purpose, as their remotest human ancestors hundreds of thousands of years ago. The raft, like the log, is now a self-carrying cargo, not a passenger craft. But there it is, much as it always was. Indeed, it is simpler now than it used to be some years ago, before the days of tugs and railways. Then it was craft and cargo in one. It was steered by immense oars, as sailing vessels were before the days of rudders; other gigantic oars were occasionally used to propel it, like an ancient galley; it carried loose-footed square sails, like the ships of Tarshish; and its crew lived aboard in shacks and other simple kinds of shelter, like the earliest Egyptian cabins ages before the captivity of Israel.

The dug-out has the humblest, though the longest, history of any craft the hand of man has ever shaped. At one time it rose to the dignity of being the liner and the man-of-war of the Pacific coast; for the giant trees there favoured a kind of dug-out that the savage world has never seen elsewhere, except in certain parts of equatorial Africa. At another time, only a century or two ago, dug-outs of twenty feet or so were used in trade between the St Lawrence and the Hudson. They were of white pine, red or white cedar, or of tulip tree; and their crews poled standing or paddled kneeling, for they had no thwarts. They carried good loads, went well, with their canoe-shaped ends, and lasted ten or twelve years if tarred or painted. They were, indeed, one-piece canoes, which they had a perfect right to be, as the word canoe comes from the name the West Indian natives gave their dug-outs when questioned by Columbus. Nowadays the dug-out is generally used for the dirtier work of 'longshore fisheries. It has lost its elegance of form, and may be said to have reverted to a lower type. But this reversion only serves the better to remind the twentieth century of what all sorts of craft were like, not twenty, but two hundred, centuries ago.

Secondly comes the Indian bark canoe, so justly famous in the history, romance, and poetry of Canada. As in the case of other craft, its form, size, and material have never been what we call 'standardized.' Indians living outside the birch belt had to use inferior kinds of bark. But the finest type was always made, and is still made, with birch-bark. At least three kinds of tree are necessary for the best results: the birch for the skin, the fir to caulk it with, and the cedar for the sewing fibres and the frame. Only a single tool is needed—a knife; and many a good canoe was built before the whites brought metal knives from Europe. The Indian looks out for the biggest, soundest, and smoothest birch tree in his neighbourhood. He prefers to strip it in the early summer, when the bark is supple with the sap. Sap is as good for the bark as it is bad for the woodwork of canoes and every other kind of craft. The soft inside of the bark is always scraped as clean as a tanner scrapes a hide. If the Indian has to build with dry or frozen bark he is careful to use hot water in stripping the trunk, and he warms the bark again for working. Of course, it is a great advantage to have as few strips as possible, since every seam must first be sewn together by the squaws and then gummed over. Occasionally a tree will be found big and suitable enough to yield a single strip from which a seamless twenty-footer can be built. But this is very rare.

The next thing is the frame—the gunwale, ribs, and cross-bars. Where many canoes are building there is generally some sort of model round which the ribs are bent. But a skilled Indian can dispense with any model when making the ribs with every requisite degree of curve, from the open ribs amidships, where the bottom is nearly flat, to the close ribs at the ends, where the shape becomes halfway between the letter 'U' and the letter 'V.' The gunwale is quite the most important part of the canoe, as it holds all the other parts together and serves some of the constructional purposes of a keel. The voyageurs, recognizing this, call it *le maître*. It is laid on the ends of the ribs, which are made fast to it. Then the frame is completed by the three or more cross-bars, which keep the two sides of the gunwale from spreading apart. After this the birch-bark skin is stretched on the frame as tightly as possible, turned in over the gunwale, and clamped on there by the *faux maître* or super-gunwale. The two ends, both as sharp as an ordinary bow, are then sewn together by a sort of criss-cross fibre lacing, and every hole or seam in the bark is well gummed with melted rosin. The finishing touches are equally important, each in its own way. Thin boards are laid in lengthwise, either between the ribs and the skin or over the ribs, so as to protect the bark bottom from being injured by the cargo. The ends of the canoe are reinforced inside by the Indian equivalent for a collision bulkhead. This bulkhead sometimes rises well above the gunwale and is carved like a figurehead, which accounts for its voyageur name of *le petit bonhomme*. A third finishing touch, very common in earlier days, is the decoration of the outsides of both ends, which used to rise with a sharp sheer, and sometimes actually curved back. The usual decorations here were totem signs, generally made of porcupine quills, dyed in many colours, and serving the original purpose of a coat of arms.

The familiar shape has never been greatly varied, though some canoes are built on finer lines for speed, and others on fuller lines for carrying cargo. But there has always been plenty of variety in size and material. The smallest canoe would hardly hold two persons, and could be carried in one hand. The big war canoes would hold more than twenty well-armed paddlers and required four men to carry them. The very biggest canoe probably did not exceed forty feet in length, six in breadth, and two in depth amidships. Fifty men or five tons of cargo could have been carried in it. But perhaps one quite so large was never built. When white cedar and birch were not to be had, all sorts of substitutes were used. Any roots with tough fibres would do for the sewing, and any light and tough wood served its turn as a more or less efficient substitute for the white cedar framing. But elm and other alternative barks were all bad. The elm bark was used inside out, because the outside was too rough and brittle for the bottom of a canoe. It made dull paddling and never lasted the whole of a hard season, unlike the birch-bark, which sometimes had a life of six or seven years. The most modern material is canvas, which is generally painted red or green. It is light, easily repaired, and has much to recommend it, though trappers think it gives a taint which scares their game away. The paddles were and are of all shapes and sizes, long and short, broad and narrow, spoon-blade and square; and they were and are made of all kinds of wood, from the lightest spruce to the much heavier but handsomer bird's-eye maple. Sails were and are only used with light winds dead aft, and not often in birch-barks even then, because there is no 'stiffness' without a keel.

There were skin as well as bark canoes among the Indians. But the typical skin canoe is the Eskimo kayak. This is a shuttle-shaped craft, about fifteen feet long and just wide enough to let its single paddler sit flat on the bottom. It differs from the Indian canoe in being entirely decked over. The skin of the grey seal, when that best of canoe skins can be found, is carefully sewn, so as to be quite waterproof, and then stretched as tightly as a drumhead all over the frame, except for the little 'well' where the Eskimo sits with his double-bladed paddle. As he tucks himself in so closely that water cannot enter he does not fear to be capsized, for he can right himself with a sweep of his paddle. Kayaks are very light and handy, as the frame is made either of whalebone or spruce. The oomiak is the Eskimo's family boat and cargo carrier, flat-bottomed, not decked in, and sometimes big enough for twenty people with their gear. It is made of much the same materials.

The white man's canoes, so well known—outside of Canada—as 'Canadian canoes,' are partly true canoes and partly a cross between canoes and boats. The fact that the skin is not made of bark or hide, but of canvas, wood, or metal, and the further innovation that machinery is freely used, make no essential difference, provided always that there is no semblance of a keel. But once the keel is introduced the whole constructional idea is changed and the ways of savages are left behind. A first-rate keeled canoe, built of white cedar, brass shod and copper fastened, fitted with air tanks and life-line, a lateen sail and portage handles, is the very perfection of a handy little cruiser for all sorts of inland waters. One like this, but built of basswood, proved quite serviceable after more than ten years' work, in the course of which it covered several thousand miles along the Lower St Lawrence, where the seas are often rough and the low-tide landings always hard.

But all similar craft, though looking like canoes afloat, are no more like the true canoes and kayaks in their constructional detail than a bird is like a butterfly. The keel makes all the difference. Everything in naval architecture springs from and is related to the keel. 'Laying the keel' means beginning the ship in the only possible way, and 'two keels to one' is an expression which every one understands as meaning a naval preponderance in that proportion. The keel is to the ribs of a ship exactly what the backbone is to the ribs of a man, and any craft built up from a keel, no matter how small and simple it may be, belongs to the third and apparently final type of craft, which is as far ahead of the canoe type as that is ahead of the dug-out, raft, and log.

An intermediate type that once did much service, and still does a little, is the white man's flat-bottomed boat, which could be paddled, rowed, or sailed, according to build and circumstances. The common punt is the best known form of it; the dory by far the handiest all round; the cargo barge the biggest; and the old-fashioned 'bateau' the most characteristically Canadian. The modern 'bateau' is to be found only among keeled sailing craft. But the old 'bateau,' which Wolfe's local transport officers spelt *battoe*, was more of a rowboat. It was sharp at both ends, wall-sided, and fitted with oars, poles, and a square sail. The bottom had some sheer—that is, it was curved up at each end—but less than the top. Four men rowed, the fifth steered, and three tons of miscellaneous goods or thirty-five barrels of flour made a fair cargo. Bateaux like this were the craft in which the United Empire Loyalists went up the St Lawrence to settle Upper Canada. Afterwards the size and crew were increased till the average cargo amounted to about four tons and a half. But the Durham boat, introduced by American traders from the Mohawk valley, soon became a successful rival, which was not itself supplanted till canals enabled still larger craft to pass from one open water to another. The Durham was larger than the bateau; long, light, and shallow. It had a not quite flat bottom and a moderate sheer in the sides. The best bateaux and Durhams were made with strong white oak bottoms and light fir sides.

The bark canoe gave place to the boat, step by step, as civilized intercourse advanced. It disappeared first from the great national highway of the St Lawrence and the Lakes, where the French began using bateaux and sailing craft as early as the seventeenth century. During the eighteenth the boat gained steadily on the canoe, which was more and more confined to the Indians. The local craft in chief civilized use on both sides during the fight for Canada was the bateau; and the best crews then and afterwards were the French-Canadian voyageurs.

But everywhere beyond the immediate spheres of French and British influence the canoe was universal. The Great West then began at the Lakes and the Mississippi, and was a land of wild adventure, rumour, and extravagant surmise. The map that formed the frontispiece to the standard authority of the time—Jefferys' *French Dominions in America*—is full of geographical romance. Once in the Kaministikwia, the map has no territorial divisions other than those between the different tribal hunting grounds, each one of which was watered by a hundred streams and marked by the 'carrying places' where the canoes had to be 'portaged.' There lived the 'Nation of the Bear' and the 'Nation of the Snake,' whose special totems of course were worked in coloured quills on every war canoe; and there flowed many a river 'the course of which is uncertain.' Along the great Assiniboine lay the 'Warrior's track from the River of the West,' and just where the prairies ran out into the complete unknown there was the vista of a second Eldorado in the hopeful suggestion that 'Hereabouts are supposed to be the Mountains of Bright Stones mentioned in the Map of ye Indian Ochagach.'

After the Conquest the tide of trade and settlement flowed faster and faster west; and with the white man's trade and settlement came the white man's boats. At last, in 1823, Sir George Simpson, the resident governor of the Hudson's Bay Company, finding that canoe transport was half as dear again as that done with boats, ordered that boats should supersede canoes all over the main trade routes of the Company's vast domain. This was the death-blow to the canoe as a real factor in Canadian life. From that time on it has been receding farther and farther, from waterway to waterway, at first before the white man's boat with oars and sails, and now before his steamer. But in distant or secluded wilds it lingers still—the same craft today that it was when the Celtic coracles were paddled on the Thames before the Romans ever heard of England—the horse, the ship, the moving home of those few remaining nomads whose life is dying with its own.

The great historic age of inland small craft—the age of dug-out, bateau, and canoe; the age of Indian, pioneer, and voyageur—was the eighteenth century, when fresh-water sailing craft were few, when steamers were unknown, and when savage and civilized men and methods were mingled with each other in the fur trade over a larger area than they used in common either before that time or since. The seventeenth century saw the slow beginnings of this age after Champlain had founded Quebec in 1608 and had taken the warpath with the Hurons against the Iroquois. The nineteenth century saw its almost equally slow decline, which began in 1815, at the close of the war with the United States, and may be said to have been practically completed with the two North-West Rebellions of 1870 and 1885. The latter year, indeed, closed a real epoch with three significant events: the end of the last Indian and half-breed war in Canada, the completion of the first trans-continental Canadian railway, and the return from Egypt of the first and last Canadians to go on an overseas campaign as professed voyageurs.

Under the French régime the fur trade reached well past Lake Superior. Nepigon and the Kaministikwia were the two most important junctions of routes at the western end of the lake. Under British rule the Montreal 'fur lords' used the 'Grand Portage,' which ends on a bay of Lake Superior some way south of the modern Fort William. It was a regular bush road, nearly ten miles long, made to avoid the falls of the Pigeon. As early as 1783, the year in which King George III first recognized the United States as an independent power, the fur lords kept no less than five hundred men in constant work at the height of the season, during the latter half of August. Horses and oxen were used later on; but the voyageur himself was the chief beast of burden here, as everywhere else. There were two kinds of voyageur. One was the mere merchant carrier, who went from Montreal to the Grand Portage in big boats of four tons burden having a crew of ten men. These were the 'pork eaters' or *mangeurs de lard*, who had nothing worse to face than well-known rapids. The others were a finer breed, the true and daring *coureurs de bois*, or pioneers of the bush, who went west in comparatively light canoes, each carrying not more than a ton and a half, who hunted their own game, risked a fight with the Indians, and were to the duller 'pork eaters' what a charger is to a cart-horse or a frigate to a barge. The regulation portage load was one hundred and fifty pounds, and many a man was known to carry this weight the whole ten miles and back within six hours.

There was need to hurry. Supplies were going west to Lake Winnipeg, up the Saskatchewan, and even on to Athabaska; while furs were coming down for the autumn trade to Europe. As a rule the traders were Scottish and the voyageurs French Canadian. Indians and half-breeds were fairly common; they manned the canoes in the farther wilds, guided the pioneers, and did the actual trapping. To speak in terms of modern transportation: the Indians and their bark canoes produced the raw material and worked the branch lines; while the voyageurs met them at the junctions and took the goods down to the head of ocean navigation, where everything was, of course, trans-shipped for Europe. The same sort of trade was carried on, in a slightly different way, in the Maritime Provinces. There are survivals of it still in Labrador. At the end of July, Nascaupees, some of whom take months to reach their hunting grounds by paddle and portage, may be seen at Seven Islands, on the north shore of the Gulf of St Lawrence, where huge modern pulp mills make paper for the New York press, and where the offing is alive with transatlantic shipping all season through.

These inland voyages are as strange to the average Canadian of today as to contemporary Englishmen and Frenchmen. So it is perhaps worth while to record the ordinary features of what must soon become altogether a thing of the past. The incidents would be much the same with every kind of small craft that has served its turn along the interlocking network of Canadian waterways, whether an old-fashioned bateau or a

Durham boat, a sharp-end dug-out, or a bark canoe. But the immemorial birch-bark is the best to choose for example, as it preceded and outlasted every other kind and is the most typically Canadian of them all.

Before starting, every broken seam and hole must be gummed over. Water is poured into the canoe and every point of exit marked for gumming. Loading must be done with unusual care, as the slightest crankness of such frail craft in such wild waters is likely to prove fatal. Crews always were their own stevedores, and it was a poor crew that could not load to perfection in a short five minutes, once the cargo had been settled. The actual paddling is not difficult to learn, that is, the paddling required from an ordinary member of the crew. But the man in the bow and, still more, the man in the stern need the highest kind of skilful daring to take them safely through. Paddling by oneself also requires a special touch, only to be learnt by long practice. Even in dead water it takes some time before a novice can send the canoe straight ahead when paddling on one side only. As the paddle goes aft the bow naturally tends to turn towards the other side. The trick of it consists in counteracting this tendency by a twist of the blade which brings the inner edge round, aftwise beside the canoe, till the blade becomes a rectifying rudder as well as a thrusting propeller at the end of every stroke. When a fall or impassable rapid is reached, the 'bowman' jumps out before the canoe touches bottom and draws her safely ashore. He and the 'steersman' then carry her over the portage, while the rest carry the cargo on their backs. A man's own weight is a fair load; but with a sling across their foreheads, and clasped hands behind their heads, strong men have carried twice as much and more. When a rapid has to be ascended the canoe is lightened as much as need be, the steel-shod poles are got out, and the bow and stern paddlers stand up to their work, balancing themselves as easily as other men would on dry land.

But it is when a rapid is to be 'run' that the finest skill is shown. If there is any doubt the steersman walks down to take a good look first. Then, if necessary, some or all of the cargo is taken out and portaged to the next 'steady' in the river. Rapids are so common in some journeys that canoemen think less of them than foxhunters think of five-barred gates. In most cases a mistake means death; so every nerve and muscle is kept tensely ready the whole run through. The current should be 'humoured'; for it does a surprising amount of the work itself. If rightly headed with the main throw of it the canoe will naturally tend to seek the deepest and safest channel just as the body of the water does. Split channels must be met by instant decision; and it is when picking out the proper one that steerage way tells. As the pace of the rapid increases, so does the danger; for the slightest false thrust of a blade is enough to make a canoe swerve or upset. But, with the expert bowman on the keenest of look-outs and the course under the knowing touch of the still more expert steersman, a rapid may be run in perfect safety through racing waves which only just fail to leap aboard, on roaring water which drowns the human voice so completely that the bowman can only make use of signals, past rocks and snags on which a single graze would mean a wreck, and, often the worst of all, from one wild 'throw' to another with quite a different set and a wrench of two fierce currents where they meet.

All the white man's boats used by the voyageurs approximated more or less to the shape of the canoe: the various kinds of Hudson river dug-out, the bateau, the 'Durham,' and the 'York,' which last became the wooden successor of the birch-bark after Governor Simpson's general inspection of the Hudson's Bay domain. Only the rather barge-like 'Mackinaw' was completely outside this venturesome class. It was a useful but humdrum cargo boat, laboriously poled along shallow, quiet waters, or rowed with lumbering sweeps; or sometimes even sailed, when it shovelled its way through the water with a very safe wind dead aft.

This completes the tale of Canadian inland small craft that depended on pole and paddle, oar and towline, and only used a simple sail as an exceptional thing. But the human interest would not be complete without some reference to the tours of inspection made by the magnates of the Hudson's Bay Company. The greatest tours of all were those of Sir George Simpson, the governor who took charge after the Company absorbed its warring rival in 1821. In modern business language he would be called the executive head of the great Canadian fur-trade 'merger.' He was a young promoted clerk, a Scotsman born, with little experience of the Canadian wilds, but with the natural faculty of rule and a good deal of diplomacy—the gauntlet in the velvet glove.

Simpson soon grasped the salient features of the people he had to deal with and very sensibly made his tours of inspection as much like a royal progress as he could. Time and money were never neglected: his 'record runs' across the wilderness and the dividends at headquarters proved that to the full. He was determined to show every one concerned that thenceforth there was only one governing company, and that he was its proper representative. Then, as always, London was the general headquarters. But the Canadian headquarters were at Montreal; and Simpson fixed what might be called the field headquarters at Norway House, near the north end of Lake Winnipeg, a commanding strategic point in the heart of the great fur territories. Here he was always busy introducing discipline, enforcing a much-needed reduction in the ration of rum given to the Indians, and reporting home. As voyageurs, he thought the French Canadians much better than the men of any other race. 'Canadians preferable to Orkneymen. Orkneymen less expensive but slow. Less physical strength and spirits. Obstinate if brought young into the service. Scotch and Irish, when numerous, quarrelsome, independent, and mutinous.' He introduced fines as a punishment. But 'this will only do for Europeans. A blow is better for Canadians.' On July 12, 1828, Simpson left York Factory on Hudson Bay for a state and business progress across the continent to Fort Vancouver on the Columbia. One of his staff, Archibald Macdonald, wrote an account of it, called *Peace River: a Canoe Voyage from the Hudson Bay to the Pacific*. The best of birch-barks were used to ensure speed; though the birch-bark had already been superseded as a cargo craft. There was a doctor in the party, which included nine voyageurs to each of the two canoes. Simpson's departure was the signal for a salute of seven guns, which was duly repeated at every subsequent fort. The whole population lined the waterside as the voyageurs struck up one of their old French folk-songs to beguile the way. The arrival at Norway House was still more imposing. The Union Jack, with the magic letters 'H. B. C.' on its fly, was hoisted, to the admiration of all the whites and Indians from that most important neighbourhood. Simpson's party had landed out of sight to put on their best clothes; after which they shot through the gorge at full speed, to the strains of the bagpipes from Simpson's canoe and bugles from the other. At Fort St James, the central point of 'New Caledonia,' the approach was made by land. 'Unfurling the British Ensign, it was given to the guide, who marched first. After him came the band, consisting of buglers and bagpipers. Next came the governor, mounted, and behind him Hamlyn and Macdonald, also on horses. Twenty men loaded like beasts of burden formed the line, and finally M'Gillivray with his wife and family brought up the rear.' On the nineteenth day out from York Factory Simpson reached Fort Langley at the mouth of the Fraser.

How far away it all seems now in this new twentieth century! And yet, as in the case of Alexander Mackenzie, there is a wonderfully intimate human link connecting that time with our own; for Lord Strathcona was born before the amalgamation of the rival companies in 1821; he became the last resident-governor of the Hudson's Bay Company while François Beaulieu, Mackenzie's centenarian voyageur, was still alive; and he lived until 1914, the year of the Great World War.

CHAPTER THREE
SAILING CRAFT: THE PIONEERS

When we call Canada a new country in the twentieth century we are apt to forget that her seafaring annals may possibly go back to the Vikings of the tenth century, a thousand years ago. Long before William the Conqueror crossed over from France to England the Vikings had been scouring the seas, north, south, east, and west. They reached Constantinople; they colonized Iceland; they discovered Greenland; and there are grounds for suspecting that the 'White Eskimos' whom the Canadian Arctic expedition of 1913 noted down for report are some of their descendants. However this may be, there is at least a probability that the Vikings discovered North America five centuries before Columbus. The saga of Eric the Red sings of the deeds of Leif Ericson, who led the discoverers and named the three new countries Helluland, Markland, and Vineland. Opinions differ as to which of the four—Labrador, Newfoundland, Nova Scotia, or New England—are to be included in the Vikings' three. In any case, the only inevitable two are Newfoundland and Nova Scotia, with which the subsequent history of Canada also begins.

But even if the Vikings never came to Canada at all, their ships could not be refused a place in any history of sailing craft; for it is the unique distinction of these famous freelances of the sea to have developed the only type of ancient and mediaeval hull which is the admiration of the naval world today. The kind of vessel they used in the tenth century is the craft of most peculiar interest to Canadian history, though it has never been noticed there except by the merest landsman's reference. The special type to which this vessel belonged was already the result of long development. The Vikings had a way of burying a chief in his ship, over which they heaped a funeral mound. Very fortunately two of these vessels were buried in blue clay, which is an excellent preserver of timber; so we are able to see them today in an almost perfect state. The one found in 1880 at the mouth of the Christiania fjord is apparently a typical specimen, though smaller than many that are described in the sagas. She is about eighty feet long, sixteen feet in the beam, and seven feet in total depth amidships, from the top of the gunwale to the bottom of the keel. The keel runs into the stem and stern-post with very gentle curves. The whole of the naval architecture is admirably done. The lines are so fine that there is almost the least possible resistance to the water when passing through it. The only point worth criticizing is the slightness of the connection between the topsides and the body of the boat. But as this was a warship, carrying little besides live ballast, such a defect would be minimized. Iron rivets, oak treenails (or pegs), clinker planking (each plank-edge overlapping the next below it), admirably proportioned frame, as well as arrangements for stepping, raising, and lowering the single mast, all show that the builders knew exactly what they were about.

The rudder is hung over on the starboard, or 'steer-board,' side and worked by a tiller. The ropes are made of bark fibre and the planking is partly fastened to the floors with ties made of tough tree roots. Only one sail, and that a simple square one, was used. Nothing could be done with this unless the wind was more or less aft. The sail, in fact, was centuries behind the hull, which, with the firm grip of its keel, would have been quite fit for a beat to windward, if the proper canvas had been carried. The thirty oars were often used, and to very good purpose, as the easy run of the lines suited either method of propulsion. The general look of these Viking craft is not unlike that of a big keeled war canoe, for both ends rise with a sharp sheer and run to a point. A classical scholar would be irresistibly reminded of the Homeric vessels, not as they were in reality, but as they appear in the eager, sea-born suggestions of the Iliad and the Odyssey—long, sharp, swift, well-timbered, hollow, with many thwarts, and ends curved high like horns.

Three Viking vessels discovered in a Danish peat-bog probably belong to the fifth century, thus being fifteen hundred years of age. Yet their counterparts can still be seen along the Norwegian coast. Such wonderful persistence, even of such an excellently serviceable type, is quite unparalleled; and it proves, if proof were needed, that the Norsemen who are said to have discovered Newfoundland and Nova Scotia were the finest seamen of their own and many a later time. The way they planned and built their vessels was the glory of their homes. The way they manned and armed and fought them was the terror of every foreign shore. War craft and crew together were the very soul and body of strength and speed and daring skill, as, with defiant figurehead and glittering, shield-hung sides, they rode to battle joyously on the wild white horses of the mediaeval sea.

Five centuries more, and the English, another great seafaring people, first arrived in Canada. Then came increasing swarms of the most adventurous fishermen of Europe. After these came many competing explorers and colonizers, all of whose fortunes directly depended on the sea.

Cabot's English crew of eighteen hands is a century nearer to our own time than Leif Ericson the Norseman was to Cabot's. Yet Cabot himself preceded Columbus in setting foot on what may fairly be called the mainland of America when he discovered Canada's eastern coast in 1497. He cleared from Bristol in May, reached the new regions on June 24, and returned safe home at the end of July. It was an age of awakening surmise. The universal question was, which is the way to the golden East? America was looked upon as a rather annoying obstruction to proper navigation, though it was allowed to have some incidental interest of its own. Vasco da Gama doubled the Cape of Good Hope in the same year that Cabot raised St George's Cross over what afterwards became British territory. Twenty-five years later Magellan found the back way through behind Cape Horn, and his ship, though not himself, went round the world. Then, twelve years later still, the French sailed into the Canadian scene on which they were to play the principal part for the next two centuries and a quarter.

Every text-book tells us that Jacques Cartier was the great French pioneer and explains his general significance in the history of Canada. But no books explain his peculiar significance from the nautical point of view, though he came on the eve of the most remarkable change for the better that was ever made in the art of handling vessels under sail. He was both the first and the last mediaeval seaman to appear on Canadian inland waters. Only four years after his discovery of the St Lawrence, an Englishman, Fletcher of Rye, astonished the seafaring world of 1539 by inventing a rig with which a ship could beat to windward with sails trimmed fore and aft. This invention introduced the era of modern seamanship. But Cartier has another, and much more personal, title to nautical fame, for he was the first and one of the best of Canadian hydrographers, and he wrote a book containing some descriptions worthy of comparison with those in the official 'Pilots' of today. This book, well called his *Brief Recit et Succincte Narration*, is quite as easy for an Englishman to read in French as Shakespeare is for a Frenchman to read in English. It abounds in acute observations of all kinds, but particularly so in its sailing directions. Compare, for instance, his remarks on Cumberland Harbour with those made in the latest edition of the *St Lawrence Pilot* after the surveys of four hundred years. Or take his few, exact, and graphic words about Isle-aux-Coudres and compare them with the entries made by the sailing masters of the British fleet that used this island as a naval base during the great campaign for the winning of Canada in 1759. In neither case will Cartier suffer by comparison. He was captain, discoverer, pilot, and surveyor, all in one; and he never failed to make his mark, whichever role he undertook.

Like all the explorers, Jacques Cartier had his troubles with his crews. The average man of any time cannot be expected to have the sustained enthusiasm, much less the manifold interest, which inspires his leader. Nearly every commander of the fifteenth, sixteenth, and seventeenth centuries had to face mutiny; and, even apart from what might be called natural causes, men of that time were quite ready to mutiny for what seem now the most absurd of reasons. Some crews would not sail past the point of Africa for fear of turning black. Others were distracted when the wind held for days together while they were outward bound, lest it might never blow the other way in North America, and so they would not be able to get back home. The ships, too, often gave as much trouble as the men. They were far better supplied with sails and accommodation than the earlier Viking ships had been; but their hulls were markedly inferior. The Vikings, as we have seen, anticipated by centuries some of the finest models of the modern world. The hulls of Cabot, Columbus, and Cartier were broader in the beam, much bluffer in the bow, besides being full of top-hamper on the deck. Nothing is known about Cabot's vessel except that she must have been very small, probably less than fifty tons, because the crew numbered only eighteen and there was no complaint of being short-handed. Cartier's *Grande Hermine* was more than twice as large, and, if the accepted illustrations and descriptions of her may be relied upon, she probably was not unlike a smaller and simplified *Santa Maria*, the ship which bore Columbus on his West Indian voyage of 1492. Such complete and authentic specifications of the *Santa Maria* still remain that a satisfactory reproduction of her was made for the Chicago World's Fair of 1893. Her tonnage was over two hundred. Her length of keel was only sixty feet; length of ship proper, ninety-three; and length over all, one hundred and twenty-eight. This difference between length of keel and length over all was not caused by anything like the modern overhang of the hull itself, which the Vikings had anticipated by hundreds and the Egyptians by thousands of years, but by the box-like forecastle built over the bows and the enormous half and quarter decks jutting out aft. These top-hampering structures overburdened both ends and produced a regular see-saw, as the Spanish crew of 1893 found to their cost when pitching horribly through a buffeting head sea. The *Santa Maria*, like most 'Spaniards,' had a lateen-rigged mizzen. But the *Grande Hermine* had no mizzen, only the square-rigged mainmast, foremast, and bowsprit. The bowsprit of those days was a mast set at an angle of forty-five; and it sometimes, as in the *Grande Hermine*, carried a little upright branch mast of its own.

Many important changes occurred in the nautical world during the two generations between the days of Jacques Cartier and those of Champlain. The momentous change in trimming sails, already referred to, came first, when Fletcher succeeded in doing what no one had ever done before. There can be no doubt that the lateen sail, which goes back at least to the early Egyptians, had the germ of a fore-and-after in it. But the germ was never evolved into a strong type fit for tacking; and no one before Fletcher ever seems to have thought it possible to lay a course at all unless the wind was somewhere abaft the beam. So England can fairly claim this one epoch-making nautical invention, which might be taken as the most convenient dividing-line between the sailing craft of ancient and of modern times.

The French had little to do with Canada for the rest of the sixteenth century. Jacques Carrier's best successor as a hydrographer was Roberval's pilot, Saint-Onge, whose log of the voyage up the St Lawrence in 1542 is full of information. He more than half believes in what the Indians tell him about unicorns and other strange beasts in the far interior. And he thinks it likely that there is unbroken land as far as Tartary. But, making due allowance for his means of observation, the claim with which he ends his log holds good regarding pilotage: 'All things said above are true.'

The English then, as afterwards, were always encroaching on the French wherever a seaway gave them an opening. In 1578 they were reported to be lording it off Newfoundland, though they had only fifty vessels there, as against thirty Basque, fifty Portuguese, a hundred Spanish, and a hundred and fifty French. Their numbers and influence increased year by year, till, in 1600, they had two hundred sail manned by eight thousand men. They were still more preponderant farther north and farther south. Frobisher, Davis, Hudson, and other Englishmen left their mark on what are now Arctic and sub-Arctic Canada. Hudson also sailed up the river that bears his name, and thus did his share towards founding the English colonies that soon began their ceaseless struggle with New France. But even before his time, which was just after Champlain had founded Quebec, two great maritime events had encouraged the English to aim at that command of the sea which they finally maintained against all rivals. In 1579 Sir Francis Drake sailed completely round the world. He was the first sea captain who had ever done so, for Magellan had died in mid-career fifty-seven years before. This notable feat was accompanied by his successful capture of many Spanish treasure ships. Explorer, warrior, enricher of the realm, he at once became a national hero. Queen Elizabeth, a patriot ruler who always loved a hero for his service to the state, knighted Drake on board his flagship; and a poet sang his praises in these few, fit words, which well deserve quotation wherever the seaborne English tongue is known:

> The Stars of Heaven would thee proclaim,
> If men here silent were.
> The Sun himself could not forget
> His fellow traveller.

Nine years later the English Navy fought the unwieldy Spanish Armada into bewildered flight and chased it to its death round the hostile coast-line of the British Isles.

Meanwhile the quickened interest in 'sea affairs' had led to many improvements in building, rigging, and handling vessels. Surprising as it may seem, most of these improvements were made by foreigners. Still more surprising is the fact that British nautical improvements of all kinds, naval as well as mercantile, generally came from abroad during the whole time that the British command of the sea was being won or held.

Belated imitation of the more scientific foreigner was by no means new, even in the Elizabethan age. It had become a national habit by the time the next two centuries were over. English men, not English vessels, won the wars. The Portuguese and Spaniards had larger and better vessels than the English at the beginning of the struggle, just as the French had till after Trafalgar, and the Americans throughout the War of 1812. Even Sir Walter Raleigh was belated in speaking of the 'new' practice of striking topmasts, 'a wonderful ease to great ships, both at sea and in the harbour.'

CHAPTER FOUR
SAILING CRAFT: UNDER THE FLEURS-DE-LIS[1]

Every one knows that when Champlain stood beside Lake Huron, wondering if it had a western outlet towards Cathay, he was discovering the Great Lakes, those fresh-water seas whose area far exceeds the area of Great Britain. Every one knows that he became the 'Father of New France' when he founded Quebec in 1608; and that he was practically the whole civil and military government of Canada in its infant days. But few know that he was also a captain in the Royal Navy of France, an expert hydrographer, and the first man to advocate a Panama canal. And fewer still remember that he lived in an age which, like our own, had its 'record-breaking' events at sea. Baffin's 'Farthest North,' reached in 1616, was latitude 77° 45'. This remained an unbroken record for two hundred and thirty-six years. Champlain's own voyage from Honfleur to Tadoussac in eighteen days broke all previous records, remained itself unbroken for a century, and would be a credit to a sailing ship today. His vessel was the *Don de Dieu*, of which he left no exact description, but which was easily reproduced for the tercentenary of Quebec in 1908 from the corresponding French merchant vessels of her day. She was about a hundred tons and could be handled by a crew of twenty. The nearest modern equivalent of her rig is that of a barque, though she carried a little square sail under her bowsprit and had no jibs, while her spanker had a most lateenish look. Her mainsail had a good hoist and spread. She had three

[1] The nautical history of New France is all parts and no whole; brilliant ideas and thwarted execution; government stimulus and government repression; deeds of daring by adventurers afloat and deeds of various kinds by officials ashore: everything unstable and changeable; nothing continuous and strong. It cannot, therefore, make a coherent narrative, only a collection of half-told tales.

masts and six sails altogether. The masts were 'pole,' that is, all of one piece. The tallest was seventy-three feet from step to truck, that is, from where the mast is stepped in over the keel to the disc that caps its top. She carried stone ballast; her rudder was worked by a tiller, with the help of a simple rope tackle to take the strain; and the poop contained three cabins.

Not long after the death of Champlain (1635) there was a world-wide advance in shipbuilding. Perhaps it would not be too much to say that the modern school of wooden sailing-ship designers began with Phineas Pett, who was one of a family that served England well for nearly two hundred years. He designed the *Sovereign of the Seas*, which brought English workmanship well to the front in the reign of Charles I. She surpassed all records, with a total depth from keel to lanthorn of seventy-six feet, which exceeds the centre line, from keel to captain's bridge, of modern 'fliers' with nearly twenty times her tonnage. The Cromwellian period also gave birth to a most effective fleet, which in its turn was succeeded by the British fleets that won the Second Hundred Years' War with France and decided the destiny of Canada. This long war, or series of wars, begun against Louis XIV in the seventeenth century, only ended with the fall of Napoleon at Waterloo. La Hogue in 1692, Quebec in 1759, and Trafalgar in 1805 were three of the great deciding crises. La Hogue and Trafalgar were purely naval; while Quebec was the result of a joint expedition in which the naval forces far exceeded the military. The general effect of this whole Second Hundred Years' War was to confirm the British command of the sea for another century.

But the French designs in shipbuilding were generally better than the English. The French, then and afterwards, were more scientific, the English more rule-of-thumb. Yet when it came to actual handling under sail, especially in action, the positions were reversed. The English seafaring class was far larger in proportion to population and it had far more practice at sea. Besides, England had more and more at stake as her oversea trade and empire extended, till at last she had no choice, as an imperial power, but either to win or die.

The French kingdom rose to its zenith under Louis XIV, whose great minister, Colbert, did all he could to foster the Navy, the mercantile marine, and the French colonies in Canada. But the fates were against him. France was essentially a landsman's country. It had several land frontiers to attack or defend, and it used its Navy merely as an adjunct to its Army. Moreover, its people were not naturally so much inclined to colonize over-sea possessions as the British, and its despotic colonial system repressed all free development. The result was that the French dominions in America never reached a population of one hundred thousand. This was insignificant compared with the twelve hundred thousand in the British colonies; while the disparity was greatly increased by the superior British aptness for the sea.

French Canada had all the natural advantages which were afterwards turned to such good account by the British. It had timber and population along a magnificently navigable river system that tapped every available trade route of the land. Had there only been a demand for ships New France might have also enjoyed the advantage of employing the scientific French naval architects. But the seafaring habit did not exist among the people as a whole. A typical illustration is to be found in the different views the French and British colonists took of whaling. The British on Nantucket Island first learned from the Indians, next hired a teacher, in the person of Ichabod Paddock, a famous whaling master from Cape Cod, and then themselves went after whale with wonderful success. The French in Canada, like the British on Nantucket Island, had both whales and whaling experts at their very doors. The Basques kept a station at Tadoussac, and whales were seen at Quebec. But, instead of hiring Basques to teach them, the French in Canada petitioned the king for a subsidy with which to hire the Basques to do the whaling for them. Of course the difference between the two forms of government counts for a good deal—and it is not at all likely that any paternal French ruler, on either side of the Atlantic, ever wished to encourage a sea-roving spirit in Canada. But the difference in natural and acquired aptitude counts for more.

The first Canadian shipbuilding was the result of dire necessity. Pont-Gravé put together a couple of very small vessels in 1606 at Port Royal so that he might cruise about till he met some French craft homeward bound. Shipbuilding as an industry arose long after this. The Galiote, a brigantine of sorts, was built by the Sovereign Council and launched at Quebec in 1663. But it was the intendant Talon who began the work in proper fashion. In 1665, immediately after his arrival, he sent men 'timber-cruising' in every likely direction. Their reports were most encouraging. Suitable timber was plentiful along the waterways, and the cost was no more than that of cutting and rafting it down to the dockyards. Talon reported home to Colbert. But official correspondence was too slow. At his own cost he at once built a vessel of a hundred and twenty tons. She was on the most approved lines, and thus served as a model for others. A French Canadian built an imitation of her the following year. Talon vainly tried to persuade this enterprising man to form a company and build a ship of four hundred tons for the trade with the West Indies. Three smaller vessels, however, successfully made the round trip from Quebec to the West Indies, on to France, and back again, in 1670. In 1671 Colbert laid aside for Talon a relatively large sum for official shipbuilding and for the export of Canadian wood to France. The next year Talon had a five-hundred-tonner on the stocks, while preparations were being made for an eight-hundred-tonner, which would have been a 'mammoth' merchant vessel in contemporary France. Before he left Canada he had the satisfaction of reporting that three hundred and fifty hands, out of a total population of only seven thousand souls, were engaged in the shipyards.[1] But there were very few at sea.

---

[1] See in this Series The Great Intendant, chapters iv and ix.

The first vessel to sail the Great Lakes was built by La Salle seventy years after their discovery by Champlain. This was *Le Griffon*, which, from Father Hennepin's description, seems to have been a kind of brig. She was of fifty or sixty tons and apparently carried a real jib. She was launched at the mouth of Cayuga Creek in the Niagara peninsula in 1679. Her career was interesting, but short and disastrous. She sailed west across Lake Erie, on through Lakes St Clair and Huron, and reached Green Bay on Lake Michigan, where she took in a cargo of fur. On her return voyage she was lost with all hands.

In the eighteenth century shipbuilding in Quebec continued to flourish. The yards at the mouth of the St Charles had been enlarged, and even then there was so much naval construction in hand that private merchant vessels could not be built as fast as they were wanted. In 1743 some French merchants proposed building five or six vessels for the West India trade, besides twenty-five or thirty more for local trade among the West Indian islands. A new shipyard and a dry-dock were hurriedly built; and there was keen competition for ship-carpenters. In 1753 *L'Algonkin*, a frigate of seventy-two guns, was successfully launched. The shipwrights experimented freely with Canadian woods, of which the white oak proved the best. But the Canadian-built vessels for transatlantic trade never seem to have equalled in number those that came from France.

The restrictions on colonial trade were rigidly enforced; no manufacture of goods was allowed in the colonies, and no direct trade except with France and French possessions. Canada imported manufactured goods and exported furs, timber, fish, and grain. The deep-water tonnage required for Canada was not over ten or twelve thousand, distributed among perhaps forty vessels on the European route and twenty more that only visited the French West Indies. A complete round trip usually meant a cargo of manufactures from France to Canada, a cargo of timber, fish, and grain from Canada to the West Indies, and a third cargo—of sugar, molasses, and rum—from the West Indies home to France. Quite half the vessels, however, returned direct to France with a Canadian cargo. Louisbourg was a universal port of call, the centre of a partly contraband coasting trade with the British Americans, and a considerable importing point for food-stuffs from Quebec.

French commerce on the sea had, however, a mighty rival. The encroaching British were working their way into every open water in America. The French gallantly disputed their advance in Hudson Bay and won several actions, of which the best victory was Iberville's in 1697, with his single ship, the *Pélican*, against three opponents. In Labrador and Newfoundland the British ousted all rivals from territorial waters, except from the French Shore. The 'Bluenose' Nova Scotians crept on from port to port. The Yankees were as supreme at home as the other British were in Hudson Bay, though on occasion both were daringly challenged. All the French had was the line of the St Lawrence; and that was increasingly threatened, both at its mouth and along the Great Lakes.

The British had in their service a powerful trading corporation. The Hudson's Bay Company was flourishing even in the seventeenth century. In one sense it was purely maritime, as its posts were all on the Bay shore, while the French traded chiefly in the hinterlands. The Company's fleet, usually three or four ships, sailed regularly from Gravesend or Portsmouth about June 1, rounded the Orkneys and made for Hudson Bay. The return cargo of furs arrived home in October. This annual voyage continues to the present day. [1]

As Hudson Bay was the place for fur, so Newfoundland, and all the waters round it, was the place for fish. 'Dogs, fogs, bogs, and codfish,' was the old half-jeering description of its products. Standing in the gateway of Canada, Newfoundland was always a menace to New France. Thirty years before Champlain founded Quebec a traveller notes that, among the fishing fleets off Newfoundland, 'the English rule all there.' In other quarters, too, there was a menace to France. The British colonies were always feeling their way along the coast as well as along the Great Lakes. In spite of ordinances on both sides, forbidding trade between colonies of different powers, little trading craft, mostly British, would creep in with some enticing contraband, generally by way of Lake Champlain.

The first attempt in the English colonies to trade with Canada by way of the open sea was made in 1658, when Captain John Perel sailed from New York for Quebec in the French barque *St Jean*, and was wrecked on Anticosti, with the total loss of a cargo of sugar and tobacco. The sloop *Mary* managed to reach Quebec in 1701 with a miscellaneous cargo, containing, among many other items, '166 cheses, 20+81+101 Rols of tobacko, 2 hogheds of botls marckt SR, 70 bunches of arthen waire pots, 8 barels of beaire, 19 caskes of schotte.' Her return cargo included '14 barels of brandy, 4 hogsds of Claret, 2 bondles of syle skins, etc.' She was wrecked before she reached home, but most of her cargo was saved. Her owner, Samuel Vetch, the son of a 'Godly Minister and Glorifier of God in the Grass Market' in Edinburgh, was a great local character in New York. Four years after this voyage he was sent to Quebec to arrange a truce between New France and New England. But his return was as unlucky as that of his sloop *Mary*, for he was arrested and fined £200 on a charge of having traded with his own country's official enemies.

The fashion in ships changed very slowly. As we have seen, what may be called the ancient period of sailing ships closed about the time Jacques Cartier appeared in Canada. When the fore-and-aft-trimmed sails were invented in 1539, the modern age began. This has three distinctive eras of its own. The first lasted for about a century after the time of Jacques Cartier; and its chief work was to free itself of ancient and mediaeval limitations.

The second, or central, modern era lasted twice as long, from the middle of the seventeenth century to the middle of the nineteenth. It thus

---

[1] For the narrative of the Hudson's Bay Company the reader is referred to The Adventurers of England on Hudson Bay, in this Series.

covered one century under the Fleurs-de-lis in Canada and another under the Union Jack. It also exactly corresponded with the long era of the famous British navigation laws, of which more will presently be heard. During this period sails were improved in size, cut, and setting. The changes can be described only in technical language. Jibs became universal, adding greatly to handiness in general and the power of tacking in particular. Four sails were used on a mast—main, top, topgallant, and royal. Naval architecture was greatly improved, especially by the French. But this improvement did not extend to giving the hull anything like its most suitable shape. The Vikings were still unbeaten in this respect. Even the best foreign three-deckers were rather lumbering craft.

The third era began with the introduction of the clippers about 1840, and will not end till deep-sea sailing craft cease to be a factor in the world's work altogether. It was in this present era, when steamers were gaining their now unquestioned victory, and not during previous eras, when steam was completely unknown, that sailing craft reached their highest development. Sails increased to eight on the mainmast of a full-rigged ship, and they were better cut and set than ever before. Yachts and merchantmen cannot be fairly compared in the matter of their sails. But it is worth noting that the old 'white-winged days' never had any sort of canvas worth comparing with a British yachting 'Lapthorn' or a Yankee yachting 'Sawyer' of our own time. Hulls, too, have improved far beyond those of the old three-decker age, beyond even the best of the Vikings'.

Such broad divisions into eras of shipbuilding are, of course, only to be taken as marking world-wide nautical advances in the largest possible sense. One epoch often overlaps another and begins or ends at different times in different countries. A strangely interesting survival of an earlier age is still to be seen along the Labrador, in the little Welsh and Devonshire brigs, brigantines, and topsail schooners which freight fish east away to Europe. These vessels make an annual round: in March to Spain for salt; by June along the Labrador; in September to the Mediterranean with their fish; and in December home again for Christmas. They are excellently handled wherever they go; and no wonder, as every man aboard of them is a sailor born and bred.

CHAPTER FIVE
SAILING CRAFT: UNDER THE THE UNION JACK

When Canada finally became a British possession in 1763 she was, of course, subject to the navigation laws, or the Navigation Act, as this conglomeration of enactments was usually called. The avowed object of these laws was to gain and keep the British command of the sea. They aimed at this by trying to have British trade done in British ships, British ships manned by British crews, and British crews always available if wanted for British men-of-war. The first law was enacted under the Commonwealth in 1651. The whole series was repealed under Victoria in 1849. Exceptions were often made, especially in time of war; and there was some opposition to reckon with at all times. But, generally speaking, and quite apart from the question of whether they were wise or not, the British government invariably looked upon these navigation laws as a cardinal point of policy down to the close of the wars with the French Empire and the American Republic in 1815.

The first laws only put into words what every sea-power had long been practising or trying to practise: namely, the confining of all sea trading to its own ships and subjects. They were first aimed at the Dutch, who fought for their carrying trade but were crushed. They operated, however, against all foreigners. They forbade all coastwise trade in the British Isles except in British vessels, all trade from abroad except in British ships or in ships belonging to the country whence the imported merchandise came, all trade between English colonies by outsiders, and all trade between the colonies and foreign countries, except in the case of a few enumerated articles. The manning clauses were of the same kind. Most of the crew and all the officers were to be British subjects—an important point when British seamen were liable to be 'pressed' into men-of-war in time of national danger.

The change of rule in 1763 meant that Canada left an empire that could not enforce its navigation laws and joined an empire that could. Whatever the value of the laws, Canadian shipping and sea trade continued to grow under them. In the eighteenth century there was little internal development anywhere in America; and less in Canada than in what soon became the United States. People worked beside the waterways and looked seaward for their profits. Elias Derby, the first American millionaire, who died in 1799, made all his money, honestly and legally, out of shipping. Others made fortunes out of smuggling. An enterprising smuggler at Bradore, just inside the Strait of Belle Isle, paved his oaken stairs with silver dollars to keep the wood from wearing out; and he could well afford to do so.

The maritime provinces of Nova Scotia (then including New Brunswick) and Prince Edward Island had been gradually growing for a quarter of a century before the United Empire Loyalists began to come. Halifax was a garrison town and naval station. There was plenty of fish along the coast; and the many conveniently wooded harbours naturally invited lumbering and shipbuilding. Fish and furs were the chief exports up to the War of 1812; after that, timber. The Loyalists came in small numbers before 1783; in larger numbers during the five years following. From twenty to thirty thousand altogether are said to have settled in the Maritime Provinces.

They were poor, but capable and energetic, and by the end of the eighteenth century their 'Bluenose' craft began to acquire a recognized place at sea. Quebec and Montreal did an increasing business. Quebec was the great timber-trade and shipbuilding centre; Montreal the point where furs were collected for export. From Quebec 151 vessels took clearance in 1774. In 1800 there were 21 Quebec-built vessels on the local register. Ten years later there were 54.

The Great Lakes had no such early development. Moreover, the days of their small beginnings were full of retarding difficulties. Nor were they free from what was then a disaster of the first magnitude; for in 1780 a staggering loss happened to the infant colony. The *Ontario* foundered with one hundred and seventy-two souls on the lake after which she was named. During the fourteen years between the Conquest and the Revolution only a few small vessels appeared there. On the outbreak of the Revolution the British government impressed crews and vessels alike, and absolutely forbade the building of any craft bigger than an open boat except for the government service. Subsequently the strained relations on both sides, lasting till after the War of 1812, and the tendency of the Americans to encroach on the frontier trade and settlements, combined to prevent the government from giving up the power it had thus acquired over shipping. The result was that trade was carried on in naval vessels, some of which had originally been built as merchantmen and others as men-of-war. There were frequent complaints of non-delivery from the business community, both on the spot and in England. But 'defence was more important than opulence,' and the burden was, on the whole, cheerfully borne by the Loyalists. In 1793 twenty-six vessels cleared from Kingston. Two years later a record trip was made by the sloop *Sophia*, which sailed from there to Queenston, well over two hundred miles, in eighteen hours. Two years later again a traveller counted sixty wagons carrying goods from Queenston, beyond the other end of Lake Ontario, to Chippawa, so as to get them past Niagara Falls. Anywhere west from Montreal the unit of measurement for all freight was a barrel of rum, the transport charge for which was over three dollars as far as Kingston, where it was trans-shipped from the bateau to a schooner.

There was very little shipping on Lake Erie till after the War of 1812. The first American vessel launched in these waters had a curious history. After a season's work in 1797 she was carted past Niagara and launched on Lake Ontario, where she plied between Queenston and Kingston under the British flag with the name of *Lady Washington*. The rival Hudson's Bay and North-West Companies each had a few boats on the western Lakes at the beginning of the nineteenth century, and the government maintained there a tiny flotilla of its own. But shipping was a very small affair west of Niagara for several years to come.

While the War of 1812 killed out the feeble trade on the Lakes, it greatly stimulated the well-established trade in sea-going craft from Quebec and the Maritime Provinces. The British command of the sea had become so absolute by 1814 that the whole American coast was practically sealed to trade, which was thus forced to seek an 'underground' outlet by way of Canada, in spite of the state of war. This, in addition to the transport required by the British forces in Canada, sent freights and tonnage up by leaps and bounds. The only trouble was to find enough ships and, harder still, enough men.

Canadian sailing craft in the nineteenth century had a chequered career. Many disturbing factors affected the course of trade: the cholera of '32; the Rebellion of '37; the Ship Fever of '47; the great gold finds in California in '49 and in Australia in '53; Reciprocity with the United States in '54; Confederation in '67; the triumph of steam and steel in the seventies; and the era of inland development which began in the eighties.

The heyday of the Canadian sailing ship was the third quarter of the nineteenth century. This period, indeed, was one of great activity in the history of mast and sail all the world over. There was intense rivalry between steam and sail. The repeal of the Navigation Act in England had brought the whole of British shipping into direct competition with foreigners. The Americans were pushing their masterful way into every sea. The rush to California was drawing eager fleets of Yankee, Bluenose, and St Lawrence vessels round the Horn. India, China, and Australia were drawing other fleets round the Cape. The American clippers threatened to oust the slower 'Britishers' and throw the comparatively minor Canadians into the shade. For the first and only time in history American tonnage actually began to threaten British supremacy.

But the challenge was met in the proper way, by building to beat on even terms. The British had already regained their lead before the Civil War of the sixties; and the subsequent inland development of the United States, with the momentous change from wood and sails to steel and steam, combined to depress the American mercantile marine in favour of its British rival.

Canada played a great part in this brief but stirring era, when the wooden sailing vessel was making its last gallant stand against steam, and the sun of its immemorial day was going down in a blaze of glory which will never fade from the memories of those who love the sea. Canada built ships, sailed ships, owned ships, and sold ships. She became one of the four greatest shipping centres in the world; and this at a time when she had less than half as many people and less than one-tenth as much realized wealth as she has now. Quebec had more than half its population dependent on shipbuilding in the fifties and sixties. In 1864 it launched sixty vessels, many of them between one and two thousand tons. About the same time Nova Scotia launched nearly three hundred vessels and New Brunswick half as many. The Nova Scotians, however, only averaged two hundred tons, and the New Brunswickers four hundred. If the Lakes, Prince Edward Island, the rest of Canada, and Newfoundland are added in, the total tonnage built in the best single year is found to be close on a quarter of a million. Allowing for the difference in numbers of the respective populations, this total compares most favourably with the highest recent totals built in the British Isles, where the greatest shipbuilding the world has ever seen is now being carried on.

It was the change from wood to metal that caused the decline of shipbuilding in Canada. It was also partly the change to steam; but only partly, for Canada started well in the race for building steamships. What proves that the disuse of wood was the real cause of the decline is the fact that Canada never even attempted to compete with other countries in building metal sailing vessels. If Canada had developed her metal industries a generation sooner she would have had steel clippers running against 'Yankees,' 'Britishers,' and German 'Dutchmen'; for there was a steel-built sailing-ship age that lasted into the twentieth century and that is not really over yet. Indeed, even wooden and composite sailers are still at work; and with their steel comrades they still make a very large fleet. Singular proof of this is sometimes found. Nothing collects sailing ships like a calm; vessels run into it from all quarters and naturally remain together till the breeze springs up. But, even so, most readers will probably be surprised to learn that, only a few years ago, a great calm off the Azores collected a fleet of nearly three hundred sail.

Canadian shipbuilders had some drawbacks to contend with. One was of their own making. Certain builders in the Maritime Provinces, especially at Pictou and in Prince Edward Island, turned out such hastily and ill constructed craft as to give 'Bluenoses' a bad name in the market. By 1850, however, the worst offenders were put out of business, and there was an increasing tendency for the builders to sail their own vessels instead of selling them.

A second, and this time a general, drawback was the difficulty of getting Canadian-built vessels rated A1 at Lloyd's. 'Lloyd's,' as every one knows, is the central controlling body for most of the marine insurance of the world, and its headquarters are in London. There were very few foreign 'Lloyd's' then, and no colonial; so it was a serious matter when the English Lloyd's looked askance at anything not built of oak. Canada tried her own oak; but it was outclassed by the more slowly growing and sounder English oak. Canada then fell back on tamarac, or 'hackmatac,' as builders called it. This was much more buoyant than oak, and consequently freighted to advantage. But it was a soft wood, and Lloyd's was slow to rate it at its proper worth. Tamarac hulls went sound for twenty years, and sometimes forty, especially when hardwood treenails were used—a treenail being a bolt that did the service of a nail in woodwork or a rivet in steel plating. At first Canadian vessels were only rated Al for seven years, as compared with twelve for those built of English oak. A year was added for hardwood treenails, and another for 'salting on the stocks.' In 1852 Lloyd's sent out its own surveyor, Menzies, who would guarantee work done under his own eye for twenty-five cents a ton; while Lloyd's, for its part, would give preferential rates to any vessels thus 'built under special survey.' Perhaps Canadian timber is not as lasting as the best European. Certainly it has no such records of longevity; though there is no reason why Canadian records should not be better than they are in this respect. Few people know how long a well-built and well-cared-for ship can live. Lloyd's register for 1913 contains vessels launched before Queen Victoria began to reign. Merchantmen have often outlived their century. Nelson's *Victory* still flies the flag at Portsmouth, though she was laid down the year before Wolfe took Quebec. And the *Konstanz,* a thirty-five-ton sloop, still plies along the Danish coast, although her launch took place in 1723—a hundred and ninety years ago.

A third drawback for Canadian builders was the lack of capital. Shipbuilding fluctuates more than most kinds of business, and requires great initial outlay as well; so failures were naturally frequent. The firm of Ross at Quebec did much to steady the business by sound finance. But the smaller yards were always in difficulties, and no shipbuilder ever made a fortune.

Excellent craft, however, came out of Canadian yards: notable craft wherever they sailed. One of the best builders at Quebec was a French Canadian, whose beautiful clipper ship *Brunelle,* named after himself, logged over fourteen knots an hour and left many a smart sailer, and steamer too, hull down astern. Mackenzie of Pictou was builder and skipper both. With the help of a friend he began by cutting down the trees and doing all the rest of the work of building a forty-five-ton schooner. By 1850 he had built a fourteen-hundred-tonner, the famous *Hamilton Campbell Kidston,* which greatly astonished Glasgow, for she was then the biggest ship the Clyde had ever seen. His last ship was launched in the 'record' year of 1865. The Salter Brothers did some fine work at the 'Bend,' as Moncton was then called. Their first vessel, a barque of eight hundred tons, was sold at once in England. Next year they built a clipper ship called the *Jemsetgee Cursetgee* for an East Indian potentate, who sent out an Oriental figurehead supposed to be a likeness of himself. A peculiar feat of theirs was rigging as a schooner and sending across the Atlantic a scow-like coal barge ordered by a firm in England.

The decline of Canadian sailing craft was swifter than its rise; and with the sailing craft went the Canadian-built steamers, because wood was the material used for both, and the use of iron and steel in the yards of the British Isles soon drove the wooden hulls from the greater highways of the sea. Once the palmy days of the third quarter of the century were over the decline went on at an ever-increasing rate. In 1875 Canada built nearly 500 vessels, and, if small craft are included, the tonnage must have nearly reached 200,000. In 1900 she built 29 vessels, of 7751 tons—steam, steel, wood, and sail. Shipowning does not show such a dramatic contrast, but the decline has been very marked. Within twenty-two years, from 1878 to 1900, the Canadian registered tonnage was almost exactly halved. The drop was from a grand total, sail and steam together, of a million and a third, which then made Canada the fourth ship owning country in the world and put her ahead of many nations with more than ten times her population.

CHAPTER SIX
SAILING CRAFT: THE BUILDING OF THE SHIP

Shipbuilding was and is a very complex industry. But only the actual construction can be noticed here, and that only in the briefest general way. The elaborate methods of European naval yards were not in vogue anywhere in Canada, not even in Quebec, much less in Nova Scotia. It was not uncommon for a Bluenose crew to make everything themselves, especially in the smaller kinds of vessels. They would cut the trees, draft the plan, build the ship and sail her: being thus lumbermen, architects, builders, and seamen all in one. The first step in building is to lay the blocks on which the keel itself is laid. These blocks are short, thick timbers, arranged in graduated piles, so that they form an inclined plane of over one in twenty, from which the completed hull can slide slowly into the water, stern first. Then comes the laying of the keel, that part which is to the whole vessel what the backbone is to a man. A false keel is added to the bottom of this in order to increase its depth and consequent grip. This prevents the side drift which is called making leeway. The false keel is only fastened to the keel itself from underneath, because such a fastening is strong enough to resist water pressure and weak enough to allow of detachment in case of grounding. The slight projection of the keel itself then gives too little purchase for a dangerous amount of leverage on the frame. A long keel is made up of several pieces of square timber, with their ends shaped into scarfs, an overlapping and interlocking arrangement of great strength. The foremost keel piece is scarfed into the stem, which is the fore-end of the vessel's bow. The aftermost keel piece joins the stern-post, on which the rudder hangs. Elm makes a good keel, especially with oak for stem and stern-post.

The frame, to pursue our simile, is to the ship what ribs are to our bodies. In the same way the planking is the skin. The frame, or ribs, determines the vessel's form. There were, and still are, many varieties of frame. In a very small vessel there are very few timbers. The keel is probably all in one piece, and the planks may possibly run from stem to stern without a break. In this case the unity of each piece supplies enough longitudinal resistance to strains. But when a vessel is large, and more especially when she is long, the strains known as hogging and sagging are apt to rack her timbers apart.

A ship is not built for mere passive resistance, like a house, or even for resistance only to pressures and vibrations, like a bridge. She is built to resist every imaginable strain of pitching and rolling, and so requires architectural skill of a far higher kind than is required (in the constructional, not the aesthetic, sense) for any structure on the land. When a ship is on the top of a single wave she tends to hog, because there is much less support for her ends than for her centre, and so her ends dip down, racking her upper and compressing her lower parts amidships. When the seas are shorter she often has her ends much more waterborne than her centre, and this in spite of the fact that the extreme ends are not naturally waterborne themselves. Then she sags, and the strains of racking and compressing are reversed, because her centre tends to sink and her ends to rise. Now, a series of hogging and sagging strains alternately compresses and opens every resisting join in every timber, with the inevitable result of loosening the whole. To meet these strains longitudinal strength must be supplied. The keel supplies much of it, so does the planking (or skin) to a lesser degree; but not enough; and the ribs, by themselves, are for transverse stiffening only. Four means are therefore employed to hold the parts together lengthwise—keelsons, shelf-pieces, fillings, and some form of truss.

The keelson is an inverted keel inside the vessel. The floors, which are the timbers uniting the two sides of the frame (or ribs), are given a middle seating on the keel. The keelson is then placed over them, exactly in line with the keel, when bolts as long as the thickness of all three are used to unite the whole in one solid backbone, and this backbone with the ribs. Side or 'sister' keelsons were used in the Navy on either side of the mainmast for a distance equal to about a third of the length of the keelson. But they were little used in merchant vessels, and their longitudinal resistance was only partial and incidental. Shelf-pieces and waterways were adapted from French models by Sir Robert Seppings, who became chief constructor to the Navy some years after Trafalgar. They are thick timbers running continuously under and over the junctions of the deck beams with the ship's sides, to both of which they are securely fastened.

The keelson was an old invention and shelf-pieces and waterways were soon in vogue. But fillings and trusses, both expensive improvements, were not much favoured in any mercantile marine. The truss is even older than the keelson, having been used by the ancient Egyptians at least thirty-five centuries ago, and probably earlier. Four to eight pillars rose in crutches from the bottom amidships to about six feet above the gunwale. The Egyptians ran a rope over the crutches and round the mast, and then used its ends to brace up the stem and stern. The moderns discarded the rope, took the strains on connecting timbers, and modified the truss, sometimes out of recognition. But many Canadian and American river steamers of the twentieth century A.D. employ the same principle for the same object as the Egyptians of the seventeenth century B.C. Fillings came from the French, like shelf-pieces and waterways. Seppings put them between the ribs, in the form of thick timbers. The whole frame thus became almost solid against any tendency of the ribs to close together, and quite strong enough against their other tendency to draw apart.

All means that strengthen a well-built hull longitudinally have also been made to add their quota to its transverse strength. The ribs spring from the solid mass of their own floors bolted in between the keelson and the keel; and the planking, or skin, is let into the rabbets, or side grooves, of the keel and firmly fastened to the ribs throughout by hardwood pegs called treenails. The decks are, in themselves, a source of weakness. The beams supporting them are like the rafters of a house, which, of course, work the walls apart under pressure from the floors—and here, as in every other detail, the stability required for a house is nothing to what is required for a ship. The way to overcome this difficulty is to make the decks and beams so many bridges holding the sides together. At the point of junction of every beam-end with a shelf-piece, waterway, and rib there is an arrangement of bolts and dowellings (or dovetailings) which makes the whole as solid as possible. An extra bolt through the waterway, rib, and outside planking adds to the strength; and a knee, or angular piece of wood or iron connecting the shelf with the under side of the beam, almost completes the beam-end connection. The final touches are the clamps below the shelves and the spirketing above the waterways, with short-stuff between the clamps of one deck and the spirketing of the next below.

All this is only the merest suggestion of what is done for the main part of the vessel's hull. The ends require many modifications, because the shape there approaches a V, and so the floors cannot cross the keel as holding bodies. But the breast-hooks forward and crutches aft, the deck transom, which is the foundation for the deck abaft as well as the assemblage of timbers uniting the stern to the body of the vessel, with all the other parts that make up the ends, cannot be more than mentioned here. Then come the decks, which are quite complex in themselves, and still more complex by reason of the mast-holes and hatchways cut out of them all, and the windlass, bitts, and capstan built into the one that is exposed to the storm. To make sure that whatever strength is taken out by cutting is restored in some other way, and that the exposed deck which has to resist the strains put upon the structures built into it is specially reinforced, the most careful provision must be made for the mast-holes; for the hatchways with their coamings fore and aft on carlings that reach from beam to beam; for the riding bitts, which are posts to hold the cable when the vessel is at anchor, and which must therefore be immensely strong; for the windlass, which in the merchant service often did the double duty of the bitts and capstan; and for a multiplicity of other parts.

A landsman could hardly believe what a marvellous adjustment of co-operating parts is required for a ship unless he actually watches its construction. He will then understand why it is by far the most wonderful structure man has ever built throughout all the ages of his evolution. It represents his first success in mastering an element not his own; and, whatever the future may see in the way of aviation, the priority of seamanship will always remain secure by thousands and thousands of known and unknown years.

But we are still no farther than a few parts of the hull. There is the stepping of the masts, with their heels set firm and square above the keel, and their rake 'right plim' throughout. Then there is the whole of the rigging—a perfect maze to look at, though an equally perfect device to use; the sails, which require the most highly expert workmanship to make; the rudder, and many other essentials. Finally, there is all that is needed in every well-found vessel which is 'fit to go foreign.' No vessel would go far unless its under-water parts were either sheathed, tarred, or tallowed; for sea-worms burrow alarmingly, and 'whiskers' grow like the obnoxious weeds they are. These particulars, of course, leave many important gaps in the process.

Then the hull has to be transferred from the inclined plane of block piles, on which it was built, to a cradle, on which it moves down the sliding-ways into the water.

When everything is ready, the christening of the ship takes place. A bottle of wine is broken against her bows and her name is pronounced by some distinguished person in a formula which varies more or less, but which is generally some version of the good old English benediction: 'God bless the *Dreadnought* and all who sail in her.' No matter what the name may be, the ship herself is always 'she.' Many ingenious and mistaken explanations have been given of this supposedly female 'she.' The schoolboy 'howler' on the subject is well known: 'All ships are "she" except mail boats and men-of-war.' Had this schoolboy known a very little more he might have added jackass brigs to his list of male exceptions. The real explanation may possibly be that the English still spoken at sea is, in some ways, centuries older than the English spoken on land, and that the nautical 'she' comes down to us from the ancient days in which all inanimate objects were endowed with life in everyday speech and neuters were as yet unknown.

Immediately this most stirring ceremony ceases, the stentorian order comes to 'Down dog-shore!' on which the dog-shore trigger is touched off, the dog-shores fall, an awakening quiver runs through the sliding-ways and cradle; and then the whole shapely vessel, still facing the land from which she gets her being, moves majestically into the water, where her adventurous life begins.

CHAPTER SEVEN
SAILING CRAFT: FIT TO GO FOREIGN

We will suppose that the ship is complete in hull, successfully launched, and properly rigged and masted. The two questions still remaining are: what is her crew like, and how does she sail?

The typical British North American crew of the nineteenth-century sailing ship is the Bluenose crew. Newfoundlanders were too busy fishing in home waters, though some of them did ship to go foreign and others sailed their catch to market. Quebeckers built ships, but rarely sailed them; while the Pacific coast had no shipping to speak of. Thus the Bluenoses had the field pretty well to themselves. Bluenoses were so called because the fog along the Nova Scotian and New Brunswick coast was supposed to make men's noses bluer than it did elsewhere. The name was generally extended by outsiders to all sorts of British North Americans; and, of course, was also applied to any vessel, as well as any crew, that hailed from any port in British North America, because a vessel is commonly called by the name of the people that sail her. 'There's a Bluenose,' 'that's a Yankee,' 'look at that Dago,' or 'hail that Dutchman' apply to ships afloat as well as to men ashore. And here it might be explained that 'Britisher' includes anything from the British Isles, 'Yankee' anything flying the Stars and Stripes, 'Frenchie' anything hailing from France, 'Dago' anything from Italy, Spain, or Portugal, and 'Dutchman' anything manned by Hollanders, Germans, Norsemen, or Finns, though Norwegians often get their own name too. A 'chequer-board' crew is one that is half white, half black, and works in colour watches.

Hard things have often been said of Bluenose crews. Like other general sayings, some of them are true and some of them false. But, mostly, each of them is partly true and partly false: and—'circumstances alter cases.' The fact is, that life aboard a Bluenose was just what we might expect from crews that lived a comparatively free-and-easy life ashore in a sparsely settled colony, and a very strenuous life afloat in ships which depended, like all ships, on disciplined effort for both success and safety. When national discipline is not very strong ashore it has to be enforced by hook or by crook afloat. The general public never bothered its head much about seamen's rights or wrongs in a rather 'hard' new country managing its own maritime affairs. So there certainly were occasional 'hell ships' among the Bluenoses, though very rarely except when there were Bluenose officers with a foreign crew.

This was quite in accordance with the practice all along the coast of North America. Even aboard the famous Black Ball Line of Yankee transatlantic packets in the forties there was plenty of 'handspike hash' and 'belaying-pin soup' for shirkers or mutineers. The men before the mast were mostly foreigners and riff-raff Britishers; very few were Yankees or Bluenoses. Discipline had to be maintained; and it was maintained by force. But these were not the real hell ships. 'Hell ships' were commonest among deep-watermen on long voyages round the Horn, or among the whalers when the best class of foremast hands were not to be had. Many of them are much more recent than is generally known; and even now they are not quite extinct. 'Black Taylor,' 'Devil Summers,' and 'Hell-fire Slocum' are well within living memory. Black Taylor came to a befitting end. Because the rope surged at the capstan he kicked the nearest man down, and was jumping to stamp his ribs in, when the man suddenly whipped out his knife and ripped Black Taylor up with a New Orleans nigger trick-twist for which he got six months, though really deserving none.

But such mates and skippers always were exceptions; and, as a general rule, no better crews and vessels have ever sailed the sea than the Yankees at their prime. Their splendid clippers successfully challenged the slower Britishers on every trade route in the world. At the very time that the *America* was beating British yachts hull-down, the old British East Indiamen were still wallowing along with eighty hands to a thousand tons, while a Yankee thousand-tonner could sail them out of sight with forty. The British excuse was that East Indiamen required a fighting crew as well as a trading one, and that British vessels were built to last, not simply put together to make one flashy record. But after the Napoleonic wars the British Navy could police the world of waters; so double numbers were no longer needed; and if East Indiamen were built to last, how was it they only went an average of six times out and six times home before being broken up?

Nor was it only in speed that the Yankees were so far ahead. They paid better wages, they gave immeasurably better food, they were smarter to look at and smarter to go, their rigging was tauter, their sails better cut and ever so much flatter on a wind, their cargo more quickly and scientifically stowed, and, most important point of all, their discipline quite excellent. Woe betide the cook or steward whose galley or saloon had a speck of dirt that would make a smudge on the skipper's cleanest cambric handkerchief! It was the same all through, from stem to stern and keel to truck, from foremast hand to skipper. Aboard the best clippers the system was well-nigh perfect. Each man had found, or had the chance of finding, the position for which he was most fit. The best human combination of head and heart and hand was sure to come to the top. The others would also find their own appropriate levels. But shirkers, growlers, flinchers, and mutineers were given short shrift. The officers were game to the death and never hesitated to use handspikes, fists, or firearms whenever the occasion required it.

As for sea-lawyers—the canting equivalent of ranting demagogues ashore—they could hardly have got a hearing among any first-rate crew. No admiralissimo ever was a greater hero to a junior midshipman than the best Yankee skippers were to the men before the mast. There's no equalitarian nonsense out at sea.

This digression springs from and returns to the main argument; because the Yankee excellence is so little understood and sometimes so grudgingly acknowledged by British and foreign landsmen, and because Bluenose and Yankee circumstances and practice were so much alike. Britishers were different in nearly all their natural circumstances, while, to increase the difference, their practice became greatly modified by a deal of good but sometimes rather lubberly legislation. And yet all three—Britisher, Bluenose, and Yankee—are so inextricably connected with each other that it is quite impossible to understand any one of them without some reference to the other two.

Bluenose discipline was good, very good indeed. When the whole ship's company was Bluenose, discipline was partly instinctive and mostly went well, as it generally did when Yankees and Bluenoses sailed together. The whole population of the little home port—men, women, and children—knew every vessel's crew and all about them. The men were farmers, fishermen, lumbermen, shipbuilders, and 'deepwatermen,' often all in one. Among other peoples, only Scandinavians ever had such an all-round lot as this. Even in the present century, with its increasing multiformity of occupation, books full of nauticalities can be read and understood in these countries by everybody, though such books cannot be read elsewhere except by the seafaring few. Business meant ships or shipping; so did politics, peace and war, adventure and ambition.

But there is a different tale to tell when the tonnage outran the Bluenose ability to man it, and Dutchmen, Dagos, miscellaneous wharf-rats, and 'low-down' Britishers had to be taken on instead. If the crew was mixed and the officers Bluenose there was sure to be trouble of graduated kinds, all the way up from simple knock-downs to the fiercest gun-play of a real hell ship. The food was inferior to that aboard the Yankees. But in discipline there was nothing to choose. An all-Bluenose or all-Yankee sometimes came as near the perfection of seamanship and discipline as anything human possibly can. But aboard a mixed Bluenose the rule of bend or break was enforced without the slightest reference to what was regarded as landlubber's law. The Britisher's Board of Trade regulations were regarded with contempt; and not without reason; for, excellent as they were, they struck the Bluenose seamen as being an interference made solely in the supposed interests of the men against the officers.

The mistake was that the old injustices were repeated in a new way. Formerly the law either sided with the officers and owners or left them alone; now it either sided with the men or left the officers and owners in the lurch. The true balance was not restored. Here is a thoroughly typical instance of the difference between a Britisher and a Bluenose under the new dispensation. The second mate of a Britisher asked for his discharge at Bombay because he could not manage the men, who had shirked disgracefully the whole way out. The skipper got a good Bluenose for his new second mate. The first day the Bluenose came aboard one of the worst shirkers slung a bucket carelessly, cut the deck, and then proceeded to curse the ship and all who sailed in her, as he had been accustomed to do under the Britisher. The Bluenose mate simply said, 'See here, just shut your head or I'll shut it for you,' on which the skulker answered by threatening to 'cut his chicken liver out.' In a flash the Bluenose had him naped, slung, and flying across the rail. A second man rushed in, only to be landed neatly on the chin and knocked limp against the scuppers. The rest of the watch, roused by this unwonted assertion of authority, came on, but stopped short, snarling, when the Bluenose swung an iron bar from the windlass in a way that showed he knew how to handle it effectively. The skipper and mate now appeared, and, seeing a clear case of actual fight, at once ranged themselves beside the capable Bluenose. The watch, a mixed lot, then slunk off; and, from that day out, the whole tone of the ship was changed, very much for the better.

It is pleasanter, however, to take our last look at a Bluenose vessel, under sail, with Bluenose skipper, mates, and crew, and a Bluenose cargo, all complete. But a word must first be said about other parts and other craft, lest the Maritime-Province Bluenose might be thought the only kind of any consequence. There were, and still are, swarms of small craft in Canada and Newfoundland which belong mostly or entirely to the fisheries, and which, therefore, will be noticed in another chapter. The schooners along the different coasts, up the lower St Lawrence, and round the Lakes; the modern French-Canadian sailing bateaux; the transatlantic English brigs that still come out to Labrador; the many Britishers and Yankees that used to come to Bluenose harbours and to Quebec; the foreigners that come there still; and the host of various miscellaneous little vessels everywhere—all these are by no means forgotten. But only one main thread of the whole historic yarn can be followed here.

Before starting we might perhaps remember what a sailing vessel cannot do, as well as what she can, when the proper men are there and circumstances suit her. She is helpless in a calm. She needs a tow in crowded modern harbours or canals. She can only work against the wind in a laborious zigzag, and a very bad gale generally puts her considerably off her course. But, on the other hand, she could beat all her best records under perfect modern conditions of canvas, scientific metal hull, and crew; and the historic records she actually has made are quite as surprising as they are little known. Few people realize that 'ocean records' are a very old affair, even in Canada, where they begin with Champlain's voyage of eighteen days from Honfleur to Tadoussac and end with King George V's sixty-seven hours from land to land, when he speeded home in H.M.S. *Indomitable* from Champlain's tercentenary at Quebec in 1908, handling his shovel in the stokehole by the way.

Here are some purely sailing records worth remembering. A Newfoundland schooner, the *Grace Carter*, has sailed across to Portugal, sold her fish there, gone to Cadiz for all the salt that she could carry, and then reported back in Newfoundland within the month. A Canadian schooner yacht, the *Lasca*, has crossed easterly, the harder way, in twelve days from the St Lawrence. In 1860 the Yankee *Dreadnought* made the Atlantic record by going from Sandy Hook to Liverpool in nine days and seventeen hours, most of the time on the rim of a hurricane. Six years later the most wonderful sea race in history was run when five famous clippers started, almost together, from the Pagoda Anchorage at Fu-chau for the East India Docks in London. This race was an all-British one, as the civil war, the progress of steam everywhere except in the China trade, and the stimulus of competition, had now given Britishers the lead in the East, while putting them on an even footing with Yankees in the West. The course was sixteen thousand miles; the prize was the world's championship in clipper-racing. Three ships dropped considerably astern. But the *Ariel* and *Taeping* raced up the Channel side by side, took in their pilots at the same time, and arrived within eight minutes of each other. The *Ariel* arrived first; but the *Taeping* won, as she had left twenty minutes later. The total time was ninety-nine days. A very different, but still more striking, record is the longest daily run ever made entirely under sail. This was, in one sense at least, an Anglo-American record; for the ship, appropriately called the *Lightning*, was built by that master craftsman, Donald M'Kay of Boston, and sailed by a British crew. She made no less than 436 sea miles, or 502 statute miles, within the twenty-four hours.

There are no individual Bluenose rivals of these mighty champions. But the Bluenoses more than held their own, all round, in any company and on any sea. So it is well worth our while to end this story of a thousand years—from the Vikings till today—by going aboard a Bluenose vessel with a Bluenose crew when both were at their prime.

The *Victoria* is manned by the husbands, fathers, sons, and brothers of the place where she was built. Her owners are the leaders of the little neighbourhood, and her cargo is home-grown. She carries no special carpenter and sailmaker, like a Britisher, because a Bluenose has an all-round crew, every man of which is smart enough, either with the tools or with the fid and palm and needle, for ordinary work, while some are sure to be equal to any special job. She of course carries two suits of canvas, her new best and older second best. Each sail has required more skill than tailors need to make a perfect fit in clothes, because there is a constant strain on sails, exceeding, if possible, the strains on every other part. But before sail is made her anchor is hove short, that is, the ship is drawn along by her cable till her bows are over it. 'Heave and she comes!' 'Heave and she must!' 'Heave and bust her!' are grunted from the men straining at the longbars of the capstan, which winds the tightening cable in. 'Click, click, clickety, click' go the pawls, which drop every few inches into cavities that, keeping them from slipping back, prevent the capstan from turning the wrong way when the men pause to take breath. 'Break out the mud-hook!' and a tremendous combined effort ensues. Presently a sudden welcome slack shows that the flukes have broken clear. The anchor is then hove up, catted, and fished.

'All hands make sail!' sings out the mate. The wind is nicely on the starboard quarter, that is, abaft the beam and forward of the stern, which gives the best chance to every sail. A wind dead aft, blanketing more than half the canvas, is called a lubber's wind. A soldier's wind is one which comes square on the beam, and so makes equally plain sailing out and back again. What sail a full-rigged ship can carry! The Yankee *Great Republic* could spread nearly one whole acre of canvas to the breeze. Another Yankee, the *R. C. Rickmers*, the largest sailing vessel in the world today, exceeds this. But her tonnage is much greater, more than eleven thousand gross, and her rig is entirely different. A full-rigged clipper ship might have twenty-two square sails, though it was rare to see so many. In addition she would have studding-sails to wing her square sails farther out. Then, there were the triangular jibs forward and the triangular staysails between the masts, with the quadrangular spanker like an aerial rudder on the lower mizzenmast. All the nine staysails would have the loose lower corner made fast to a handy place on deck by a sheet (or rope) and the fore and aft points connected by the stays to the masts, the fore point low and the aft high. This is not the nautical way of saying it. But 'points' and 'corners' and other homely land terms sometimes save many explanations which, in their turn, lead on to other explanations.

The heads of square sails are made fast to yards, which are at right angles to the masts on which they pivot. Sails and yards are raised, lowered, swung at the proper angle to catch the wind, and held in place by halliards, lifts, braces, and sheets, which can be worked from the deck. Sheets are ropes running from the lower corners of sails. All upper sails have their sheets running through sheave-holes in the yardarms next below, then through quarter-blocks underneath these yards and beside the masts, and then down to the deck. Braces are the ropes which swing the yards to the proper angle. Halliards are those which hoist or lower both the yards and sails. The square sails themselves are controlled by drawlines called clew-garnets running up from the lower corners, leechlines running in diagonally from the middle of the outside edges, buntlines running up from the foot, and spilling lines, to spill the wind in heavy weather. When the area of a sail has to be reduced, it is reefed by gathering up the head, if a square sail, or the foot, if triangular, and tying the gathered-up part securely by reef points, that is, by crossing and knotting the short lines on either side of this part. The square sails on the mainmast are called, when eight are carried, the mainsail, lower and upper maintopsails, lower and upper maintopgallants, main-royal, mainskysail, and the moonsail. The standing rigging is the whole assemblage of ropes by which the masts are supported.

These few words are very far from being a technically full, or even quite precise, description. But, taken with what was previously said about the hull, they will give a better general idea than if the reader was asked to make a realizable whole out of a mazy bewilderment embracing every single one of all the multitudinous parts.

'All hands make sail!' Up go some to loose the sails aloft, while others stay on deck to haul the ropes that hoist the sails to the utmost limit of the canvas. The jibs and spanker generally go up at once, because they are useful as an aid to steering. The staysails generally wait. The jibs and staysails are triangular, the spanker a quadrangular fore-and-after. The square sails made fast to wide-spreading yards are the ones that take most hauling. But setting the sails by no means ends the work at them. Trimming is quite as important. Every time there is the slightest shift in the course or wind there ought to be a corresponding shift of trim so as to catch every breath the sail can hold. To effect this with the triangular sails a sheet must be slacked away or hauled more in; while, in the case of the square sails on the yards, a brace must be attended to.

Our Bluenose mate now thinks he can get more work from his canvas. His voice rings out: 'Weather crossjack brace!' which means hauling the lowest and aftermost square sail more to windward. 'Weather crossjack brace!' sings out the timekeeper, whose duty it is to rouse the watch as well as strike the bells that mark the hours and halves. The watch tramp off and lay on to the weather brace, the A.B.'s (or able-bodied seamen) leading and the O.S.'s (ordinary seamen) at the tail. Some one slacks off the lee braces and sings out 'Haul away!' Then the watch proceed to haul, with weird, wild cries in minor keys that rise and fall and rise again, like the long-drawn soughing of the wind itself.

Eh—heigh—o—az! Eh—heigh—ee! Eh—hugh! In comes the brace till the trim suits the mate, when he calls out 'Turn the crossjack brace!' which means making it fast on a belaying pin. The other braces follow. By the time the topgallant braces are reached only two hands are needed, as the higher yards are naturally much lighter than the lower ones.

Sheets and braces are very dangerous things to handle in a gale of wind. Every movement of the rope must be closely watched with one vigilant eye, while the other must be looking out for washing seas. The slightest inattention to the belaying of a mainsheet while men are hanging on may mean that it breaks loose just as the men expect it to be fast, when away it goes, with awful suddenness and force, dragging them clean overboard before their instinctive grip can be let go. The slightest inattention to the seas may mean an equally fatal result. Not once, nor twice, but several times, a whole watch has been washed away from the forebraces by some gigantic wave, and every single man in it been drowned.

Squalls need smart handling. Black squalls are nothing, even when the ship lays over till the lee rail's under a sluicing rush of broken water. But a really wicked white squall requires luffing, that is, bringing her head so close to the wind that it will strike her at the acutest angle possible without losing its pressure in the right direction altogether. The officer of the watch keeps one eye to windward, makes up his mind what sail he'll shorten, and then yells an order that pierces the wind like a shot, 'Stand by your royal halliards!' As the squall swoops down and the ship heels over to it he yells again, 'Let go your royal halliards, clew 'em up and make 'em fast!' Down come the yards, with hoarse roaring from the thrashing canvas. But then, if no second squall is coming, the mate will cut the clewing short with a stentorian 'Masthead the yards again!' on which the watch lay on to the halliards and haul—*Ahay! Aheigh! Aho—oh!* Up she goes!

The labour is lightened, as hand labour always has been lightened, by singing to the rhythm of the work. The seaman's working songs are chanties, a kind of homespun poetry which, once heard to its rolling music and the sound of wind and wave, will always bring back the very savour of the sea wherever it is heard again.[1] There are thousands of chanties in scores of languages, which, like the men who sing them, have met and mingled all round the world. They are the folklore of a class apart, which differs, as landsmen differ, in ways and speech and racial ambition, but which is also drawn together, as landsmen never have been, by that strange blend of strife and communing with man and nature which is only known at sea. They will not bear quotation in cold print, where they are as pitiably out of place as an albatross on deck. No mere reader can feel the stir of that grand old chanty

Hurrah! my boys, we're homeward bound!

unless he has heard it when all hands make sail on leaving port, and the deck begins pulsating with the first throb of the swell that sets in landward across the bar. And what can this chorus really mean to any one who has never heard it roared by strong male voices to the running accompaniment of seething water overside?

What ho, Piper! watch her how she goes!
Give her sheet and let her rip.
We're the boys to pull her through.
You ought to see her rolling home;
For she's the gal to go
In the passage home in ninety days
From Cal-i-for-ni-o!

But though you can no more wrest a chanty from its surroundings and then pass it off as a seaman's folk-song than you can take the blue from the water or the crimson from the sunset, yet, as some chanties have become so well known ashore, as others so richly deserve to be known there, and as all are now being threatened with extinction, perhaps a few may be mentioned in passing. *Away for Rio!* with its wild,

---

[1] For an excellent summary of the history of the sea shanty, with 65 authentic examples, see: *The Way of the Ship: Sailor's, Shanties, and Shantymen* by Richard Runciman Terry, Fireship Press, 2009

queer wail in the middle of its full-toned chorus, has always been a great favourite afloat:

For we're bound for Rio Grande,
And away Rio! ay Rio!
Sing fare-ye-well, my bonny young girl,
We're bound for Rio Grande.

The *Wide Missouri* is a magnificent song for baritones and basses on the water:

Oh, Shenando'h, I love your daughter,
'Way-ho, the rolling river!
Oh, Shenando'h, I long to hear you,
'Way-ho, we're bound away,
Down the broad Missouri.

A famous capstan chanty is well known on land, whence, indeed, it originally came:

And it's hame, dearie, hame; oh! it's hame I want to be.
My topsails are hoisted and I must out to sea;
But the oak and the ash and the bonnie birchen tree,
They're all a-growin' green in the North Countree.

—which is quite as appropriate to the Nova Scotia as to the one beyond the North Atlantic. A favourite sail-setting chanty is

Solo: Haul on the bowlin', the fore and maintop bowlin'—
Chorus. Haul on the bowlin', the bowlin' haul!

A good pumping-out chanty after a storm is

Solo: Old Storm has heard the angel call.
Chorus: To my ay! Old Storm along!

Reuben Ranzo is a grand one for a good long haul. The chorus comes after every line, striking like a squall, with a regular roar on the first word, Ranzo.

Solo: Hurrah for Reuben Ranzo!
Chorus: Ranzo, boys, Ranzo!

Ranzo's progress from a lubberly tailor to a good smart sailor is then related with infinite variations, but always with the same gusto. Ranzo is only really popular afloat. But Blow the man down is a universal favourite.

Solo: Blow the man down, blow the man down,
Chorus: 'Way-ho! Blow the man down.
Solo: Blow the man down from Liverpool town;
Chorus: Give us some wind to blow the man down.

When every sail is set and every stitch is drawing, there is no finer sight the sea can show. The towering masts; the canvas gleaming white, with its lines of curving beauty drawn by the touch of the wind; the whole ship bounding forward as if just slipped from her leash—all this makes a scene to stir the beholder then and for ever after. The breeze pipes up.

She's doing ten knots now; eleven, twelve; and later on, fifteen. This puts the lee rail under; for she lays over on her side so far that her deck is at a slope of forty-five. Her forefoot cuts through the water like the slash of a scimitar; while her bows throw out two seething waves, the windward one of which breaks into volleying spray a-top and rattles down like hail-stones on the fore-deck.

But next day the wind has hauled ahead, and she has to make her way by tacking. She loses as little as possible on her zigzag course by sailing close to the wind, that is, by pointing as nearly into it as she can while still 'keeping a full on' every working sail. Presently the skipper, having gone as far to one side of his straight course as he thinks proper, gives the caution; whereupon the braces are taken off the pins and coiled down on deck, all clear for running, while the spanker-boom is hauled in amid-ships so that the spanker may feel the wind and press the stern a-lee, which helps the bow to windward. Then the 'old man' (called so whatever his age may be) sings out at the top of his voice, 'Ready, oh!' The helm is eased down on his signal, so as not to lose way suddenly. When it is quite down he shouts again, 'Helm's a-lee!' on which the fore and head sheets (holding the sails attached to the foremast and bowsprit) are let go and overhauled. The vessel swings round, the spanker pressing her stern in one direction and the sails at the bows offering very little resistance now their sheets are let go. The skipper's eye is on the mainsail, which is the point of pivoting. Directly the wind is out of it and it begins to shiver he yells, 'Raise tacks and sheets!' when, except that the foretack is held a bit to prevent the foresail from bellying aback, all the remaining ropes that held the ship on her old tack are loosed. A roar of wind-waves rushes through the sails, and a tremor runs through the whole ship from stem to stern. The skipper waits for the first decided breath on her new tack and then shouts, 'Mainsail haul!' when the yards come swinging round so quickly that the men can hardly take in the slack of the braces fast enough. The scene of orderly confusion is now at its height. Every one hauling sings out at the very top of his pipes. The sails are struggling to find their new set home; while the headsheets forward thrash about like mad and thump their blocks against the deck with force enough to dash your brains out.

Mates and boatswain work furiously, for the skipper's eye is searching everywhere, and the skipper's angry words cut the delinquent like the lash of a well-aimed whip. The boatswain forward has the worst of it, for the restive sheets and headsails won't come to trim without a fight when it's breezing up and seas are running. But presently all the yards get rightly trimmed, tacks boarded, and bowlines hauled out taut. She's on a bowline taut enough to please the old man now; that is, the ropes leading forward from the middle of the forward edge of every square sail are so straight that she is sailing as near the wind as she can go and keep a full on. 'Go below, the watch!' and the men off duty tramp down, the cook and boatswain with their 'oilies' streaming from their scuffle with the flying spray and slapping dollops at the bows.

When a quartering trade wind is picked up sailing is at its easiest; for a well-balanced suit of canvas will keep her bowling along night and day with just the lightest of touches at the wheel. Then is the time to bend her old sails on; for, unlike a man, a ship puts on her old suit for fair weather and her new suit for foul. Then, too, is the time for dog-watch yarning, when pipes are lit without any fear of their having to be crammed half-smoked into the nearest pocket because all hands are called. Landsmen generally think that most watches aboard a wind-jammer are passed in yarns and smoking. But this is far from being the case. The mates and skipper keep everybody busy with the hundred-and-one things required to keep a vessel shipshape: painting, graining, brightening, overhauling the weak spots in the rigging, working the 'bear' to clean the deck with fine wet sand, helping whomever is acting as 'Chips' the carpenter, or the equally busy 'Sails'; or 'doing Peggy' for 'Slush' the cook, who much prefers wet grub to dry, slumgullion coffee to any kind of tea, ready-made hard bread to ship-baked soft, and any kind of stodge to the toothsome delights of dandyfunk and crackerhash. And all this is extra to the regular routine, with its lamp-lockers, binnacles, timekeeping, incessant lookout, and trick at the wheel. Besides, every man has to look after his own kit, which he has to buy with his own money, and his quarters, for which he alone is responsible.

So there is never much time to spare, with watch and watch about, all through the voyage; especially when all the ills that badly fed flesh is heir to on board a deepwaterman incapacitate some hands, while falls from aloft and various accidents knock out others.

The skipper, boatswain, cook, steward, Chips, and Sails keep no watches, and hence are called 'the idlers,' a most misleading term, for they work a good deal harder than their counterparts ashore; though the mates and seamen often work harder still. There are seven watches in a day, reckoned from noon to noon: five of four hours each and two of two hours each. These two, the dog watches, are from four to six and six to eight each afternoon. The crew are divided into port and starboard watches, each under a mate. In Bluenose vessels the port watch was always called by the old name of larboard watch till only the other day. The starboard and larboard got their names because the starboard was the side on which the steering oar was hung before the rudder was invented, and the larboard was the side where the lading or cargo came in.

Bluenoses have no use for nippers, as Britishers call apprentices. But if they had, and the reader was a green one, he would just about begin to know the ropes and find his sea legs by the time that our *Victoria* had run her southing down to within another day's sail of the foul-weather zone in the roaring forties round the Horn, which seamen call 'Old Stiff.' Sails are shifted again, and the best new suit is bent; for the coming gales have a clear sweep from the Antarctic to the stormiest coast of all America, and the enormous, grey-backed Cape Horners are the biggest seas in the world.

The best helmsmen are on duty now. Not even every Bluenose can steer, any more than every Englishman can box or every Frenchman fence. There are a dozen different ways of mishandling a vessel under sail. Let your attention wander, and she'll run up into the wind and perhaps get in irons, so that she won't cast either way. Let her fall off when you're running free, and she'll broach to and get taken aback. Or simply let her yaw about a bit instead of holding true, and you'll lose a knot or two an hour. But do none of these careless things, observe all the rules as well, and even then you will never make a helmsman unless it's born in you. Steering is blown into you by the wind and soaked into you by the water. And you must also have that inborn faculty of touch which tells you instinctively how to meet a vessel's vagaries—and no two vessels are alike—as well as how to make her fall in with all the humours of a wayward ocean.

The hungry great Antarctic wind comes swooping down. The *Victoria* lays over to it, her forefoot slashing, her lee side hissing, the windward rigging strained and screaming, and every stitch of canvas drawing full. Still the skipper carries on. He and his vessel have a name to keep up; and he has carried on till all was blue ere this, and left more than one steam kettle panting. Every timber, plank, mast, yard, and tackle wakes to new life and thrills in response to the sails. She answers her helm quickly, eagerly. She rides the galloping waters now as you ride her. And as she rises to each fresh wave you also rise, with the same exultant spring, and take the leap in your stride.

The wind pipes up: a regular gale is evidently brewing; and most of the canvas must come off her now or else she'll soon be stripped of it. 'Stand by your royal halliards!' yells the second mate. 'Let go your royal halliards!' The royals are down for good. The skysails have been taken in before. Another tremendous blast lays her far over, and the sea is a lather of foam to windward. The skipper comes on deck, takes a quick look round, and shouts at the full pitch of his lungs: 'All hands shorten sail!' Up come the other watch in their oilskins, which they have carefully lashed round their wrists and above their knees to keep the water out. Taking in sail is no easy matter now. Every one tails on, puts his back into it, and joins the chorus of the hard-breathed chanty. The human voices sound like fitful screams of seabirds, heard in wild snatches between the volleying gusts; while overhead the sails are booming like artillery, as the spilling lines strain to get the grip. 'Now then, starboard watch, up with your sail and give the larboard watch a dressing down!' *Yo—ho! Yo—hay! Yo—ho—oh!* Up she goes! A hiss, a crash, a deafening thud, and a gigantic wave curls overhead and batters down the toiling men, who hang on for their lives and struggle for a foothold. 'Up with you!' yells the mate, directly the tangled coil of yellow-clad humanity emerges like a half-drowned rat, 'Up with you, boys, and give her hell!' *Yo—ho! To—hay! Yo—ho—harrhh!* 'Turn that!' 'All fast, sir!' 'Aloft and roll her up! Now then, starbowlines, show your spunk!' Away they go, the mate dashing ahead; while the furious seas shoot up vindictive tongues at them and nearly wash two men clean off the rigging on a level with the lower topsails. Out on the swaying yard, standing on the foot-rope that is strung underneath, they grasp at the hard, wet, struggling canvas till they can pass the gaskets round the parts still bellying between the buntlines. 'One hand for the ship and one for yourself' is the rule aloft. But exceptions are more plentiful than rules on a day like this. Both hands must be used, though the sail and foot-ropes rack your body and try their best to shake you off. If they succeed, a sickening thud on deck, or a smothered scream and a half-heard *plopp!* overside would be the end of you.

All hands work like fury, for a full Antarctic hurricane is on them. This great South Polar storm has swept a thousand leagues, almost unchecked, before venting its utmost rage against the iron coasts all round the Horn. The South Shetlands have only served to rouse its temper. Its seas have grown bigger with every mile from the Pole, and wilder with every mile towards the Horn. Now they are so enormous that even the truck of the tall Yankee clipper staggering along to leeward cannot be seen except when both ships are topping the crest. Wherever you look there seems to be an endless earthquake of mountainous waves, with spuming volcanoes of their own, and vast, abysmal craters yawning from the depths. The *Victoria* begins to labour. The wind and water seem to be gaining on her every minute. She groans in every part of her sorely racked hull; while up aloft the hurricane roars, rings, and screeches through the rigging.

But suddenly there is a new and far more awful sound, which seems to still all others, as a stupendous mother wave rears its huge, engulfing bulk astern. On it comes, faster and higher, its cavernous hollow roaring and its overtopping crest snarling viciously as it turns forward, high above the poop. 'Hold on for your lives!' shout the mates and skipper. They are not a moment too soon. The sails are blanketed, and the ship seems as if she was actually being drawn, stern first, into the very jaws of the sea. A shuddering pause ... and then, with a stunning crash, the whole devouring mass bursts full on deck. The stricken *Victoria* reels under the terrific shock, and then lies dead another anxious minute, utterly helpless, her deck awash with a smother of foaming water, and her crew apparently drowned. But presently her stern emerges through the dark, green-grey after-shoulder of the wave. She responds to the lift of the mighty barrel with a gallant effort to shake herself free. She rises, dripping from stem to stern. Her sails refill and draw her on again. And when the next wave comes she is just able to take it—but no more.

The skipper has already decided to heave to and wait for the storm to blow itself out. But there is still too much canvas on her. Even the main lower topsail has to come in. The courses, or lowest square sails, have all come in before. The little canvas required for lying to must neither be too high nor yet too low. If it is too high, it gives the wind a very dangerous degree of leverage. If it is too low, it violently strains the whole vessel by being completely blanketed when in the trough of the sea and then suddenly struck full when on the crest. The main lower topsail is at just the proper height. But only the fore and mizzen ones are wanted to balance the pressure aloft. So in it has to come. And a dangerous bit of work it gives; for it has to be hauled up from right amidships, where the deck is wetter than a half-tide rock. The yellow-oilskinned crew tail on and heave. *Yo—ho! Yo—hay!* 'Hitch it! Quick, for your lives, hang on, all!' A mountainous wall of black water suddenly leaps up and crashes through the windward rigging. The watch goes down to a man, some hanging on to the rope as if suspended in the middle of a waterfall, for the deck is nearly perpendicular, while others wash off altogether and fetch up with a dazing, underwater thud against the lee side. Inch by inch the men haul in, waist-deep most of the time and often completely under. *Yo—ho! Yo—hay! harrhh*, and they all hold breath till they can get their heads out again. *Yo—ho! Yo—hay!* 'In with her!' *Heigh—o—oh!* 'Turn that!' 'All fast!'

"Way aloft and roll her up quick!' The tossing crests are blown into spindrift against the weather yardarm, while a pelting hailstorm stings the wet, cold hands and faces. The men tear at the sail with their numb fingers till their nails are bleeding. They hit it, pull it, clutch at it for support. Certain death would follow a fall from aloft; for the whole deck is hidden under a surging, seething mass of water. You would swear the water's boiling if it wasn't icy cold. The skipper's at the wheel, watching his chance. There is no such thing as a good chance now. But he sees one of some kind, just as the men get the sail on the yard and are trying to make it fast. Down goes the helm, and her head comes slowly up to the wind. 'She's doing it—— No! Hang on, all! Great snakes, here comes a sea!' Struck full, straight on her beam, by wind and sea together, the *Victoria* lays over as if she would never stop. Over she heels to it—over, over, over! A second is a long suspense at such a time as this. The sea breaks in thunder along her whole length, and pours in a sweeping cataract across her deck, smashing the boats and dragging all loose gear to leeward. Over she heels—over, over, over! The yards are nearly up and down. The men cling desperately, as if to an inverted mast. And well they may, especially on the leeward arm that dips them far under a surge of water which seems likely to snap the whole thing off. But the *Victoria's* cargo and ballast never shift an inch. Her stability is excellent. And as the heaving shoulder eases down she holds her keel in, just before another lurch would send her turning turtle. A pause ... a quiver ... and she begins to right. 'Now then,' roars the indomitable mate, the moment his dripping yardarm comes from under, 'turn to, there—d' y' think we 're going to hang on here the whole damn' day?' Whereupon the men turn to again with twice the confidence and hearty goodwill that any other form of reassurance could possibly have given them.

As she comes back towards an even keel the wind catches the sails. The skipper is still at the wheel, to which he and the two men whose trick it is are clinging. 'Hard-a-lee!' and round she goes this time, till she snuggles into a good lie-to, which keeps her alternately coming up and falling off a little, by the counteraction of the sails and helm. Here she rides out the storm, dipping her lee rail under, climbing the wild, gigantic seas, and working off her course on the cyclone-driven waters; but giving watch and watch about a chance to rest before she squares away again.

Next morning the skipper hardly puts his head out before he yells the welcome order to set the main lower topsail—from the lee yardarm of which a dozen men had nearly gone to Davy Jones's locker only yesterday. He takes a look round; then orders up reefed foresail and the three upper topsails, also reefed. Up goes the watch aloft and lays out on the yard. 'Ready?' comes the shouted query from the bunt. 'Ay, ay, sir!' 'Haul out to windward!' *Eh—hai, o—ho, o—ho—oh!* 'Far enough, sir?' 'Haul out to leeward!' *Eh—hai, o—ho, o—ho—oh!* 'That'll do! Tie her up and don't miss any points!' 'Right-oh! Lay down from aloft and set the sail!' *Yo—ho, yo—hai, yo—ho—oh!* Then the chanty rises from the swaying men, rises and falls, in wavering bursts of sound, as if the gale was whirling it about:

> Blow the man down, blow the man down,
> Way-ho! Blow the man down.
> Blow the man down from Liverpool town;
> Give us some wind to blow the man down.

And so the gallant ship goes outward-bound; and homeward-bound the same. At last she's back in Halifax, after a series of adventures that would set an ordinary landsman up for life. But the only thing the Nova Scotian papers say of her is this: 'Arrived from sea with general cargo—ship Victoria, John Smith, master, ninety days from Valparaiso. All well.'

No mention of that terrible Antarctic hurricane? No 'heroes'? No heroics?

It's all in the day's work there.

CHAPTER EIGHT
STEAMERS

Steamers and all other machine-driven craft are of very much greater importance to Canada now than canoes and sailing craft together. But their story can be told in a chapter no longer than the one devoted to canoes alone; and this for several reasons. The tale of the canoe begins somewhere in the immemorial past and is still being told today. The story of the sailing ship is not so old as this. But it is as old as the history of Canada. It is inseparably connected with Canada's fortunes in peace and war. It is Canada's best sea story of the recent past. And, to a far greater extent than the tale of the canoe, it is also a story of the present and the immediate future. Moreover, sailing craft helped to make turning points of Canadian history as only a single steamer ever has. Sailing craft made Canada known distinctively among every great seafaring people as steamers never have.

And while the building, ownership, and actual navigation of sailing craft once made Canada fourth among the shipping countries of the world, the change to steam and steel, co-inciding with the destruction of the handiest timber and the development of inland forms of business, put no less than eight successful rivals ahead of her.

Every one knows that James Watt turned the power of steam to practical use in the eighteenth century. But it was not till the first year of the nineteenth that a really workable steamer appeared, though the British, French, and Americans had been experimenting for years, just as ingenious men had been experimenting with stationary engines long before Watt. This pioneer steamer was the *Charlotte Dundas*, which ran on the Forth and Clyde Canal in Scotland in 1801. Six years later Fulton's *Clermont*, engined by the British firm of Boulton and Watt, ran on the Hudson from New York to Albany. Two years later again the *Accommodation*, the first steamer in Canada, was launched at Montreal, and engined there as well. She was built for John Molson by John Bruce, a shipbuilder, and John Jackson, an engineer. She was eighty-five feet over all and sixteen feet in the beam. Her engine was six horse-power, and her trial speed five knots an hour. She was launched, broadside on, behind the old Molson brewery. She was fitted up for twenty passengers, but only ten went on her maiden trip. The fare was eight dollars down to Quebec and ten dollars back. The following is interesting as a newspaper account of the first trip made by the first Canadian steamer. It is taken, word for word, from an original copy of the *Quebec Gazette* of November 9, 1809:

> The Steam Boat, which was built at Montreal last winter, arrived here on Saturday last, being her first trip. She was 66 hours on the passage, of which she was at anchor 30. So that 36 hours is the time which, in her present state, she takes to come down from Montreal to Quebec [over 160 statute miles]. On Sunday last she went up against wind and tide from Brehault's wharf to Lymburner's; but her progress was very slow. It is obvious that her machinery, at present, has not sufficient force for this River. But there can be no doubt of the possibility of perfectioning it so as to answer every purpose for which she was intended; and it would be a public loss should the proprietors be discouraged from persevering in their undertaking.

They did not fail to persevere. When Molson found that ox-teams were required to tow her up St Mary's Current, below Montreal, he ordered a better engine of thirty horse-power from Boulton and Watt in England, and put it into the *Swiftsure* in 1811. This steamer was twice the size of the *Accommodation*, being 120 by 24 feet; and the *Quebec Gazette* waxed eloquent about her:

> The Steam Boat arrived here from Montreal on Sunday. She started from Montreal at 5 o'clock on Saturday morning, and anchored at Three Rivers, which she left on Sunday morning at 5 o'clock, and arrived at the King's Wharf, Quebec, at half-past two; being only 24 hours and a half under way between the two cities, with a strong head wind all the way. She is most superbly fitted up, and offers accommodation for passengers in every respect equal to the best hotel in Canada. In short, for celerity and security, she well deserves the name of *Swiftsure*. America cannot boast of a more useful and expensive undertaking by one individual, than this of Mr Molson's. His Excellency, the Governor-in-chief, set out for Montreal on Tuesday afternoon, in the Steam Boat.

The following letter from Molson, for the information of Sir George Prevost, governor-general during the War of 1812, refers to one of the first tenders ever made, in any part of the world, to supply steamer transport for either naval or military purposes. It was received at Quebec by Commissary-General Robinson on February 6, 1813:

> I received a letter from the Military Secretary, under date of the 15th Decr. last, informing me of His Excellency's approval of a Tender I had made of the Steam Boat for the use of Government; wherein I am likewise informed that you would receive instructions to cause an arrangement to be made for her Service during the ensuing Season. For the Transport of Troops and conveyance of light Stores, it will be necessary to fit her up in a manner so as to be best adapted for the purpose, which will be in my opinion something after the mode of a Transport. For a passage Boat she would have to be fitted up quite in a different manner. If you wish her to be arranged in any particular manner under the direction of any Person, I am agreeable. I should be glad to be informed if His Excellency wishes or expects that I shall sail in her myself, whether Government or I furnish the Officers and men to Navigate and Pilot her, the Engineer excepted, the fuel and all other necessarys that may be required for her use. I imagine the arrangement must be for the Season, not by the Trip, as Government may wish to detain her for particular purposes. Ensurance I do not believe can be effected for less than 30 p. cent for the Season, therefore I must take the risque upon myself.

Within five years of this tender Molson's St Lawrence Steamboat Company had six more steamers running. In 1823 a towboat company was formed, and the *Hercules* towed the *Margaret* from Quebec to Montreal. The well-known word 'tug' was soon brought into use from England, where it originated from the fact that the first towboat in the world was called *The Tug*. In 1836, before the first steam railway train ran from La Prairie to St Johns, the Torrance Line, in opposition to the Molson Line, was running the *Canada*, which was then the largest and fastest steamer in the whole New World. Meanwhile steam navigation had been practised on the Great Lakes for twenty years; for in 1817 the little *Ontario* and the big *Frontenac* made their first trips from Kingston to York (now Toronto). The *Frontenac* was built at Finkles Point, Ernestown, eighteen miles from Kingston, by Henry Teabout, an American who had been employed in the shipyards of Sackett's Harbour at the time of the abortive British attack in 1813. She was about seven hundred tons, schooner rigged, engined by Boulton and Watt, and built at a total cost of $135,000. A local paper said that 'her proportions strike the eye very agreeably, and good judges have pronounced this to be the best piece of naval architecture of the kind yet produced in America.'

Canals and steamers naturally served each other's turn. There was a great deal of canal building in the twenties. The Lachine Canal, opening up direct communication west of Montreal, was dug out by 1825, the Welland, across the Niagara peninsula, by 1829, and the Rideau, near Ottawa, by 1832. A few very small canals had preceded these; others were to follow them; and they were themselves in their infancy of size and usefulness. But the beginning had been made.

The early Canadian steamers and canals did credit to a poor and thinly peopled country. But none of them ranked as a pioneering achievement in the world at large. This kind of achievement was reserved for the *Royal William*, a vessel of such distinction in the history of shipping that her career must be followed out in detail.

She was the first of all sea-going steamers, the first that ever crossed an ocean entirely under steam, and the first that ever fired a shot in action. But her claims and the spurious counter-claims against her must both be made quite clear. She was not the first steamer that ever put out to sea, for the Yankee *Phoenix* made the little coasting trip from Hoboken to Philadelphia in 1809. She was not the first steamer in Canadian salt water, for the *St John* crossed the Bay of Fundy in 1826. And she was not the first vessel with a steam engine that crossed an ocean, for the Yankee *Savannah* crossed from *Savannah* to Liverpool in 1819. The *Phoenix* and *St John* call for no explanation. The *Savannah* does, especially in view of the claims so freely made and allowed for her as being the first regular steamer to cross an ocean. To begin with, she was not a regular sea-going steamer with auxiliary sails like the *Royal William*, but a so-called clipper-built, full-rigged ship of three hundred tons with a small auxiliary engine and paddle-wheels made to be let down her sides when the wind failed. She did not even steam against head winds, but tacked. She took a month to make Liverpool, and she used steam for only eighty hours altogether. She could not, indeed, have done much more, because she carried only seventy-five tons of coal and twenty-five cords of wood, and she made port with plenty of fuel left. Her original log (the official record every vessel keeps) disproves the whole case mistakenly made out for her by some far too zealous advocates.

The claims of the *Royal William* are proved by ample contemporary evidence, as well as by the subsequent statements of her master, John M'Dougall, her builder, James Goudie, and John Henry, the Quebec founder who made some castings for her engines the year after they had been put into her at Montreal.

M'Dougall was a seaman of indomitable perseverance, as his famous voyage to England shows. Goudie, though only twenty-one, was a most capable naval architect, born in Canada and taught his profession in Scotland. His father was a naval architect before him and had built several British vessels on the Great Lakes for service against the Americans during the War of 1812. Both Goudie and Henry lived to retell their tale in 1891, when the Canadian government put up a tablet to commemorate what pioneering work the *Royal William* had done, both for the inter-colonial and inter-imperial connection.

The first stimulus to move the promoters of the *Royal William* was the subsidy of $12,000 offered by the government of Lower Canada in 1830 to the owners of any steamer over five hundred tons that would ply between Quebec and Halifax. Half this amount had been offered in 1825, but the inducement was not then sufficient. The Quebec and Halifax Navigation Company was formed by the leading merchants of Quebec joined with a few in Halifax. The latter included the three Cunard brothers, whose family name has been a household word in transatlantic shipping circles from that day to this. On September 2, 1830, Goudie laid the keel of the *Royal William* in the yard belonging to George Black, a shipbuilder, and his partner, John Saxton Campbell, formerly an officer in the 99th Foot, and at this time a merchant and shipowner in Quebec. The shipyard was situated at Cape Cove beside the St Lawrence, a mile above the citadel, and directly in line with the spot on which Wolfe breathed his last after the Battle of the Plains.

The launch took place on Friday afternoon, April 29, 1831. Even if all the people present had then foreknown the *Royal William*'s career they could not have done more to mark the occasion as one of truly national significance. The leaders among them certainly looked forward to some great results at home. Quebec was the capital of Lower Canada; and every Canadian statesman hoped that the new steamer would become a bond of union between the three different parts of the country—the old French province by the St Lawrence, the old British provinces down by the sea, and the new British province up by the Lakes.

The mayor of Quebec proclaimed a public holiday, which brought out such a concourse of shipwrights and other shipping experts as hardly any other city in the world could show.

Lord Aylmer was there as governor-general to represent King William IV, after whom the vessel was to be named the *Royal William* by Lady Aylmer. This was most appropriate, as the sailor king had been the first member of any royal house to set foot on Canadian soil, which he did at Quebec in 1787, as an officer in H.M.S. *Pegasus*. The guard and band from the 32nd Foot were drawn up near the slip. The gunners of the Royal Artillery were waiting to fire the salute from the new citadel, which, with the walls, was nearing completion, after the Imperial government had spent thirty-five million dollars in carrying out the plans approved by Wellington. Lady Aylmer took the bottle of wine, which was wreathed in a garland of flowers, and, throwing it against the bows, pronounced the historic formula: 'God bless the *Royal William* and all who sail in her.' Then, amid the crash of arms and music, the roaring of artillery, and the enthusiastic cheers of all the people, the stately vessel took the water, to begin a career the like of which no other Canadian vessel ever equalled before that time or since.

Her engines, which developed more than two hundred horse-power, were made by Bennett and Henderson in Montreal and sent to meet her a few miles below the city, as the vessel towing her up could not stem St Mary's Current. Her hull was that of a regular sea-going steamer, thoroughly fit to go foreign, and not the hull of an ordinary sailing ship, like the *Savannah*, with paddles hung over the sides in a calm. Goudie's master, Simmons of Greenock, had built four steamers to cross the Irish Sea; and Goudie probably followed his master's practice when he gave the *Royal William* two deep 'scoops' to receive the paddle-boxes nearer the bows than the stern. The tonnage by builder's measurement was 1370, though by net capacity of burden only 363. The length over all was 176 feet, on the keel 146. Including the paddle-boxes the breadth was 44 feet; and, as each box was 8 feet broad, there were 28 feet clear between them. The depth of hold was 17 feet 9 inches, the draught 14 feet. The rig was that of a three-masted topsail schooner. There were fifty passenger berths and a good saloon.

The three trips between Quebec and Halifax in 1831 were most successful. But 1832 was the year of the great cholera, especially in Quebec, and the *Royal William* was so harassed by quarantine that she had to be laid up there. The losses of that disastrous season decided her owners to sell out next spring for less than a third of her original cost. She was then degraded for a time into a local tug or sometimes an excursion boat. But presently she was sent down to Boston, where the band at Fort Independence played her in to the tune of 'God Save the King,' because she was the first of all steamers to enter a seaport of the United States under the Union Jack.

Ill luck pursued her new owners, who, on her return to Quebec, decided to send her to England for sale. She left Quebec on August 5, 1833, coaled at Pictou, which lies on the Gulf side of Nova Scotia, and took her departure from there on the 18th, for her epoch-making voyage, with the following most prosaic clearance: '*Royal William*, 363 tons. 36 men. John M'Dougall, master. Bound to London. British. Cargo: 254 chaldrons of coals [nearly 300 tons], a box of stuffed birds, and six spars, produce of this province. One box and one trunk, household furniture and a harp, all British, and seven passengers.' The fare was fixed at £20, 'not including wines.'

The voyage soon became eventful. Nearly three hundred tons of coal was a heavy concentrated cargo for the tremendous storm she encountered on the Grand Banks of Newfoundland.

She strained; her starboard engine was disabled; she began to leak; and the engineer came up to tell M'Dougall she was sinking. But M'Dougall held his course, started the pumps, and kept her under way for a week with only the port engine going. The whole passage from Pictou, counting the time she was detained at Cowes repairing boilers, took twenty-five days. M'Dougall, a sturdy Scotsman, native of Oban, must have been sorely tempted to 'put the kettle off the boil' and run her under sail. But either the port or starboard engine, or both, worked her the whole way over, and thus for ever established her claim to priority in transatlantic navigation under steam alone.

In London she was sold for £10,000, just twice what she had fetched at sheriff's sale in Quebec some months before. She was at once chartered, crew and all, by the Portuguese government, who declined to buy her for conversion into a man-of-war. In 1834, however, she did become a man-of-war, this time under the Spanish flag, though flying the broad Pennant of Commodore Henry, who was then commanding the British Auxiliary Steam Squadron against the Carlists in the north of Spain. Two years later, on May 5, 1836, under her Spanish name of *Isabella Se-*

gunda, she made another record. When the British Legion, under Sir de Lacy Evans, was attacking the Carlists in the bay of St Sebastian, she stood in towards the Carlist flank and thereupon fired the first shot that any steam man-of-war had ever fired in action.

Strangely enough, she cannot be said to have come to any definite end as an individual ship. She continued in the Spanish service till 1840, when she was sent to Bordeaux for repairs. The Spaniards, who are notorious slovens at keeping things shipshape, had allowed her to run down to bare rot after her Britisher-Canadian crew had left her. So the French bought her for a hulk and left her where she was. But the Spaniards took her engines out and put them into a new *Isabella Segunda*, which was wrecked in a storm on the Algerian coast in 1860.

Her career of record-making is well worth a general summary: the *Royal William* was the first steamer built to foster inter-colonial trade in Canada; the first Canadian steamer specially designed for work at sea; the first sea-going steamer to enter a port in the United States under the British flag; the first steam transport in Portugal; the first steam man-of-war in Spain; the first naval steamer that ever fired a shot in action; and the first vessel in the world that ever crossed an ocean under steam alone.

The next step in the history of Canadian steamers is not concerned with a ship but with a man. Sir Hugh Allan, who, though the greatest, was not the first of the pioneers. The Cunard brothers preceded the Allan brothers in establishing a transatlantic line. Samuel Cunard had been one of the shareholders in the *Royal William*. He had wonderful powers of organization. He knew the shipping trade as very few have ever known it; and his name has long since become historical in this connection. The first 'Cunarder' to arrive in Canada was the *Britannia*, 1154 tons, built on the Clyde, and engined there by Napier. From that time on till Confederation, that is, from 1840 to 1867, Cunarders ran from Liverpool to Halifax. But Halifax was always treated as a port of call. The American ports were the real destination. And after 1867 the Cunarders became practically an Anglo-American, not an Anglo-Canadian, line. During their connection with Canada, partially renewed in the present century, the Cunards never did anything really original. They were not among the first to make the change from wood to iron or from paddle-wheels to screws. But they did business honestly and well and always took care of their passengers' safety.

The Cunards were Canadians. Sir Hugh Allan was a Scotsman. But he and the line he founded are unchallengeably first in their services to Canada. Hugh Allan was born in 1810, the son of a Scottish master mariner who about that time was mate of a transport carrying supplies to the British Army in the Peninsular War. He arrived in Canada when he was only fifteen, entered the employ of a Montreal shipping firm when he came of age, and at forty-eight obtained complete control of it with his brother Andrew. From that day to this the Allan family have been the acknowledged leaders of Canadian transatlantic shipping.

Hugh Allan was a man of boundless energy, iron will, and consummate business ability. The political troubles of the Pacific Scandal in 1873 prevented him from anticipating the present Canadian Pacific Railway in making a single united service of trains and steamers to connect England with China and both with Canada. But what he did succeed in carrying through, against long odds, was quite enough for one distinguished business lifetime. He began by running a line of sailing craft between Montreal and the mother country in conjunction with his father's firm in Glasgow. Then, in 1853, he and his brother headed a company which ordered two iron screw steamers to be built in Scotland for the St Lawrence. The first of these, the *Canadian*, came out to Quebec on her maiden voyage in 1854; but both she and her sister ship were soon diverted to the Crimea, where high rates were being paid for transports during the war.

In 1858 the Allans contracted with the government for a weekly mail service and bought out all their partners, as they alone considered that the time had come for such a venture. The subsidy was doubled the next year to prevent the collapse of the service after a widespread financial panic. But heavy forfeits were imposed for lateness in delivering mails, an adverse factor in the greatest fight against misfortune ever known to Canadian shipping history. Within eight years the Allans lost as many vessels. In every case there was disastrous loss of property; in some, a total loss of everything—vessel, cargo, crew, and passengers.

No other firm has ever had to face such a storm of persistent adversity. But the indomitable Allans emerged triumphant; and by the time of Confederation, in 1867, the worst was over. Thenceforth they were first in all respects till very recently. In the introduction of shipbuilding improvements they are without a rival still. Their *Bavarian* was the first Atlantic liner entirely built of steel; their *Parisian* the first to be fitted with bilge keels; their *Virginian* and *Victorian* the first to use the turbine.

There are only two other salient features of Canadian steamer history that can be mentioned beside the *Royal William* and the Allans: the Richelieu and Ontario Navigation Company and the Canadian Pacific Railway's merchant fleet. True, neither of these comes into quite the same class. The *Royal William* occupies an absolutely unique position in the world at large. The Allans are more intimately connected with the history of Canadian shipping than any other family or firm. Both the *Royal William* and the Allans are landmarks. But the Richelieu and Ontario Navigation Company and the Canadian Pacific Railway Company have also shown abundant energy; turned to effective national account.

The Richelieu Steamboat Company was formed in 1845, and took its other title thirty years later, when it made its first great 'merger.' It began in a very humble way, by running two little market boats between Sorel and Montreal. From the first it had to fight for its commercial life. The train was beginning to be a formidable competitor. But the fight to a finish was the fight of boat against boat. Fares were cut and cut again. At last the passengers were offered bed, board, and transportation for the price of a single meal. Every day there was a desperate race on the water.

The rival steamers shook and panted in their self-destroying zeal to be the first to get the gangway down. Clouds of fire-streaked smoke poured from their funnels. More than once a cargo that would burn well was thrown into the furnaces to keep the steam up. The public became quite as keen as any of the crews or companies, and worked excitement up to fever pitch by crowding the wharves to gamble madly on this daily river Derby. The stress was too much for the weaker companies. One by one they either fell out or 'merged in.' After the merger with the Ontario Company in 1875 things went on, with many ups and downs, more in the usual way of competition. Finally, in 1913, a general 'pooling merger' was effected by which practically all Canadian lines came under one control, from the lower Great Lakes, down the St Lawrence, through the Gulf, and south away to the West Indies. The title of this new merger is the Canada Steamship Lines Limited. The Canadian Pacific Railway Company has half a dozen different fleets at work: one on the Atlantic, another as a trans-Pacific line, a third on the Pacific coast, a fourth on the lakes of British Columbia, a fifth on the upper Great Lakes, and a sixth as ferries for its trains. Thus, by taking the upper Great Lakes and the West, it divides the trans-Canadian waters with the Canada Steamship Lines, which latter take the lower Great Lakes and the East. A company whose annual receipts and expenditure are balanced at not far short of two hundred millions of dollars might well seem to be all-important in every way, especially when its shipping tonnage exceeds that of the Allans by over thirty thousand. But this Chronicle is a history of at least four hundred years; while the famous 'C.P.R.' has not as yet been either forty years a railway line or twenty years a shipping firm. There is only one great C.P.R. disaster to record. But that is of appalling magnitude. Over a thousand lives were lost when the Norwegian collier *Storstad* sank the *Empress of Ireland* off Rimouski in 1914.

The five principal features of Canadian steamship history have now been pointed out: John Molson's pioneer boats, the *Royal William*, the Allan line, the 'R. and O.' (now the Canada Steamship Lines), and the 'C.P.R.' No other individual feature has any noteworthy Canadian peculiarities. Nor does the general evolution of steam navigation in or around Canada differ notably, in other respects, from the same evolution elsewhere. Steamers have adapted themselves to circumstances in Canada very much as they have in other countries, pushing their persistent way step by step into all the navigable waters, fresh or salt. The Canadian waters, especially the fresh waters, certainly have some marked characteristics of their own, but the steamers have acquired no special character in consequence.

Both Canadian and visiting steamers have always had their duplicates on many other oceans, lakes, and rivers. There is the ubiquitous tug; stubby, noisy, self-assertive, small; but, in its several varieties, the handiest all-round little craft afloat. It is worth noting that in the special class of sea tugs the Dutch, and not the British, are easily first: a curious exception to the general rule of British supremacy at sea. Then, with many variations and several intermediate types, there are the two main distinctive kinds of inland vessels: the long, low, grimy, cargo-carrying whale-back, tankship, barge, or other useful form of ugliness, simply meant to nose her way through quite safe waters with the utmost bulk her huge stuffed maw will hold; and, at the opposite end of the scale, the high, white, gaily decorated 'palace' steamer, with tier upon tier of decks, and a strong suggestion of the theatre all through. Sea-going craft show the same variations within a given type and the same intermediate types between the two ends of the scale. But the general distinction is quite as well marked, though the necessity for seaworthy hulls brings about a closer resemblance along the water-line. There is the cargo boat, long, comparatively low, and rather dingy; with derricks and vast holds, which remind one of the tentacles and stomach of an octopus. The opposite extreme is the great passenger liner, much larger and more shapely in the hull; but best distinguished, at any distance, by her towering, white, superstructural decks, with their clean-run symmetry fore and aft.

The 'Britisher' is the predominant type in Canadian waters. This is natural enough, considering that the British Isles build nearly all 'Britishers,' most 'Canadians,' and many foreigners, and that the tonnage actually under construction there in 1913 exceeded the total tonnage owned by any other country except Germany and the United States, while it greatly exceeded the total tonnage under construction in all other countries of the world put together, including Germany and the United States. The British practice is naturally the prevailing one both in shipbuilding and marine engineering. But there is a general conformity to certain leading ideas everywhere. The engine is passing out of the stage in which the fuel-made steam worked machinery, which, in its turn, worked propellers; and passing into the stage in which the latent forces of the fuel itself are brought to bear more directly on propellers, that is to say, into the stage of internal combustion engines and the turbine-driven screw. The hull has changed more and more in its proportions between length and breadth since the supplanting of wood by steel.

Instead of a length equal at most to five beams there are lengths of more than ten beams now. This means a radical change in framing. The old wooden vessel, as we have seen, had a frame looking like the skeleton of a man's body, with the keel for a backbone and multitudinous ribs at right angles to it. But the new steel vessel, especially if built on the excellent Isherwood principle, looks entirely different. The transverse ribs are there, of course, but in a modified form. They do not catch the eye, which now, instead of being drawn from side to side, is led along from end to end by what looks like, and really is, a complete ribbing of internal keels. The whole system has, in fact, been changed from the transverse to the longitudinal.

The subject is well worth pursuing for its own sake. But the modern developments of naval architecture and waterborne trade which Canada shares with the rest of the world do not concern us any further here.

CHAPTER NINE
FISHERIES

The fisheries of Canada are the most important in the world. True as this statement is, it needs some explanation. In the first place, Newfoundland is included, in accordance with its inclusion under all other headings in this book. Then, all the wholly or partly unexploited waters are taken into consideration, including Hudson Bay and the Arctic ocean. And, thirdly, the catch made by foreigners in all waters neighbouring the Canadian coasts is not left out. Thus the Canadian fisheries are held to mean all the fisheries, fresh and salt, in or nearest to the whole of British North America. This is a perfectly fair basis to start from. It is, indeed, the fairest basis that can be found, as it affords a fixed territorial standard of comparison with other countries; and standards of comparison are particularly hard to fix in regard to fishing. French and Americans fish round Newfoundland, in waters closely neighbouring British territory and far removed from their own; and the fishing fleets of the British Isles work grounds as far asunder as the White Sea is from Africa. Yet all their catches figure in official reports as being French, American, or British. And so they legally are, if the men who make them observe the three-mile open-water distance-limit fixed by international agreement as the proper territorial boundary of government control. Beyond three miles from shore all 'nationals' are on an equal footing.

Now, taking the word Canadian in the sense just defined, it is safe to say that Canadian waters contain a greater quantity of the principal food fishes than those of any other country. The truth of this statement depends on three facts. The first is that practically all fish landed in Canada are caught in Canadian waters. This is a marked contrast to what happens in the other great fishing countries, like the United States, the British islands, Germany, Norway, and France, all of which send some of their fleets very far afield. The second fact is the statistics of totals caught. Canada at present catches fifty million dollars' worth of fish from her own waters in a single year. The 'Britisher' and 'Yankee' totals each exceed this, though not by much. But the Yankee total includes a good deal, and the Britisher total a very great deal, caught far outside their own waters. No other country is even worthy of comparison with these. The third fact is that the Canadian total, already advancing more rapidly than any other total, must continue to advance more rapidly still, because Canada has the greatest area of unexploited fish-bearing waters in the world.

If the amount caught per head of the total population is made the standard of comparison, then the Canadian catch is more than five times greater than the Britishers', and more than ten times greater than the Yankees'. And if, still keeping to this standard, the comparison is made between totals caught in strictly territorial waters, Canada surpasses both Britishers and Yankees, put together, ten times over.

There are nearly 120,000 fishermen in Canada and Newfoundland. The proportion in Newfoundland is, of course, by far the higher of the two. About 60,000 people are engaged in handling fish ashore, and many thousands more are concerned in trading with fish products. One way and another, the livelihood of at least one Canadian in every fifteen, and one Newfoundlander in every two, is entirely dependent on fishing. Statistics are apt to become bewildering unless carefully marshalled in tabular form. But one or two items might be added. There is a fishing craft of some kind, however small most of them are, to every single family in Newfoundland, a proportion immeasurably higher than in any other country in the world. But even more astonishing is the statistical fact that the fishermen of all nations in Newfoundland waters catch each year nearly 1000 cod-fish for every single individual person there is in the whole population of the island. After this, numbers seem rather to weaken than strengthen the argument. But it is worth mentioning that there are nearly 80,000 local fishing boats of all sorts actually counted by the governments of Canada and Newfoundland, from little rowboats up to full-powered steamers of considerable tonnage; that nearly a quarter of the whole number in 1913 already had gasoline or other motors; that the total length of all the Canadian and Newfoundland coastlines is nearly equal to that of the equator; that, excluding all parts of the Great Lakes within the American sphere of influence, the fresh-water fishing area of Canada exceeds the total area of the British Isles by more than 100,000 square miles; and, finally, that the mere increase of value in the fisheries of the single province of British Columbia, within a single year, has exceeded the value of the total catch marketed in several of the smaller states of Europe and America.

The two principal salt-water craft that have a history behind them and a sphere of active usefulness today are the schooner and its tender, the little dory. A schooner is a fore-and-aft-rigged vessel with at least two masts and four sails—mainsail, foresail, jib, and the staysail generally called a wind-bag. The schooner rig makes the handiest all-round vessel known. It can be managed by fewer hands in proportion to its tonnage than any other, and its sails do the greatest amount of work under the most varied conditions. Other rigs may beat it on special points; but the general sum of all the sailing virtues is decidedly its own. It takes you more nearly into a head wind than most others, and scuds before a lubber's wind dead aft with a maximum of canvas spread out 'wing-and-wing'—one big sail to port and the other out to starboard.

The dory is a two-man rowboat which possesses as many of the different, and sometimes contradictory, good points of the canoe, skiff, punt, and lifeboat as it is possible to combine in a single craft. It can be rowed, sculled, sailed, or driven by a motor. It is the first aquatic plaything for the boys, and often the last salvation for the men. The way it will ride out a storm that makes a liner labour and sinks any ill-found vessel like a stone is little short of marvellous. It has a flattish bottom, sheering up at both ends, which are high in the gunwale. The flat stern, which looks like a narrow wedge with the point cut off, is a good deal more waterborne than the bow and rises more readily to the seas without presenting too much resisting surface to either wind or wave. Each schooner has several dories, which fish all round it, thus suggesting what is often called the hen-and-chickens style. At dark, or when the catch has filled the dory, the men come back on board, 'nesting' half a dozen dories, one inside the other. But sometimes a sudden storm, especially if it follows fog, will set the chickens straying; and then the men must ride it out moored to some sort of drogue or floating anchor. The usual drogue is a trawl tub, quite perfect if filled with oil-soaked cotton waste to make a 'slick' which keeps the crests from breaking. The tub is hove into the water, over the stern, to which it is made fast by a bit of line long enough to give the proper scope. And there, with the live ballast of two expert men, whose home has always been the water, the dory will thread its perilous way unharmed through spume and spindrift, across the engulfing valleys and over the riven hill-tops of the sea.

These schooners and their attendant dories have a long and stirring history of their own. But they are not the only craft, nor yet the oldest; and though their history would easily fill a volume twice the size of this, it would only tell us a very little about Canadian fisheries as a whole, from first to last. Even if we went back by hasty steps, of quite a century each, we should never get into the wild days of the early 'fishing admirals' before our space gave out. All we can do here is simply to mention the steps themselves, and then pass on. First, the red men, few in number, and fishing from canoes. Then the early whites, dispossessing the red men and steadily increasing. They came from all seafaring peoples, and had no other form of justice than what could be enforced by 'fishing admirals,' who won their rank by the order of their arrival on the Banks—admiral first, vice-admiral second, rear-admiral third. Then government by men-of-war began, and Newfoundland itself became, officially, a man-of-war, under its own captain from the Royal Navy. Finally, civil self-government followed in the usual way.

All through there was a constantly growing and apparently inextricable entanglement of international complications, which were only settled by The Hague agreement in the present century. And only within almost as recent times has what may be called the natural history of Canadian fisheries begun to follow the inevitable trend of evolution which gradually changes the civilized fisherman from a hunter into a farmer. As man increases in number, and his means of hunting down game increase still faster, a time inevitably comes when he disturbs the balance of nature to such an extent that he must either exterminate his prey or begin to 'farm' it, that is, begin to breed and protect as well as kill it. Fisheries are no exception to this rule; and what with close seasons, prohibitions, hatcheries, and other means of keeping up the supply of fish, the fishing population is beginning, though only to a very small extent as yet, to make the change. Some day we shall talk of our pedigree cod, but the men of this generation will not live to see it.

The change is beneficial for the mere mouths there are to fill. But it means less and less demand for those glorious and most inspiring qualities of courage, strength, and bodily skill which are required by all who pit themselves against Nature in her wildest and most dangerous moods. The fisherman and sealer have only the elements to fight; though this too often means a fight for life. A hundred men were frozen to death on the ice, and two hundred more were drowned in the Gulf, during the great spring seal hunt blizzard of 1914. Whalemen still occasionally fight for their lives against their prey as well. And all three kinds of deep-sea fishery have bred so many simple-minded heroes that only cowards attract particular attention.

No modern reader needs reminding that whales are not fish but mammals, belonging to the same order of the animal kingdom as monkeys, dogs, and men. They include the most gigantic of all creatures, living or extinct. The enormous 'right' whales of the story-books have been driven far north in greatly diminished numbers. The equally famous sperm whales have always been very rare, as they prefer southern waters. But the 'finners,' which are still fairly common, include the 'sulphurs,' among which there have been specimens far exceeding any authentic sperms or 'rights.' Even the humpbacks and common finbacks, both well known in Canadian waters, occasionally surpass the average size of sperms and 'rights.' But the sulphur is probably the only kind of whale which sometimes grows to a hundred feet and more.

Whaling is done in three different ways: from canoes, from boats sent off by sailing ships, and from steamers direct. The Indians whaled from canoes before the white man came, and a few Indians, Eskimos, and French Canadians are whaling from canoes today. Eskimos sometimes attack a large whale in a single canoe, but oftener with a regular flotilla of kayaks, and worry it to death; as the Indians once did with bark canoes in the Gulf and lower St Lawrence. Modern canoe whaling is done from a North-Shore wooden canoe of considerable size and weight with a crew of two men. It is now chiefly carried on by a few French Canadians living along the north shore of the lower St Lawrence. It is not called whaling but porpoise-hunting, from the mistaken idea that the little white whale is a porpoise, instead of the smallest kind of whale, running up to over twenty feet in length. It is dangerous work at best, and a good many men are drowned. As a rule they are very skilful, and they nearly always jab carefully while sitting down. Sometimes, however, the rare occasion serves the rare harpooner, when the whale and canoe appear as if about to meet each other straight head-on. Then, in a flash, the man in the bow is up on his feet, with the harpoon so poised that the rocking water, the mettlesome canoe, and his watchful comrade in the stern, all form part of the concentrated energy with which he brings his every faculty to a single point of instantaneous action. There, for one fateful moment, he stands erect, his whole tense body like the full-drawn bow before it speeds the arrow home. He throws: and then, for some desperate minutes, it is often a fight to a finish between the whale's life and his own.

The old wooden whaling vessel under mast and sail is almost extinct. But it had a long and splendid career. The Basques, who were then the models for the world, began in the Gulf before Jacques Cartier came; and worked the St Lawrence with wonderful success as high as the basin of Quebec. The French never whaled in Canada; but the 'Bluenose' Nova Scotians did, and held their own against all comers. 'A dead whale or a stove boat' was the motto for every man who joined the chase. Discipline was stern; and rightly so. A green hand was allowed one show of funk; but that was all. However, there was very little funking so long as Britishers, Bluenoses, and Yankees could pick their crews from among the most adventurous of their own populations.

Hardly had the long-drawn clarion call of the look-out's *B—l—o—w!* sounded aloft than the boats were lowered from the davits and began pulling away towards the likeliest spot for a rise. Two barbed harpoons, always known as 'irons,' were carried on the same line, always called the 'warp.' It both could be used, so much the better, especially as they were some distance apart on the warp, the bight of which formed a considerable drag in the water. Other drags, usually called 'drugs,' were bits of wood made fast thwart-wise on the warp, so as to increase the pull on a sounding whale. The coiling and management of the warp was of the utmost importance. Many a man has gone to Davy Jones with a strangling loop of rope around him. Everything, of course, had to be made shipshape in advance, as there was no time for finishing touches once the cry of *Blow!* was raised. And if there was haste at all times, what was there not when fleets of whalers under different flags were together in the same waters?

The approach, often made by changing the oars for silent paddles; the strike; the flying whale; the snaking, streaking, zipping line; the furious tow, with the boat almost leaping from crest to crest; the long haul in on the gradually slackening warp; the lancing and the dying flurry, were all exciting enough by themselves. And when a whale showed fight, charged home, and smashed a boat to splinters, it took a smart crew to escape and get rescued in time. A Greenland whale once took fifteen harpoons, drew out six miles of line, and carried down a boat with all hands drowned before it was killed. Old sperms that had once escaped without being badly hurt were always ready to fight again. One fighting whale took down the bow oarsman in its mouth, drowned the next two, and sent the rest flying with a single snap of its jaws. Another fought nine hours, took five harpoons and seven bombs, smashed up three boats, and sank dead—a total loss. A third, after smashing a boat, charged the ship and stove her side so badly that she sank within five minutes.

Yet accidents like these only spurred the whalemen on to greater efforts, not of mere bravado, but of daring skill. Perhaps the most wonderful regular feat of all was 'spading,' which meant slewing the boat close in, as the whale was about to sound, and cutting the tendons of its tremendous death-dealing tail by a slicing blow from the two-handed razor-edged 'spade.' Perhaps the most wonderful of all exceptional escapes was that of a boat which was towed by one whale right over the back of another. And perhaps the most exciting finish to any international race was the one in which the Yankee, who came up second, got 'first iron' by 'pitchpoling' clear over the intervening British boat, whose crew were nearly drowned by this 'slick' Yankee's flying warp.

No wonder old whalemen despise the easier and safer methods of steam whaling practised by the Norwegians in Canadian and other waters at the present day. And yet steam whaling is not without some thrilling risks. The steamers are speedy, handy, small, about one hundred tons or so, with the latest pattern of the explosive harpoon gun originally invented by Sven Foyn in 1880. The range is very short, rarely over fifty yards. The harpoon may be compared to the stick of an umbrella, with four ribs that open when the bomb in the handle explodes inside the whale, which it thus anchors to the steamer. The whole steamer then plays the whale as an angler plays a fish, letting out line—sometimes two miles of it—towing with stopped engines at first, and then winding in while giving quarter, half, and three-quarter speed astern, as the steamer gains on the whale. Even a steamer, however, has been charged, stove, and sunk. And a fighting humpback in the Gulf of St Lawrence is no easy game to tackle with a hand-lance in a pram. Norwegians are thrifty folk, and bomb harpooning is expensive. So when the whale and steamer meet, at the end of the chase, a tiny pram is launched with two men rowing and a third standing up in the stern to wield the fifteen-foot lance. As the humpback's flippers are also fifteen feet long, and as they thrash about with blows that have sunk several prams and killed more than one crew, it still requires the fittest nerves and muscles to give the final stroke.

But whaling, in this and every other form, is bound to come to an untimely end very soon unless the whales are protected by international game laws rigidly enforced. At present the only protection is the exhaustion of a whaling ground below a paying yield; when whaling stops till the whales breed back. But soon they won't breed back at all. Modern steam whaling spares no kind of whale in any kind of sea. It has one good point. It is more humane, as a rule. But the odds against the whale are simply annihilating. And the extermination of whales, those magnificent leviathans of the mighty deep, would be a loss from every point of view. Their own commercial value counts for a good deal. Their value to the fisherman by driving bait inshore counts for a good deal more. And their admirable place in nature counts for most of all. Like elephants, lions, and deer, like birds of paradise and eagles, the whales are among those noblest forms of life, without whose glorious strength and beauty this world would be a poorer, tamer, meaner place for proper men to live in.

CHAPTER TEN
ADMINISTRATION

Administration is used here for want of a better general term to cover every form of management that is done ashore, as well as every form of what might be called, by analogy with fleets and armies, non-combatant work afloat. It falls into two natural divisions: the first includes all private management, the second all that concerns the government. Here, even more than in the other chapters, we are face to face with such complex and enormous interests that we can only take the merest glance at what those interests principally are.

The privately managed interests have both their business and their philanthropic sides. Let us take the philanthropic first. Seamen's Institutes have grown from very small beginnings, and are now to be found in every port where English-speaking seamen congregate. They began when, as the saying was, the sailor earnt his money like a horse and spent it like an ass. They flourish when the sailor is much better able to look after himself. But their help is needed still; and what they have done in the past has not been the least among the influences which have made the common lot of the seaman so very much better than it was. Another excellent influence is that of the Royal National Mission to Deep Sea Fishermen. This mission sends its missioners afloat in its own steamers to tend the sick and bring some of the amenities of shore life within the reach of those afloat. Religion is among its influences, but only in an unsectarian way. Its work in Canadian waters is directed by two able and self-sacrificing men: Dr Grenfell, whose base is at St Anthony's in North-East Newfoundland, and whose beat goes straight down north along the Newfoundland Labrador, which faces the Atlantic; and Dr Hare, whose base is Harrington, in the centre of the Canadian Labrador, which runs in from the Strait of Belle Isle to Natashquan, more than two hundred miles along the north shore of the Gulf, among a perfect labyrinth of islands.

Next, the business side. As only a single instance can be given, and as ordinary business management in shipping circles more or less resembles what is practiced in other commercial affairs, the special factor of marine insurance will alone be taken, as being the most typically maritime and by far the most interesting historically. Ordinary insurance on land is a mere thing of yesterday compared with marine insurance, which, according to some, began in the ancient world, and which was certainly known in the Middle Ages. It is credibly reported to have been in vogue among the Lombards in the twelfth century, and on much the same principles as are followed by Canadians in the twentieth. It was certainly in vogue among the English before Jacques Cartier discovered the St Lawrence. And in 1613, the year Champlain discovered the site of Ottawa, a policy was taken out, in the ordinary course of business, on that famous old London merchantman, the *Tiger*, to which Shakespeare twice alludes, once in *Macbeth* and again in *Twelfth Night*.

Modern practice is based on the Imperial Marine Insurance Act of 1906, which is a development of the Act of 1795, which, in its turn, was a codification of the rules adopted at Lloyd's in 1779. Nothing shows more unmistakably how supreme the British are in every affair of the sea than these striking facts: that 'A1 at Lloyd's' is an expression accepted all the world over as a guarantee of prime efficiency, that nearly every shipping country in the world has its own imitation of Lloyd's, nearly always including the name of Lloyd, and that the original Lloyd's at the Royal Exchange in London is still unassailably first. Most people know that Lloyd's originated from the marine underwriters who used to meet for both business and entertainment at Lloyd's coffee-house in the seventeenth century. But comparatively few seem to know that Lloyd's, like most of its imitators, is not a gigantic insurance company, but an association of carefully selected members, who agree to carry on their completely independent business affairs in daily touch with each other. Lloyd's' method differs from that of ordinary insurance in being conducted by 'underwriters,' each one of whom can write his name under any given risk for any reasonable part of the whole. Thus, instead of insuring a million with a company or a single man, the owner lays his case before Lloyd's, whereupon any members who choose to do so can sign for whatever proportion they intend to assume. In this way individual losses are spread among a considerable number of underwriters. Long experience has proved that the individual and associated methods of doing business have nowhere been more happily combined than they are at Lloyd's today, and that this special form of combination suits both parties in a shipping risk better than any other known.

Canadian shipping has often resented Lloyd's high rates against the St Lawrence route, and threatened to establish a Lloyd's of its own. Yet, on the whole, the original Lloyd's is the fairest, the soundest, and incomparably the most expert association of its kind the world has ever seen.

Business administration in marine affairs is complex enough. Lloyd's alone is not the subject of one text-book, nor of several, but of a regular and constantly increasing library. What, then, can usefully be said in a very few words about the still more complex affairs of government administration? The bare enumeration of the duties performed by a single branch of the department of Marine and Fisheries in Canada will give some faint idea of what the whole department does. There are Naval, Fisheries, and Marine branches, each with sub-branches of its own. Among the duties of the Marine branch are the following: the construction of lighthouses and fog-alarms, the maintenance of lights and buoys, the building and maintenance of Dominion steamers, the consideration of all aids to navigation, the maintenance of the St Lawrence ship channel, the weather reports and forecasts, investigations into wrecks, steamboat inspection, cattle-ship inspection, marine hospitals, submarine signals, the carrying out of the Merchant Shipping Act and other laws, humane service, subsidies to wrecking plant, winter navigation, removal of obstructions, examinations for masters' and mates' certificates, control of pilots, government of ports and harbours, navigation of Hudson Bay and northern waters generally, port wardens, wreck receivers, and harbour commissioners.

Besides all this there are, in the work of the department, items like the Dominion registry of more than eight thousand vessels, the administration of the enormous fisheries, and the hydrographic survey. Then, quite distinct from all these Canadian government activities, is the British consular service, maintained by the Imperial government alone, but available for every British subject. And round everything, afloat and ashore, supporting, protecting, guaranteeing all, stands the oldest, most glorious, and still the best of all the navies in the world—the Royal Navy of the motherland.

This is only a glance at the conditions of the present; while each Imperial and Canadian service, department, branch, and sub-division has a long, romantic, and most important history of its own. The lighthouse service alone could supply hero-tales enough to fill a book. The weather service is full of absorbing interest. And, what with wireless telegraphy, submarine bells, direction indicators, micro-thermometers as detectors of ice, and many other new appliances, the whole practice of navigation is becoming an equally interesting subject for a book filled with the 'fairy tales of science.' Even hydrography—that is, the surveying and mapping (or 'charting') of the water—has an appealing interest, to say nothing of its long and varied history. Jacques Cartier, though he made no charts, may be truly called the first Canadian hydrographer; for his sailing directions are admirably clear and correct. In the next century we find Champlain noting the peculiarities of the Laurentian waters to good effect; while in the next again, the eighteenth, we come upon the famous Captain Cook, one of the greatest hydrographers of all time. Cook was at Quebec with Wolfe, and afterwards spent several years in making a wonderfully accurate survey of the St Lawrence and Gulf. His pupil, Vancouver, after whom both a city and an island have been named, did his work on the Pacific coast equally well. The principal hydrographer of the nineteenth century was Admiral Bayfield, who extended the survey over the

Great Lakes, besides re-surveying all the older navigational waters with such perfect skill that wherever nature has not made any change his work stands today, reliable as ever. And it should be noted that all the successful official surveys, up to the present century, were made by naval officers—another little known and less remembered service done for Canada by the British guardians of the sea.

CHAPTER ELEVEN
NAVIES

This is not the place to discuss the naval side of craft and waterways in Canada. That requires a book of its own. But no study of Canada's maritime interests, however short, can close without a passing reference to her naval history.

When the Kirkes, with their tiny flotilla, took Quebec from Champlain's tiny garrison in 1629 the great guiding principles of sea-power were as much at work as when Phips led his American colonists to defeat against Frontenac in 1690, or as when Saunders and Wolfe led the admirably united forces of their enormous fleet and little army to victory in 1759. In the same way the decisive influence of sea-power was triumphantly exerted by Iberville, the French naval hero of Canada, when, with his single ship, the *Pélican*, he defeated his three British opponents in a gallant fight; and so, for the time being, won the absolute command of Hudson Bay in 1697. Again, it was naval rather than political and military forces that made American independence an accomplished fact. The opposition to the war in England counted for a good deal; and the French and American armies for still more. But the really decisive anti-British force consisted of practically all the foreign navies in the world, some—like the French, Spanish, Dutch, and the Americans' own—taking an active part in the war, while the others were kept ready in reserve by the hostile armed neutrality of Russia, Sweden, Denmark, Prussia, and the smaller sea-coast states of Germany. Once again, in the War of 1812, it was the two annihilating American naval victories on Lakes Erie and Champlain that turned the scale far enough back to offset the preponderant British military victories along the Canadian frontier and prevent the advance of that frontier beyond Detroit and into the state of Maine.

There were very few people in 1910 who remembered that the Canadian navy then begun was the third local force of its kind in Canada, though the first to be wholly paid and managed locally. From the launch of La Salle's *Griffon* in 1679 down to the Cession in 1763 there was always some sort of French naval force built, manned, and managed in New France, though ultimately paid and directed from royal headquarters in Paris through the minister of Marine and Colonies. It is significant that 'marine' and 'colonies' were made a single government department throughout the French régime. The change of rule did not entail the abolition of local forces; and from 1755, when a British flotilla of six little vessels was launched on Lake Ontario, down to and beyond the peace with the United States sixty years later, there was what soon became a 'Provincial Marine,' which did good service against the Americans in 1776, when it was largely manned from the Royal Navy, and less good service in 1812, when it was a great deal more local in every way. Two vestiges of those days linger on to the present time, the first in the Canadian Militia Act, which provides for a naval as well as a military militia, permanent forces included, and the second in one of the governor-general's official titles—'Vice-Admiral' of Canada.

The Canadian privateers are even less known than the Provincial Marine. Yet they did a good deal of preying on the enemy at different times, and they amounted altogether to a total which will probably surprise most students of Canadian history. At Halifax alone eighteen Nova Scotian privateers took out letters of marque against the French between 1756 and 1760, twelve more against the French between 1800 and 1805, and no less than forty-four against the Americans during the War of 1812.

The century of peace which followed this war gradually came to be taken so much as a matter of course that Canadians forgot the lessons of the past and ignored the portents of the future. The very supremacy of a navy which protected them for nothing made them forget that without its guardian ships they could not have reached their Canadian nationality at all. Occasionally a threatened crisis would bring home to them some more intimate appreciation of British sea-power. But, for the rest, they took the Navy like the rising and the setting of the sun.

The twentieth century opened on a rapidly changing naval world. British supremacy was no longer to go unchallenged, at least so far as preparation went. The German Emperor followed up his pronouncement, 'Our future is on the sea,' by vigorous action. For the first time in history a German navy became a powerful force, fit to lead, rather than to follow, its Austrian and Italian allies. Also for the first time in history the New World developed a sea-power of first-class importance in the navy of the United States. And, again for the first time in history, the immemorial East produced a navy which annihilated the fleet of a European world-power when Japan beat Russia at Tsu-shima in the centennial year of Nelson at Trafalgar.

These portentous changes finally roused the oversea dominions of the British Empire to some sense of the value of that navy which had been protecting them so efficiently and so long at the mother country's sole expense. But the dawn of naval truth broke slowly and, following the sun, went round from east to west. First it reached New Zealand, then Australia, then South Africa, and then, a long way last, Canada; though Canada was the oldest, the largest, the most highly favoured in population and resources, the richest, and the most expensively protected of them all.

There was a searching of hearts and a gradual comprehension of first principles. Colonies which had been living the sheltered life for generations began to see that their immunity from attack was not due to any warlike virtue of their own, much less to any of their 'victories of peace,' but simply to the fact that the British Navy represented the survival of the fittest in a previous struggle for existence. More than two centuries of repeated struggle, from the Armada in 1588 to Trafalgar in 1805, had given the British Empire a century of armed peace all round the Seven Seas, and its colonies a century's start ahead of every rival. But in 1905 the possible rivals were beginning to draw up once more, thanks to the age-long naval peace; and the launch of her first modern Dreadnought showed that the mother country felt the need of putting forth her strength again to meet a world of new competitors.

The critical question now was whether or not the oversea dominions would do their proper share. They had grown, under free naval protection, into strong commercial nations, with combined populations equal to nearly a third of that in the mother country, and combined revenues exceeding a third of hers. They had a free choice. Canada, for instance, might have declared herself independent, though she could not have made herself more free, and would certainly not have been able to maintain a position of complete independence in any serious crisis. Or she could have destroyed her individual Canadian characteristics by joining the United States; though in this case she would have been obliged to pay her share towards keeping up a navy which was far smaller than the British and much more costly in proportion. As another alternative she could have said that her postal and customs preferences in favour of the mother country, taken in conjunction with what she paid for her militia, were enough. This would have put her far behind New Zealand and Australia, both of whom were doing much more, in proportion to their wealth and population.

There was a very natural curiosity to see what Canada would do, because she was much the senior of the other dominions, while in size, wealth, and population she practically equalled all three of them together. But whatever the expectations were, they were doomed to disappointment, for, while she was last in starting, she did not reach any decisive result at all. Australia, New Zealand—and even South Africa, so lately the scene of a devastating war—each gave money, while Canada gave none. New Zealand, with only one-seventh of Canada's population, gave a Dreadnought, while Canada gave none. Australia had a battle-worthy squadron of her own—but Canada had nothing but a mere flotilla.

The explanation of this strange discrepancy is to be found, partly, in geographical position. The geographical position of Canada differs widely from that of any other dominion. She lives beside the United States, a country with a population ten times greater than her own, a country, moreover, which holds the Monroe Doctrine as an article of faith in foreign policy. This famous doctrine simply means that the United States is determined to be the predominant power in the whole New World and to prevent any outside power from gaining a foothold there. Consequently the United States must defend, if necessary, any weaker nation in America whenever it is attacked by any stronger nation from outside. Of course the United States would exert its power only on its own terms, to which any weaker friend would be obliged to submit. But so long as there was no immediate danger that the public could actually feel, the Monroe Doctrine provided a very handy argument for all those who preferred to do nothing. Another peculiarity of Canada's position is that she is far enough away from the great powers of Europe and from the black and yellow races of Africa and Asia to prevent her from realizing so quickly as the mother country the danger from the first, or so quickly as her sister dominions the danger from the second.

For five successive years, from 1909 to 1913, the naval policy of Canada was the subject of debate in parliament, press, and public meetings. In 1909 the building programme for the German navy brought on a debate in the Imperial parliament which found an echo throughout the Empire. The Canadian parliament then passed a loyal resolution with the consent of both parties. In 1910 these parties began to differ. The Liberals, who were then in power, started a distinctively Canadian navy on a very small scale. In 1911 naval policy was, for the first time, one of the vexed questions in a general election. In 1912 the new Conservative government passed through the House of Commons an act authorizing an appropriation of thirty-five million dollars for three first-class Dreadnought battleships. This happened to be the exact sum paid by the Imperial government for the fortification of Quebec in 1832, and considerably less than one-thirtieth part of what the Imperial government had paid for the naval and military protection of Canada during the British régime. The Senate reversed the decision of the Commons in 1913, with the result that Canada's total naval contribution up to date consisted of five years' discussion and a little three-year-old navy which had far less than half the fighting power of New Zealand's single Dreadnought.

The two great parliamentary parties agreed on the general proposition that Canada ought to do something for her own defence at sea, and that, within the British Empire, she enjoyed naval advantages which were unobtainable elsewhere. But they differed radically on the vexed question of ways and means. The Conservatives said there was a naval emergency and proposed to give three Dreadnoughts to the Imperial government on certain conditions. The principal condition was that Canada could take them back at any time if she wished to use them for a navy of her own. The Liberals objected that there was no naval emergency, and that it was wrong to let any force of any kind pass out of the control of the Canadian government. Nothing, of course, could be done without the consent of parliament; and the consent of parliament means the consent of both Houses, the Senate and the Commons of Canada. There was a Conservative majority in the Commons and a Liberal majority in the Senate. The voting went by parties, and a complete deadlock ensued.

PART II
THE RAILWAY BUILDERS: A CHRONICLE OF OVERLAND HIGHWAYS

BY OSCAR D. SKELTON

CHAPTER ONE
THE COMING OF THE RAILWAY

On the morning of October 6, 1829, there began at Rainhill, in England, a contest without parallel in either sport or industry. There were four entries :

Braithwaite and Ericsson's *Novelty.*
Timothy Hackworth's *Sans-pareil.*
Stephenson and Booth's *Rocket.*
Burstall's *Perseverance.*

These were neither race-horses nor stagecoaches, but rival types of the newly invented steam locomotive. To win the £500 prize offered, the successful engine, if weighing six tons, must be able to draw a load of twenty tons at ten miles an hour, and to cover at least seventy miles a day. Little wonder that an eminent Liverpool merchant declared that only a parcel of charlatans could have devised such a test, and wagered that if a locomotive ever went ten miles an hour, he would eat a stewed engine-wheel for breakfast! The contest had come about as the only solution of a deadlock between the stubborn directors of the Liverpool and Manchester Railway, or tramway, then under construction, and their still more stubborn engineer, one George Stephenson. The railway was nearly completed, and the essential question of the motive power to be used had not yet been decided. The most conservative authorities thought it best to stick to the horse ; others favoured the use of stationary steam-engines, placed every mile or two along the route, and hauling the cars from one station to the next by long ropes ; Stephenson, with a few backers, urged a trial of the locomotive. True, on the Stockton and Darlington Railway, the first successful public line ever built, opened four years before, a Travelling Engine, built by the same dogged engineer, had hauled a train of some forty light carriages nearly nine miles in sixty-five minutes, and had even beaten a stage-coach, running on the highway alongside, by a hundred yards in the twelve miles from Darlington to Stockton. But even here the locomotive was only used to haul freight; passengers were still carried in old stage-coaches, which were mounted on special wheels to fit the rails, and were drawn by horses. The best practical engineers in England, when called into consultation, inspected the Stockton road, and then advised the perplexed directors to install twenty-one stationary engines along the thirty-one miles of track, rather than to experiment with the new Travelling Engine.

'What can be more palpably absurd and ridiculous,' the *Quarterly Review* had declared in 1825, 'than the prospect held out of locomotives travelling twice as fast as stagecoaches! We should as soon expect the people of Woolwich to suffer themselves to be fired off upon one of Congreve's ricochet rockets as trust themselves to the mercy of such a machine, going at such a rate.' And the *Quarterly* was not alone in its scepticism. The directors of the new railway had found great difficulty in obtaining a charter from parliament—a difficulty registered in a bill for parliamentary costs reaching £27,000, or over $4000 a mile. Canal proprietors and toll-road companies had declaimed against the attack on vested rights. Country squires had spluttered over the damage to fox covers. Horses could not plough in neighbouring fields.

Widows' strawberry-beds would be ruined. What would become of coachmen and coach-builders and horse-dealers ? 'Or suppose a cow were to stray upon the line; would not that be a very awkward circumstance ?' queried a committee member, only to give Stephenson an opening for the classic reply in his slow Northumbrian speech: 'Ay, verra awkward for the coo.' And not only would the locomotive as it shot along do such varied damage; in truth, it would not go at all; the wheels, declared eminent experts, would not grip on the smooth rails, or else the engines would prove top-heavy.

To decide the matter, the directors had offered the prize which brought together the *Novelty*, the *Sans-pareil*, the *Rocket*, and the *Perseverance*, engines which would look almost as strange to a modern crowd as they did to the thousands of spectators drawn up along the track on that momentous morning. The contest was soon decided. The *Novelty*, an ingenious engine but not substantially built, broke down twice. The *Sans-pareil* proved wasteful of coal and also met with an accident. The *Perseverance*, for all its efforts, could do no better than five or six miles an hour. The *Rocket* alone met all requirements. In a seventy-mile run it averaged fifteen miles an hour and reached a maximum of twenty-nine. Years afterwards, when scrapped to a colliery, the veteran engine was still able, in an emergency, to make four miles in four and a half minutes. 'Truly,' declared Cropper, one of the directors who had stood out for the stationary engine and the miles of rope, 'now has George Stephenson at last delivered himself.'

Stephenson had the good fortune, he had earned it indeed, to put the top brick on the wall, and he alone lives in popular memory. But the railway, like most other great inventions, came about by the toil of hundreds of known and unknown workers, each adding his little or great advance, until at last some genius or some plodder, standing on their failures, could reach success. Both the characteristic features of the modern railway, the iron road and the steam motive power, developed gradually as necessity urged and groping experiment permitted.

The iron road came first. When men began to mine coal in the north of England, the need grew clear of better highways to bear the heavy cartloads to market or riverside. About 1630 one Master Beaumont laid down broad wooden rails near Newcastle, on which a single horse could haul fifty or sixty bushels of coal. The new device spread rapidly through the whole Tyneside coal-field. A century later it became the custom to nail thin strips of wrought iron to the wooden rails, and about 1767 cast-iron rails were first used. Carr, a Sheffield colliery manager, invented a flanged rail, while Jessop, another colliery engineer, took the other line by using flat rails but flanged cart-wheels. The outburst of canal building in the last quarter of the eighteenth century overshadowed for a time the growth of the iron road, but it soon became clear that the 'tramway' was necessary to supplement, if not to complete, the canal. In 1801 the first public line, the Surrey Iron Railway, was chartered, but it was not until 1825 that the success of the Stockton and Darlington Railway proved that the iron way could be made as useful to the general shipping public as to the colliery owner. At the outset this road was regarded as only a special sort of toll-road upon which any carrier might transport goods or passengers in his own vehicles, but experience speedily made it necessary for the company to undertake the complete service. It took longer to find the new motive power, but this, too, first came into practical use in the land where peace and liberty gave industry the fostering care which the warrent Continent could never guarantee. Nowadays it seems a simple thing to turn heat energy into mechanical energy, to utilize the familiar expansive power of water heated to vapour. Yet centuries of experiment, slowly acquired mechanical dexterity, and an industrial atmosphere were needed for the development of the steam-engine, and later of the locomotive. Inventiveness was not lacking in the earlier days. In the second century before Christ, Hero of Alexandria had devised steam fountains and steam turbines, but they remained scientific toys, unless for the miracle-working purposes to which legend says that eastern priests adapted them. So in the seventeenth century, when the Norman, Solomon de Caus, claimed that with the vapour of boiling water he could move carriages and navigate ships, Cardinal Richelieu had him put in prison as a madman. About 1628 an Italian, Giovanni Branca, invented an engine which had the essential features of the modern turbine, but his crude apparatus lacked efficiency.

Once more the coal-mines of England set invention working on a definite, continuous object. As the shafts were sunk to lower and lower levels, it became impossible to pump the water out of the mines by horse power, and the aid of steam was sought. Just at the close of the seventeenth century Savery devised the first commercial steam-engine, or rather steam fountain, which applied cold water to the outside of the cylinder to condense the steam inside and produce a vacuum; while Papin, one of the Huguenot refugees to whom industrial England owed so much, planned the first cylinder and piston engine. Then in 1705 Newcomen and Cawley, working with Savery, took up Papin's idea, separated boiler from cylinder, and thus produced a vacuum into which atmospheric pressure forced the piston and worked the pump. Next Humphrey Potter, a youngster hired to open and shut the valves of a Newcomen engine, made it self-acting by tying cords to the engine-beam, had his hour for play or idling, and proved that if necessity is the mother of invention, laziness is sometimes its father. Half a century passed without material advance; even as perfected in detail by Smeaton, the Newcomen engine required thirty-five pounds of coal to produce one horse-power per hour, as against one pound today. Then James Watt, instrument-maker in Glasgow, seeing that much of the waste of steam was due to the alternate chilling and heating of the cylinder, added a separate condenser in which to do the chilling, and kept the temperature of the cylinder uniform by applying a steam-jacket. Later, by applying steam and a vacuum to each side of the piston alternately, and by other improvements, Watt, with his partner Boulton, brought the reciprocating steam-engine to a high stage of efficiency.

It took fifty years longer to combine the steam-engine and the rail. French and American inventors devised steam carriages, which came to nothing. England again led the way. At Redruth in Cornwall Boulton and Watt had a branch for the erection of stationary engines in Cornish tin mines, in charge of William Murdock, later known as inventor of the system of lighting by gas. Murdock devised a steam carriage to run upon the ordinary highway, but was discouraged by his employers from perfecting the machine. Another mechanic at Redruth, Richard Trevithick, captain in a tin mine, took up the torch, built a 'Dragon' for use on the common highway, but was baffled by the hopeless badness of the roads, and turned to making a locomotive for use on the iron ways of the Welsh collieries. Two years later, in 1803, he had constructed an ingenious engine, which could haul a ten-ton load five miles an hour, but the engine jolted the road to pieces, and the versatile inventor was diverted to other schemes. Blenkinsop of Leeds in 1812 had an engine built with a toothed wheel working in a racked rail, which did years of good service; and next year at Wylam on the Tyne a colliery owner, Blackett, had the *Puffing Billy* built, and proved that smooth wheels would grip smooth rails. Still another year, and an enginewright in a Tyneside colliery, George Stephenson, himself born at Wylam, devised the *Blucher*, doubling effectiveness by turning the exhaust steam into the chimney to create a strong draught. Using this steam blast, and adopting the multi-tubular boiler from a French inventor, Seguin, Stephenson finally scored a triumph, due not so much to unparalleled genius as to dogged perseverance in working out his own ideas and in adapting the ideas of other men.

Thus by slow steps the steam railway had come. It was a necessity of the age. Crude means of transport might serve the need of earlier days when each district was self-contained and self-sufficing. But now the small workshop and the craftsman's tool were giving way to the huge factory and the power-driven machine. The division of labour was growing more complex. Each district was becoming more dependent on others for markets in which to buy and to sell. Traffic was multiplying. The industrial revolution brought the railway, and the railway quickened the pace of the industrial revolution.

To some critics, as to Ruskin, railways have appeared 'the loathesomest form of deviltry now extant, animated and deliberate earthquakes, destructive of all nice social habits or possible natural beauty.' Animated and deliberate earthquakes they were indeed to prove, transforming social and industrial and political structures the world over. With the telegraph and the telephone, they greatly widened the scope and quickened the pace of business operations, making it possible, and therefore necessary, for the captain of industry or finance of the twentieth century to have under control ten times the press of affairs which occupied his eighteenth-century forerunner. The railway levelled prices and levelled manners. It enabled floods of settlers to sweep into all the waste places of the earth, clamped far-flung nations into unity, and bound country to country.

Nowhere was the part played so momentous as in the vast spaces of the North American continent, and not least in the northern half. The railway found Canada scarcely a geographical expression, and made it a nation.

CHAPTER TWO
EARLY TRAVEL IN CANADA

British North America before the railway came was a spring of scattered provinces. Lake Huron was the western boundary of effective settlement: beyond lay the fur trader's preserve. Between Upper and Lower Canada and the provinces by the Atlantic a wilderness intervened. With the peninsula of Ontario jutting southwest between Michigan and New York, and the northeastern states of the Union thrusting their borders nearly to the St Lawrence, the inland and the maritime provinces knew less of each other than of the neighbouring states.

Settlement clung close to river, lake, and sea. Till the Eastern Townships were settled, Lower Canada had been one long-drawn-out village with houses close set on each side of the river streets. Deep forest covered all the land save where the lumberman or settler had cut a narrow clearing or fire had left a blackened waste. To cut roads through swamp and forest and over river and ravine demanded capital, surplus time, and strong and efficient governments, all beyond the possibilities of early days. On the other hand, the waterways offered easy paths. The St Lawrence and the St John and all their tributaries and lesser rivals provided inevitably the points of settlement and the lines of travel.

The development of water transport in Canada furnishes a record of the interaction of route and cargo, of need and invention, of enterprise and capital. First came the bark canoe, quick to build, light to carry round the frequent gaps in navigation, and large enough to hold the few voyageurs or the rich-in-little peltry that were chief cargo in early days. It was the bark canoe that carried explorer, trader, soldier, missionary, and settler to the uttermost north and south and west. For the far journeys it long held its place. Well on into the nineteenth century fur traders were still sending in supplies from Montreal and bringing back peltry from Fort William in flotillas of great bark canoes. For shorter voyages the canoe gave place to the larger and clumsier bateau, the characteristic eighteenth-century conveyance. After the War of 1812 the increasingly heavy downward freight of grain and potash led to the introduction from the United States of the still larger Durham boats. Along the coast and on the Great Lakes the sailing schooner long filled a notable place. Finally the steamboat came. In 1809, only one year after the *Clermont* had begun its regular trips on the Hudson, and before any steamboat plied in British home waters, John Molson of Montreal with John Bruce and John Jackson—luckily for Canada not all three baptized 'Algernon'—built at Montreal the 40-ton steamer *Accommodation*. Seven years later Upper Canada's first steamboat was launched, the 740-ton *Frontenac*, built at the then thriving village of Ernestown. The fleet of river and lake steamers multiplied rapidly. The speed and certainty and comfort—relative, at least—of the steamboat at once gave a forceful impetus to settlement and to travel, and for some sections ended the pioneer period.

Meanwhile, the waterways were being improved. Little was needed or done in the great network of New Brunswick's rivers or in Nova Scotia's shorter streams, but on the St Lawrence system, with a fall of nearly six hundred feet from Lake Erie to tidewater at Three Rivers, canal construction was imperative. As early as 1779 canals were built round the rapids between Lake St Louis and Lake St Francis, on the St Lawrence, with a depth of only a foot and a half of water on the sills. Far westward, at Sault Ste Marie, the energetic North-West Company built, about 1800, a canal half a mile long. In the early twenties, after the failure of a private company, the province of Lower Canada constructed a boat canal between Montreal and Lachine, and a less successful beginning was made on a canal round the Chambly rapids on the Richelieu. In Upper Canada the British government built the Rideau Canal, chiefly for military purposes. The Welland Canal was begun by a private company in 1824, opened for small boats five years later, and taken over by the province in 1840, after a record notable alike for energy and perseverance and for jobbery and inefficiency. After the Union of 1841, when population, revenue, and credit were all growing, energetic digging was begun on the St Lawrence system of canals, and by 1848 vessels of twenty-six foot beam and drawing nine feet of water could sail from the ocean to Chicago.

Land transport came later than water transport, and developed by slower stages. Road-making was an art which the settler learned slowly. The blazed trail through the woods sufficed for the visit to the neighbour or the church, or for the tramp to the nearest gristmill with a sack of wheat on one's back. 'He who has been once to church and twice to mill is a traveller,' the common saying ran. The trail broadened to a bridle-road for pack-horse or saddle-horse. The winter, that maligned stepmother of Canada, gave the settler an excellent though fleeting road on the surface of the frozen river or across the hard-packed snow. Through the endless swamps jolting 'corduroy' roads were built of logs laid crosswise on little or no foundation. With more hands and more money there came the graded road, fenced and bridged, but more rarely gravelled. Finally, little earlier than the railway, came the macadamized road, and that peculiar invention of Upper Canada, the plank road, built of planks laid crosswise on a level way, and covered with earth to lessen the wear and noise. Upon these roads carriole or calèche, 'cutter' or 'lumber-wagon,' carried the settler or his goods to meeting-place and market. By 1816 a stage route was established from Montreal to Kingston, a year later from Kingston to York (Toronto), and in 1826 from Toronto to Niagara and from Ancaster to Detroit.

Road-making policy fluctuated between the Scylla of local neglect and the Charybdis of centralized jobbery. At first the settler was burdened with the task of clearing roughly the road in front of his own land, but the existence of vast tracts of Clergy Reserves, or other grants exempt from clearing duties, made this an ineffective system. Labour on roads required by statute, whether shared equally by all settlers or allotted according to assessed property, proved little more successful. On the other hand, the system of provincial grants for road-building too often meant log-rolling and corruption, and in the Canadas it was discontinued after the establishment of municipal institutions in 1841. The reaction to local control was perhaps too extreme, and we are today recognizing the need of more aid and control by the central provincial authorities. In the Maritime Provinces the system worked better, and when the railway came these provinces possessed a good network of great roads and by-roads, without a single toll-gate. With the passing of the Joint Stock Act by the Canadian legislature in 1849, toll-road companies were freely organized, and many of the leading roads were sold by the government to these private corporations, and without question their operations brought marked improvement for a time.

To realize more concretely the mode of travelling before the railway came, let us make the journey, say, from Quebec to Toronto, at three different periods, in 1800, in 1830, and in 1850.

'In no part of North America,' wrote an experienced traveller just at the close of the eighteenth century, 'can a traveller proceed so commodiously as along the road from Quebec to Montreal.'[1] A posting service had been established which could fairly be compared with European standards. At regular intervals along the road the traveller found post-houses, where the post-master kept four vehicles in readiness: in summer the calèche, a one-horse chaise built for two passengers, with a footboard seat for the driver and with the body hung by broad leather straps or thongs of bull's hide; in winter the carriole, or sledge, with or without covered top, also holding two passengers and a driver. The drivers were bound to make two leagues an hour over the indifferent roads, and in midwinter and midsummer the dexterous, talkative, good-humoured driver, or *marche-donc*, usually exceeded this rate for most of the jour-

1 Isaac Weld, *Travels through the States of North America and the Provinces of Upper and Lower Canada* (Fourth Edition), p. 300.

ney of three days. From Montreal onward no one travelled in winter except an occasional Indian messenger. Even in summer few thought of going by land, though some half-broken trails stretched westward. The river was the king's highway. The summer traveller at once purchased the equipment needed for a week's river journey —tent, buffalo-skins, cooking utensils, meat and drink—and secured passage on board one of the bateaux which went up the river at irregular intervals in brigades of half a dozen. The bateau was a large flat-bottomed boat, built sharp both at bow and stern, with movable mast, square sail, and cross benches for the crew of five or six. Sometimes an awning or small cabin provided shelter. In still water or light current the French-Canadian crew-—always merry, sometimes sober, singing their voyageur songs, halting regularly for the inevitable 'pipe'—rowed or sailed; where the current was strong they kept inshore and pushed slowly along by 'setting' poles, eight or ten feet long and iron shod; and where the rapids grew too swift for poling, the crews joined forces on the shore to haul each bateau in turn by long ropes, while the passengers lent a hand or shot wild pigeons in the neighbouring woods. At night the whole party encamped on shore, erecting tents or hanging skins and boughs from branches of friendly trees. With average weather Kingston could be reached in seven or eight days; the return journey down-stream was made in two or three. From Kingston westward the journey was continued in a sailing schooner, either one of the government gunboats or a private venture, as far as York, or even to the greater western metropolis, Queenston on the Niagara river. In good weather thirty or forty hours sufficed for the lake voyage, but with adverse winds from four to six days were frequently required.

Thirty years later those to whom time or comfort meant more than money could make the through journey in one-third the time, though for the leaner-pursed the more primitive facilities still lingered. For the summer trip from Quebec to Montreal the steamer had outstripped the stage-coach. Even with frequent stops to load the fifty or sixty cords of pine burned on each trip—how many Canadian business men secured their start in prosperity by supplying wood to steamers on lake or river!—the steamer commonly made the hundred and eighty miles in twenty-eight hours. The fares were usually twenty shillings a cabin and five shillings for steerage, though the intense rivalry of opposing companies sometimes brought reckless rate-cutting. In 1829, for instance, each of the two companies had one boat which carried and boarded cabin passengers for seven and sixpence, while deck passengers who found themselves in food were crowded in for a shilling.

From Montreal to Lachine the well-to-do traveller took a stage-coach, drawn by four spanking greys, leaving Montreal at five in the morning, for stage-coach hours were early and long. At Lachine he left the stage for the steamer, at the Cascades he took a stage again, and at Coteau transferred once more to a steamer for the run to Cornwall. Shortly after 1830 steamers were put on the river powerful enough to breast the current as far as Dickenson's Landing, leaving only a twelve-mile gap to be filled by stage, but in 1830 it was still necessary, if one scorned the bateau, to make the whole journey from Cornwall to Prescott by land, over one of the worst through roads in the province. The Canadian stage of the day was a wonderful contrivance: a heavy lumbering box, slung on leather straps instead of springs, and often made without doors in order that, when fording bridgeless streams, the water might not flow in. With the window as the only means of exit, heavy-built passengers found it somewhat awkward when called upon, as they often were, to clamber out in order to ease the load uphill, or to wait while oxen from a neighbouring farm dragged the stage out of a mud-hole. The traveller who 'knew the ropes' provided himself with buffalo-skins or cushions; others went without. Arrived at Prescott, the passengers shifted to a river steamer, fitted more commodiously than the little boats used in the lower stretches, but still providing no sleeping quarters except in open bunks circling round the dining-saloon.

For thousands of the immigrants who were pouring into Upper Canada the fares of the river steamer were still prohibitive. Many came on bateaux, sometimes poled along as of yore, sometimes taken in tow by a steamer. Often more than a hundred immigrants, men, women, and children, would be crowded into a single thirty-foot bateau, 'huddled together,' a traveller notes, 'as close as captives in a slave trader, exposed to the sun's rays by day, and the river damp by night, without protection.'[1] [1]Still more used the Durham boat for the river journey. This famous craft was a large, flat-bottomed barge, with round bow and square stern. With centre-board down and mainsail and topsail set on its fixed mast, it made fair progress in the wider stretches. But on the up trip it was for the most part poled or 'set' along. Each of the crew took his stand at the bow end of one of the narrow gangways which ran along both sides of the boat, set firmly in the river bottom his long, heavy, iron-shod pole, put his shoulder to it, and, bending almost double, walked along the gangway to the stern and inch by inch forced the boat up-stream. 'The noise made by the clanking of the iron against the stones, as the poles were drawn up again toward the bow, could be heard for a long distance on a calm summer's day.' Finally, at Prescott or Kingston the Durham boat was exchanged for the lower decks of the steamer, and the rest of the journey made with somewhat greater speed, if not much greater comfort.

The twenty years which followed 1830 saw the steamboat in its prime. The traveller going westward from Quebec in 1850 had a simple task before him: a change at Montreal was the only necessary break in a relatively comfortable and speedy journey. Two days now sufficed for the trip from Montreal to Toronto. In the United States, river boats had been evolved which far surpassed anything Europe had to offer in luxury and speed. Canadian business men were not far behind, and the St Lawrence lake and river route was well supplied with crack steamers, of the Royal Mail and rival lines, or with independent boats. The competition was at times intense, both in fares and in speed. Many Canadians of the day,

---

[1] 1 Shirreff, *A Tour through North America*, p. 143.

absorbed in the local or personal rivalries of these boats, and impressed by their magnificence and reliability, were convinced that the last word in transportation had been said. Yet, on the lake and river, winter barred all through traffic. The main turnpike roads of the interior were greatly improved, but even on these long distance traffic was expensive, and the by-roads, especially in the spring and autumn, were impassable except at a snail's pace. For traffic of town with town and province with province some means of transport less dependent on time and tide was urgently needed.

CHAPTER THREE
THE CALL FOR THE RAILWAY

We have seen how in England a succession of workers almost apostolic in continuity had brought the steam railway to practical success, and how in Canada, before the railway came, men were making shift with bateau and steamer, with stage-coach and cart and calèche, to carry themselves and their wares to meeting-place and market. Now we may glance for a moment at the chief hope and motive of those who brought the locomotive across the seas.

In all but the very earliest years of railway planning and building in Canada, two aims have been dominant. One has been political: the desire to clamp together the settlements scattered across the continent, to fill the waste spaces and thus secure the physical basis for national unity and strength. The other has been commercial: the desire to capture the trade and traffic of an ever-expanding and ever-receding west. Local convenience and local interests have played their part, but in the larger strategy of railway building the dominant motives have been political and commercial. They have been blended in varying proportions; each has acted against the other as well as with it, but at all times they give the key to facts which otherwise remain a meaningless jumble of dates and figures.

The political motive is familiar and needs only brief reference. That the present Canada is not a natural geographical unit is an undeniable fact. Each of the principal sections has more natural connection with the corresponding section of the United States than with the other parts of Canada. And sixty years ago it was doubtful whether any common sentiment could take the place of the physical unity which was lacking. There was, of course, no national consciousness, based on common history and common aspirations. At best the link of the scattered colonies was that of common loyalty to the British crown, and at worst a common inherited antagonism to the great republic to the south. Yet far-seeing and courageous men were not content to accept the decrees of geography or of the diplomats who had been over-generous in conceding territory to American claims. They sought unity and understanding, out of fear of aggression from their overshadowing neighbours and out of faintly shaping hope of what the northern half-continent might become.

For unity, knowledge and daily intercourse were needed; for knowledge and intercourse, speedy and cheap transportation was essential. Within each province and between the two Canadas much had been done, but neither river, canal, nor turnpike could serve to annihilate the vast distances that separated east from west and west from farthest west. Only the railway could achieve such a task.

But more was needed than patriotic sentiment. All-red speeches might adorn a banquet or win an election, but facts—or fictions —as to freight and dividends were needed to beguile the capital from investors' pockets. The hope of securing for the Canadian provinces the trade and traffic of the golden West was, in early years as in late, much the strongest factor in railway policy.

When the white man came to North America, he found himself hemmed in to the Atlantic coast by the long range of the Appalachians. These mountains, though not lofty, were rugged and covered with dense forests and tangled undergrowth. There were few doorways to the great open spaces beyond. On the far north the southward intrusion of the ocean, known as Hudson Bay, opened a precarious way, important in the early days of the white man's period, possibly to become important again in our own, but negligible during the intervening years. From the south, entrance could be had by the Mississippi and its tributaries, offering for most of the year ten thousand miles of navigable waters. In the east the St Lawrence system, stretching three thousand miles westward from the sea, and the Hudson and Mohawk rivers, passing through a gap in the Alleghanies, offered still more convenient access.

Early and late in the history of the white man's America the land and the trade of the interior have been the prize sought by rival nations and rival cities, and the possession of a speedy and convenient route has been the means of securing the prize. The later warfare was less spectacular than the old, but no less keen. The navvy took the place of the Indian, pick and shovel and theodolite the place of bow and musket, and a lower freight by a cent on a bushel of wheat became the ammunition in place of the former glass beads or fire-water. But seventeenth- or eighteenth-century Englishmen and Frenchmen on Hudson Bay, Spaniards and Frenchmen on the Mississippi, Frenchmen and Englishmen on the St Lawrence, Dutchmen and Englishmen on the Hudson, did not strive more eagerly for control than the Montreal and Halifax, Portland and Boston and New York, Philadelphia and Baltimore and New Orleans of the nineteenth century. The struggle became especially intense when the advancing flood of settlers cut their way through the Appalachian woods and burst into the prairies of the Mississippi valley. There was no longer a ten-year struggle to clear a space of forty or fifty acres; at once the soil was ready for the plough. For a few years the grain of the valley states was needed for their own in-rushing settlers, but a surplus grew rapidly and had to find an outlet in the east or in Europe. The miraculous speed of western settlement and the magnitude of the prize at stake soon centered public interest on the question of the route which was to provide this outlet. The Mississippi route was the first to be developed. In canoe and pirogue, bateau, flatboat, and ark, settlers went up and produce came down. But the winding stream, the shifting channel, the swift current, the frequent snag and sand-bar made navigation down-stream dangerous and navigation upstream incredibly slow: the heavier vessels took three months for the trip from New Orleans to Louisville. With the coming of the steamboat a strong impetus was given alike to settlement and to export trade. By the forties New Orleans ranked the fourth port in the world and the Mississippi valley exceeded the British Isles in the ownership of ships' tonnage. In 1850 the Mississippi still carried to the sea cargoes twice the value of those that sought the Lakes and the Erie Canal, though in the import trade these proportions were reversed. At this time a line drawn east and west through the centre of Ohio marked the commercial watershed. Not until after the Civil War did the glories of the Mississippi pass away.

Next, New York devised its master-stroke, the Erie Canal. Gouverneur Morris and De Witt Clinton saw the opportunity which the Mohawk- Hudson cleft in the Appalachian barrier offered, and the state rose to it.

Digging was begun in 1817, and in 1825 the first barge passed from Lake Erie to the Hudson. At first the canal was only a four-foot ditch, but it proved the greatest single factor in the development of the region south of the Lakes. Prosperous cities—Buffalo, Lockport, Rochester, Syracuse, Utica, Schenectady—sprang up all along the route. Cost of transport from Buffalo to New York was cut in four. The success of New York led Pennsylvania to build canals through the state to Pittsburg, with a portage railroad over the Alleghanies, while in the west canals were dug to connect Lake Erie with the Ohio, and Lake Michigan with the Illinois and the Mississippi. To the Canadian of that day the West meant Upper Canada or Canada West, and ' the far west' meant Illinois and Indiana. The Saskatchewan was to him little more than the Yang-tse-Kiang. But although the far west was not under his own flag, it dominated his thoughts as greatly as the North-West has dominated our thoughts half a century later. Canada sought its share of the western trade. The Canadian provinces were thinly peopled, their revenues were scanty and their credit low, but the example of New York stirred them to the effort to remove the barriers to navigation in the St Lawrence, and to offer their magnificent lake and river ship-route against the petty barge canal which was capturing the western trade. The Welland Canal was built to carry east-bound traffic beyond the point where Buffalo tapped it, and by 1848, as we have seen, canals were completed on the St Lawrence, providing a nine-foot waterway from Chicago to Montreal.

It was a magnificent effort for a struggling colony. But it was scarcely finished—the paeans of self-congratulation on the unexpected discovery of an enterprise quite Yankee in its daring were still echoing—when it was found to have been made largely in vain. So far from monopolizing the trade of the western states, the St Lawrence route was not even keeping the east-bound traffic of Upper Canada itself. The reasons were soon plain. The repeal in 1846 of the Corn Laws and in 1848 of the differential duties in favour of the St Lawrence route were temporary blows. The granting of bonding privileges by the United States in 1845 drew traffic from Canada to southern routes. Ocean rates were cheaper from New York than from Montreal; in 1850, for example, the freight on a barrel of flour from New York to Liverpool was 1s. 3 1/2d., while from Montreal it was 3s. 1/2d. This was because the majority of the vessels arriving at Montreal came in ballast, and also because on the outward voyage the offerings of timber made rates high. Timber enjoyed a preference in the British market, and, as has happened since, this preference was simply absorbed by the vessel owner. But most important of all, in the United States the railway, with its speedy, all-year service, had already taken the place of the canal. The Canadian ports were fighting with weapons obsolete before completed.

CHAPTER FOUR THE CANADIAN BEGINNINGS

From the beginning in Canada, to a much greater degree than in Great Britain or in the United States, the railway was designed to serve through traffic. But it was regarded at first as only a very minor link in the chain. River and canal were still considered the great highways of through traffic. Only where there were gaps to be bridged between the more important waterways was the railway at first thought profitable. In the phrase of one of the most distinguished of Canadian engineers, Thomas C. Keefer, the early roads were portage roads.

In 1832, two years after the completion of the Liverpool and Manchester Railway, a charter was granted by the legislature of Lower Canada to the Company of the Proprietors of the Champlain and St Lawrence Railroad, for a line from Laprairie on the St Lawrence to St Johns, sixteen miles distant on the Richelieu river, just above the rapids. From St Johns transportation to New York was easily effected, through the Richelieu to Lake Champlain and thence to the Hudson. This portage road promised to shorten materially the journey from Montreal to New York.

Construction was begun in 1835, and the road opened for traffic in July 1836. The rails were of wood, with thin flat bars of iron spiked on. These were apt to curl up on the least provocation, whence came their popular name of 'snake-rails.' At first horse power was used, but in 1837 the proprietors imported an engine and an engineer from England. Some premonition of trouble made the management decide to make the trial run by moonlight. In spite of all the efforts of engineer and officials, the *Kitten* would not budge an inch. Finally an engineer, borrowed from the Baltimore and Ohio Railroad, reported that all that was needed was 'more wood and water,' and given these the *Kitten* gambolled along at twenty miles an hour.

The Champlain and St Lawrence was at first operated only in the summer, when its services as a portage route were most needed. After a decade of moderately successful working, it was decided, significantly, to lengthen the rail and shorten the water section of the route. By 1852 the rails had been extended northward to St Lambert, opposite Montreal, and southward to Rouse's Point, on Lake Champlain. Twenty years later this pioneer road, after a period of leasing, was completely absorbed by the Grand Trunk Railway.

For ten years the sixteen-mile Champlain and St Lawrence was the sole steam railway in British North America, while by 1846 the United Kingdom had built over twenty-eight hundred miles, and the United States nearly five thousand. Political unrest, commercial depression, absorption of public funds in canals, hindered development in Canada. Many projects were formed and charters secured—for roads in the western peninsula of Upper Canada, between Cobourg and Rice Lake, on the Upper Ottawa, in the Eastern Townships, and elsewhere—but they all came to nothing. It was not until the railway mania broke out in England in the middle forties—when 'King' Hudson, first of the great promoters and speculators, turned all to gold; when ninety schemes were floated in a single week, calling for eighty million pounds; when companies capitalized at over seven hundred millions scrambled for charters and all England fought for their shares—that Canadian promoters found interest awakened and capitalists keen to listen. At the same time, the active competition of United States roads for the western traffic and the approaching completion of the St Lawrence canal system prompted further steps. A second stage in Canadian railway building had begun. First may be noted three small lines, which were in their beginnings chiefly portage roads of the most limited type. The Montreal and Lachine, begun in 1846 and completed in 1847, was the second complete road built. Its track of eight miles took the place of the earlier stage route round the Lachine rapids. Five years later an extension, the Lake St Louis and Province Line, was built from Caughnawaga, on the opposite shore of the St Lawrence, to the boundary and beyond to Mooer's Junction, where it made connection with American roads, and thus offered a route from Montreal to New York rivalling the older Champlain and St Lawrence route. A steam ferry, which could carry a locomotive and three loaded cars, was used for crossing from Lachine to Caughnawaga. The enlarged line, known as the Montreal and New York Railroad, did not prosper, and was eventually absorbed by its rival, the Champlain and St Lawrence. The third completed road, the St Lawrence and Industry Village, was also built in Lower Canada, running from Lanoraie on the north bank of the St Lawrence twelve miles to the village of Industry, later Joliette. It was opened for traffic in 1850, and was a road for use in summer only. Meanwhile, the desirability of building a road to circumvent Niagara had not escaped attention. In 1835 the Erie and Ontario Railroad was chartered, and in 1839 the line was opened from Queenston to Chippawa. The grades near Queenston were too steep for the locomotives of the day, and the road was operated by horses; even so, it halted a hundred feet above the level of the river, and failed to make good its promise as an effective portage route. In 1852 the charter was amended, and two years later the road was rebuilt from Chippawa to Niagara-on-the-Lake, and operated by steam. It was later extended to Fort Erie and absorbed by the Canada Southern.

More ambitious schemes were under way —the planning of the St Lawrence and Atlantic in Canada East, and of the Great Western and later the Northern in Canada West. These roads were all designed to secure for Canadian routes and Canadian ports a share of the through traffic of the West. They were all links in longer chains; the time of independent through roads had not yet come. The St Lawrence and Atlantic was built to secure the supremacy of the upper St Lawrence route by giving Montreal a winter outlet at Portland. The Northern, running from Lake Ontario at Toronto to Georgian Bay at Collingwood, was a magnified portage road, shortening by hundreds of miles the distance from Chicago and the upper lakes to the St Lawrence ports. The Great Western, connecting Buffalo and Detroit, was the central link in the shortest route between New York and Chicago. Not only were these roads important in themselves, but the experience acquired in the endeavour to finance and construct them largely determined the policy of the great era of railway construction which began with the chartering of the Grand Trunk.

The St Lawrence and Atlantic was the Canadian half of the first international railway ever built. At the outset much more than half of the enterprise and activity was centered in the United States, for the Canadas were still apprentices in railway promotion and construction. The ambition of an American seaport prompted the planning of the line, the untiring energy of an American promoter made it possible, and American contractors built the greater part.

The little city of Portland possessed the most northerly harbour on the Atlantic coast of the United States. Mr John A. Poor, whose lifetime was devoted to the extension of railways in northern New England, dreamed of making it, by a road to Montreal, the outlet of the trade of the West, at least so far as freight traffic went. Passengers and mails, he conceived, could best be carried to Europe from Halifax, nearly six hundred miles nearer than New York to Liverpool, but the railway connecting Halifax with the large American cities should pass through Portland, and thus make it an important divisional point, if not a terminus. His enthusiasm fired his fellow-citizens: the city subscribed for stock in the proposed road to Montreal, and guaranteed bonds, while private subscriptions mounted still higher, at least on paper. More difficulty was experienced in inducing allies in Montreal to undertake the Canadian half of the road. Before 1845, however, Montreal business men were convinced that a railway to Portland or Boston offered them the best means of recovering from the blow inflicted by the repeal of the British preference on

Canadian wheat and flour. If Montreal could not be the New York of Canada, it might at least occupy the position which Buffalo was now achieving, gathering all the trade of the interior to forward it in summer and especially in winter over the new road. The advantage of such a line in the development of the Eastern Townships was also evident.

The only question in dispute in Canada was as to the relative merits of the Boston and the Portland route. The superior energy of the Portland promoters weighed down the scale in favour of their city. In February 1845 Poor struggled five days through a northeast blizzard, and reached Montreal just in time to turn the vote of the Board of Trade against Boston. He organized a spectacular race of express sleighs to disprove the claim that, though the British packet called at Portland before going on to Boston, the route by Boston would prove speedier. Relays of teams were provided all along the rival roads from Boston and from Portland, five to fifteen miles apart; evergreen bushes were set up in the snow to mark the road, part of the Montreal mail was taken off at Portland, and part at Boston, and dispatched by the rival couriers. The Portland relay covered the distance, nearly three hundred miles, in twenty hours, and dashed into Montreal, with all colours flying, twelve hours ahead of the Boston contingent. The cheers that greeted the victors marked the definite turn of popular favour toward the Portland route. Two allied companies were incorporated—the Atlantic and St Lawrence to build the United States section of the railway, and the St Lawrence and Atlantic to build from Montreal to the border.

The St Lawrence and Atlantic was a valuable medium of experience, if not of traffic. In its management were found the leading business men of Montreal, such as Moffat, M'Gill, Molson, Stayner, and Torrance. At first all was fair. Subscriptions came in freely from Montreal and the Eastern Townships. One of the youngest of the directors, Alexander T. Galt, then commissioner of the British-American Land Company, succeeded in floating a large quantity of stock in England—the first of countless railway appeals to the London market—only to have the subscriptions with drawn in 1846 when the Hudson bubble burst. The Canadian stockholders put up what money they could. The city of Montreal took £125,000 stock. The British-American Land Company and the Montreal Seminary each lent £25,000. Country subscribers were permitted to make payments in pork or eggs for the use of the construction gang, though one director resigned because not allowed to turn in his farm. The contractors, Black, Wood and Company, as was customary in the United States at the time, took a large portion of their payment in stock. Still, funds were lacking. Internal difficulties developed; directors did not direct; and in 1849 the finances were found to be in a hopelessly tangled state. Galt then took charge as president, with John Young—forwarder and born promoter, active in all transportation schemes, whether for canal, railway, or bridge—as vice-president. Under their skillful financing the work went on, but scarcely forty miles could be opened in 1849. To complete the road to the border, in the depression which prevailed, seemed utterly beyond the unaided resources of private capitalists, and the directors turned to the government for aid.

Meanwhile, Upper Canada lagged in action, although schemes were many. Omitting merely local projects, the roads most in the public eye were those leading west and north from Lake Ontario. The Great Western project had been longest under way, and showed a significant evolution. In 1834 the legislature of Upper Canada had granted a charter to the London and Gore Railroad Company. This road was designed to carry the products of the rich western peninsula to the bordering lakes, and chiefly to Lake Ontario. The main line was to run in the direction of Governor Simcoe's great highway, Dundas Street, from Burlington Bay to London, while power was taken to extend the road to Lake Huron and the navigable waters of the Thames. Nothing was done under this charter. When it was renewed by an Act of 1845, the name was changed to the Great Western, and, more important, the route was altered to extend from the Niagara river via Hamilton to Windsor and Sarnia. For meanwhile the New York Central had reached Buflalo, and the Michigan Central was being pushed westward from Detroit toward Chicago. A road through Canada would provide a shorter link than one south of Lake Erie, and the Great Western was designed to fill this gap.

With all the possibilities of through and local traffic, and of comparatively good grades and few curves, the road was long in starting. An eminent American engineer, Charles B. Stuart, reported glowingly on the prospects. Two citizens of Hamilton, Allan MacNab, fiery politician and calculating lobbyist, and Isaac Buchanan, untiring advocate of railways, protection, and paper money, threw themselves into the campaign. Samuel Zimmermann, the best known contractor of the period, a Pennsylvanian who had come to Canada to take a Welland Canal contract, and stayed to be the power behind the scenes in the provincial legislature, was prepared to build the road. Hudson gave the scheme his approval. All to no immediate purpose. The contracts were let, ground was broken at London in 1843, but the money to build was not forthcoming. In consequence the Great Western also turned to parliament for aid.

The Toronto, Simcoe and Huron Union Railroad Company—later known as the Northern —the first road in Upper Canada on which steam locomotives were used, was still slower in emerging from the promotion stage. The idea of building a great portage road between Lake Huron and Lake Ontario was an obvious one, and proposals for its construction were frequent. It was not until the scheme was taken up by Frederick Chase Capreol, a sanguine and ingenious Englishman many years resident in Toronto, that any real progress was made. Capreol conceived the brilliant idea of combining the lure of a lottery and the increment of land values to finance a road from Toronto to Georgian Bay. His proposal was to raise funds by a lottery for the purchase of 100,000 acres of land along the route of the railroad, and to pay for the road out of the increase in the value of the land. Objections moral and financial were urged, and Capreol modified his scheme. In 1849 an Act was passed granting a charter and permitting the raising of money either by subscription or by lottery, but it was reserved by the governor-general for royal assent, on account of the lottery clause. Capreol, nothing daunted, sailed for England, and in seven weeks was back with royal assent assured. The lottery, for all its alluring promises, fell flat. Then the Northern, too, clamoured for public aid.

With these local roads under way or actively promoted, still larger projects loomed up. A line from Montreal to Toronto, paralleling the St Lawrence, and thus for the first time competing with water transport instead of merely supplementing it, began to be talked of as possible. The need of bringing the Maritime Provinces into closer touch with the Canadas lent support to plans of a road from Halifax to Quebec. But for these extensive schemes public aid was even more indispensable.

Hitherto the government of British North America had framed no definite or continuous railway policy. There had been general agreement that railway building should be left to private enterprise. In 1832, when the charter of the Champlain and St Lawrence was under discussion in the legislature of Lower Canada, some members advocated government ownership, but Papineau, the French–Canadian leader, protested against the jobbery that would follow. In the forties the government of Canada was selling its highways to toll-companies, and was not likely to embark on railway construction. In several later charters provision was made for state purchase, after a term of years, at cost plus twenty or twenty-five per cent. Control of private companies in the interest of the shipper was sometimes sought. In the charter of the Champlain and St Lawrence a maximum rate was prescribed at 3d. a mile for passengers and 9 3/4d. a mile pet ton of freight, subject to reduction when profits exceeded twelve per cent. In Upper Canada the earlier charters set no maximum, though the governor in council was given power to approve rates. It appeared to be held that different forwarding companies would make use of the iron way, and afford sufficient competition to protect shippers and passengers against extortion. New Brunswick in 1836 revealed the not modest expectations of profit which prevailed. It provided, in the St Andrews and Quebec charter, that after ten years tolls, if excessive, might be reduced to yield only twenty-five per cent profit. The same sanguine expectations were reflected in the provision made in eight charters issued by Lower Canada between 1845 and 1850, that half the profits over a minimum varying from ten to twenty-four per cent were to go to the state.

The prevalent belief in the great profits to be obtained influenced public opinion against any grant of government aid, except during a brief period before the Rebellion of 1837, when the lavish policy of state construction and state bonuses adopted by the neighbouring republic proved contagious in Upper Canada.

Under the influence of that example the Cobourg Railroad was to be granted a loan of £10,000 as soon as an equal sum was privately subscribed and one-third was paid up. The Toronto and Lake Huron was promised £3 for every £1 of private capital expended, up to £100,000, while the London and Gore was offered a loan of twice that sum; in both these cases the loan was to be secured not only by a lien on the road, but by the liability of the communities benefited to a special tax. None of these generous offers was taken up, and they were not renewed. But a growing realization of the importance of railways and of the evident difficulty of building them in Canada solely by private funds compelled the formation of a new policy of state assistance. This new policy ushered in the first great period of railway construction.

CHAPTER FIVE
THE GRAND TRUNK ERA

It has been seen that by the close of the forties British North America was realizing both the need of railway expansion and the difficulty of financing it. Other factors combined to bring about the intervention of the state on a large scale. Both in the Canadas and in the Maritime Provinces political disputes were giving place to economic activities. The battle of responsible government had been fought and won. Men's energies were no longer absorbed by constitutional strife. Baldwin and LaFontaine were making way for Hincks and Morin; Howe had turned to constructive tasks. Responsibility was bringing new confidence and new initiative, though colonial dependence still continued to hamper enterprise. British and American contractors discovered the virgin field awaiting them, and local politicians discovered the cash value of votes and influence. The example set in the United States was powerful. Massachusetts had guaranteed bonds of local roads to the extent of eight millions, without ever having to pay a cent of the interest; and though New York's experience had been more chequered, the successes were stressed and the failures were plausibly explained away.

The eight or ten years which followed 1849 are notable not only for a sudden outburst of railway construction and speculative activity throughout the provinces, but for the beginning of that close connection between politics and railways which is distinctively Canadian. In this era parliament became the field of railway debate. Political motives came to the front: 'statesmen' began to talk of links of Empire and 'politicians' began to press the claims of their constituencies for needed railway communications. Cabinets realized the value of the charters they could grant or the country's credit they could pledge, and contractors swarmed to the feast. 'Railways are my politics,' was the frank avowal of the Conservative leader, Sir Allan MacNab.

Three names are closely linked with this new policy—those of Howe in Nova Scotia, Chandler in New Brunswick, and Hincks in Canada.

Francis Hincks, merchant, journalist, and politician, moderate reformer, and Canada's first notable finance minister, took the initiative. As inspector-general in the second Baldwin-LaFontaine Cabinet, he brought down the first installment of his railway policy in 1849. In the previous session a committee of the House had considered the demand of the Great Western and of the St Lawrence and Atlantic for assistance, and had discussed the less advanced proposals for railways from Montreal to Toronto and from Quebec to Halifax. Allan MacNab, as chairman of the committee, had listened sympathetically to the plea of Allan MacNab, president of the Great Western, and the committee had reported in favour of guaranteeing the stock of the two companies to the extent of a million sterling. No action was taken at this session. Meanwhile Hincks, by instruction of his colleagues, had drawn up two memoranda— one suggesting that the crown lands in the province might be offered as security for the capital necessary to build the road within the province, and the other urging the Imperial government to undertake the road from Halifax to Quebec. Capitalists gave no encouragement to the first suggestion, and the British government had not replied to the second by the end of the session of 1848-49. Accordingly, in April 1849 Hincks brought down a new policy, based upon a suggestion of the directors of the St Lawrence and Atlantic. The proposal was, to guarantee the interest, not exceeding six per cent, on half the bonds of any railway over seventy-five miles long, whenever half the road had been constructed, the province to be protected by a first charge after the bondholders' lien. MacNab seconded the resolution; voices from Bytown and the Saguenay mildly questioned the policy, but the resolution passed unanimously.

Even with this aid construction did not proceed apace. It was still necessary for the companies to complete half the road before qualifying for government assistance. This the St Lawrence road effected slowly, in face of quarrels with contractors, repudiation of calls by shareholders, and hesitancy of banks to make advances. The Great Western did not get under way until 1851, when American capitalists, connected with the New York Central, took shares and a place on the directorate. In the same year the Toronto, Simcoe and Huron, later known as the Northern, began construction.

Meanwhile suggestions from the Maritime Provinces had brought still more ambitious schemes within practical range, and these led Hincks to take the second step in his policy of aid to railways.

In the Maritime Provinces, from 1835 to 1850, many railways had been projected, but, with the exception of a small coal tramway in Nova Scotia, built in 1839 from the Albion coal-mines to tide-water, not a mile was built before 1847. There, as elsewhere, the pamphleteer and the promoter acted as pioneers, and the capitalist and the politician took up their projects later. The plans which chiefly appealed to public attention looked to the linking up of St Andrews, St John, and Halifax with Quebec and Montreal and with the railways of Maine. From the outset the projects in these provinces were much more ambitious than the local beginnings in the Canadas. They were more markedly political and military in aim, and in consequence depended in greater measure upon the aid of the British government. When at last construction was begun, the policy of provincial ownership was more widely adopted.

When in 1876 Sandford Fleming drew up a record of the great work just completed under his direction, the Intercolonial Railway, he called attention to the first proposal for such a road, found in an article contributed to the *United Service Journal* in 1832 by Henry Fairbairn.[1] The author proposed the two chief projects which for half a century were to engross the attention of the Maritime Provinces: a road from St Andrews to Quebec, which should 'convey the whole trade of the St Lawrence, in a single day, to Atlantic waters,' and another line from Halifax through St John to the border of Maine, which should command for Halifax 'the whole stream of passengers, mails, and light articles of commerce passing into the British possessions and to the United States and every part of the continent of America.'

St Andrews was the winter port in British territory nearest to the upper provinces. If the territory in dispute on the Maine boundary fell to New Brunswick and Quebec, a road not more than 250 or 300 miles long could be built from this port to the city of Quebec. In 1835 a Railway Association was formed in St Andrews, an exploratory survey was made, and the interest of Lower Canada was enlisted.

In the following year New Brunswick gave a charter to the St Andrews and Quebec Railroad, and the Imperial government agreed to bear the cost of a survey. But the survey was speedily halted because of protests from Maine; in 1842 the Ashburton Treaty assigned to the United States a great part of the territory through which the line was projected, and the promoters gave up. Then in 1845 the railway mania in England brought a revival of all colonial schemes. Sir Richard Broun took up the plan for a line from Halifax to Quebec, along with other grandiose projects connected with his endeavour to revive the lost glories of the baronetage of Nova Scotia, but did not get past the stage of forming a provisional committee. This discussion revived the flagging hopes of St Andrews, and, as will be seen in detail later, a beginning was made by a railway from St Andrews to Woodstock, the New Brunswick and Canada, for which ground was broken in November 1847. The provincial legislature early concluded that it would be impossible to induce private capitalists to build an intercolonial road unaided. They were unanimous also, not yet having emerged from the stage of colonial dependence, in desiring to throw the burden of such aid as far as possible on the British gov-

[1] As a matter of fact, discussion of this scheme began in St Andrews in 1827, and in 1828 John Wilson convened a meeting of the citizens to further it.

ernment. In the absence of a colonial federation the United Kingdom was the main connecting-link between the colonies in British North America, and was presumably most interested in matters affecting more than a single colony. The British government, however, had by this time about decided that the old policy of treating the colonies as an estate or plantation of the mother country, protecting or developing them in return for the monopoly of their trade, did not pay. It had reluctantly conceded them political home rule; it was soon to thrust upon them freedom of trade; and it was not inclined to retain burdens when it had given up privileges. Mr Gladstone, secretary for the Colonies, agreed, however, in 1846, to have a survey made at the expense of the three colonies concerned.

This survey, the starting-point for the controversies and the proposals of a generation, was completed in 1848, under Major Robinson and Lieutenant Henderson of the Royal Engineers. 'Major Robinson's Line,' as it came to be known, ran roughly in the direction eventually followed by the Intercolonial—from Halifax to Truro, and thence north to Miramichi and the Chaleur Bay, and up the Metapedia valley to the St Lawrence. The distance from Halifax to Quebec was computed at 635 miles, and the cost at £7000 sterling a mile or about £5,000,000. Acting on the assurance of engineers that the route was feasible, each of the three colonial governments offered in 1849 to set aside for the work a belt of crown lands ten miles wide on each side of the railway, and to pledge £20,000 a year to meet interest or expenses, if the British government would undertake the project. Downing Street, however, replied politely but emphatically that no aid could be given.

After the plan of a northern route to Quebec was thus apparently given its quietus, interest shifted to the Portland connections. The building of the road from Montreal to Portland added further strength to the claims of this route. On paper, at least, it seemed possible to make the connection between Montreal and Halifax by following either the northern or the southern sides of the great square. One of the southern sides was now under way, and by building the other, from Portland to St John and Halifax, connection with the Canadas would be completed. Under the leadership once more of John A. Poor, Portland took up the latter project. The name of the proposed road, the European and North American, showed the influence of the same hope which Fairbairn had expressed—that the road from Portland to Halifax would become the channel of communication between the United States and Europe, at least for passengers, mails, and express traffic. With a line of steamers from Halifax to Galway in Ireland, it was held that the journey from New York to London could be cut to six or seven days.

In July 1850 a great convention assembled in Portland, attended by delegates from New Brunswick and Nova Scotia as well as from Maine and other New England states. Intertwined flags and fraternal unity, local development and highways to Europe, prospective profits and ways and means of construction, were the themes of the fervent orators and promoters. The convention was enthusiastically in favour of the project. The 550 miles from Portland to Halifax — 222 in Maine, 204 in New Brunswick, and 124 in Nova Scotia—would cost, it was estimated, $12,000,000, half of which might be raised by private subscription and the rest by state and provincial guarantee.

The delegates from the Maritime Provinces returned home full of enthusiasm, but increasingly uncertain about the securing of the necessary capital. At this stage Joseph Howe came to the front. He had much earlier, in 1835, before entering parliament, taken the lead in advocating a local railway from Halifax to Windsor, but had not been prominent in recent discussions. He now urged strongly that the province of Nova Scotia should itself construct the section of the European and North American which lay within its borders. He proposed further to seek from the Imperial government a guarantee of the necessary loan, in order that the province might borrow on lower terms. The Colonial Office, while expressing its approval of the Portland scheme, declined to give a guarantee any more than a cash contribution. Nothing daunted, Howe sailed for England in November 1850, and by persistent interviews, eloquent public addresses and exhaustive pamphlets, caught public favour, and in spite of Cabinet changes in London secured the pledge he desired.

In the official reply of the Colonial Office Howe was informed that aid would not be given except for an object of importance to the Empire as a whole, and that accordingly aid was contingent upon securing help from New Brunswick and Canada to build the whole road from Halifax to Quebec. Major Robinson's line need not be followed if a shorter and better could be secured; any change, however, should be subject to the approval of the British government. 'The British Government would by no means object to its forming part of the plan that it should include provision for establishing a communication between the projected railway and the railways of the United States.' The colonies were to bear the whole cost of the loan, and were to impose taxes sufficient to provide interest and sinking fund, and thus ensure against any risk of loss to the United Kingdom.

Howe returned triumphant. The British government would guarantee a loan of £7,000,000, which would build the roads to Portland and to Quebec and perhaps still farther west. He hastened to New Brunswick, and won the consent of its government to the larger plan, went on to Portland and allayed its murmurs, and with E. B. Chandler of New Brunswick reached Toronto, then the seat of government of the province of Canada, in June 1851. His eloquence and the dazzling offer of cheap and seemingly unlimited capital soon won consent. The representatives of the three provinces agreed to construct the road from Halifax to Quebec on joint account, while Canada would build the extension from Quebec to Montreal, and New Brunswick the extension to the Maine border, each at its own risk, but in all cases out of the £7,000,000 guaranteed loan.

Then suddenly the bubble burst. The Colonial Office, late in 1851, declared that Howe had been mistaken in declaring that the guarantee was to extend to the European and North American project. The British government had no objection to this road being built, but would not aid it. The officials of the Colonial Office declared that they never meant to promise anything else.

It is difficult to assign with certainty responsibility for this serious misunderstanding. Possibly Howe's optimism and oratorical vagueness led him to misinterpret the promises made, but his reports immediately after the interviews were explicit, and in dispatches and speeches sent to the Colonial Office and acknowledged with high compliments, his version of the agreement had been set forth clearly and for months had gone unchallenged. He cannot be freed from a share of the blame, but the negligence of Downing Street was at least equally the source of the misunderstanding.

The whole plan thus fell to the ground. The consent of the three provinces was essential, and New Brunswick would not support the Halifax and Quebec project if the Portland road, running through the most populous and influential sections of the province, was to be postponed indefinitely. Hincks determined to endeavour to save the situation. Accompanied by John Young and E. P. Taché, he visited Fredericton and Halifax early in 1852, and hammered out a compromise. New Brunswick agreed to join in the Halifax to Quebec project on condition that the road should run from Halifax to St John and thence up the valley of the St John river; Nova Scotia agreed to this change, which made St John rather than Halifax the main ocean terminus, on condition that New Brunswick should bear five-twelfths as against its own three-twelfths of the cost. It remained to secure the consent of the Imperial government to this change in route, and accordingly Hincks, Chandler, and Howe arranged to sail for England early in March. Hincks sailed on the day agreed ; Chandler followed a fortnight later ; Howe, repenting of his bargain, postponed sailing a fortnight, a month, six weeks, and then announced that because of election pressure he could not go at all. Hincks and Chandler found in office in London a new government which appeared biased against the valley route. Upon a peremptory request from Hincks for a definite answer within a fortnight, the British Cabinet, in spite of the previous promise to consider the route an open question, declined to aid any but a road following Major Robinson's line. The negotiations broke off, joint action between the provinces failed, and each province switched to its own separate track.

Howe steadily maintained the policy of state ownership, but had unusual difficulty in carrying Nova Scotia with him. The great English contracting firm of Peto, Brassey, Betts and Jackson, whose operations in the other provinces will be discussed at greater length, offered to find the necessary capital if given the contracts on their own terms. Many Nova Scotians were dazzled by the promises of the agents of this firm, and Howe in 1853 was forced to agree to their proposals. The contractors found themselves unable to make good their promises, in face of panics on the stock market in England, and in the following year Howe's original policy was sanctioned. He himself retired from political life for a time in order to carry through, as one of the railway commissioners, the policy he had steadfastly urged.

It was on June 13, 1854, that the first sod was turned for the construction of the Nova Scotia Railway, and a beginning made at last. The road was to run from Halifax to Truro, with a branch to Windsor. Progress was slow, but by 1858 the ninety-three miles planned had been completed. Then came a halt, when reality succeeded the glowing visions of the prospectus, the service proved poor, and the returns low. Nine years later an extension from Truro to Pictou was constructed. This gave Nova Scotia at Confederation in 1867 145 miles of railroad in all, built at a cost of $44,000 a mile, and connecting Halifax with the Bay of Fundy and the Gulf of St Lawrence. The gauge adopted was five feet six, and the Nova Scotia road led the way in Canada in using coal for fuel.

New Brunswick had a more chequered experience. After the collapse of the Halifax and Quebec project, her efforts were confined to the road running north from St Andrews and to the European and North American.

The possibilities of St Andrews as an ocean terminus had been severely hampered by the thrusting in of the Maine-wedge between New Brunswick and Quebec, but still the town struggled on. In 1847 shares in the railway had been placed both in England and in the province, and the legislature guaranteed the interest on debentures and also granted a land subsidy. Still, the money came in slowly. Operations were time and again suspended, contract after contract was made, and reorganizations were effected. In 1858 the road had reached Canterbury, and four years later its temporary terminus at Richmond; in 1866 a branch to St Stephen was opened, and in 1868 an extension to Woodstock, making 126 miles all told, costing about $20,000 a mile. At Confederation only a third of the distance between St Andrews and Rivière du Loup on the St Lawrence had been completed, and the road was in a receiver's hands.

The European and North American also had its troubles. Maine proved unable to build its section. In 1852 the New Brunswick government made a contract with the English firm already referred to, under the style of Peto, Betts, Jackson and Brassey, for the construction of a line from Maine to Nova Scotia, at $32,500 a mile. The province agreed to subscribe $6000 stock and lend $9400 in bonds per mile; the contractors were to find the rest of the money in England. This they failed to do. The firm was dissolved in 1856, and the government took over the road, completing it from St John to Shediac, 108 miles, in 1860. The western half was not begun until August 1867.

To return to the upper provinces. By 1851 the St Lawrence, the Great Western, and the Northern were under way, and more ambitious schemes proposed. The Guarantee Act of 1849, which was the first phase of Hincks' policy, assuring public aid for the second half of any road at least seventy-five miles in length, was proving inadequate, and the government was considering an extension of its policy. At this juncture the golden news arrived of Howe's success in securing the £7,000,000 loan at bargain rates. All hesitation was removed. No doubt was felt that the roads would pay, once they were built; the only difficulty had been to find the money to build them. And now £7,000,000 was available—£4,000,000 of it for Canada, at probably 3 1/2 per cent. Paper computations soon proved that £4,000,000 would suffice not only to build Canada's third of the Quebec-Halifax route, but to build a trunk line from Quebec or Montreal through to Hamilton, whence the Great Western ran to Windsor on the frontier opposite Detroit.

At once a struggle began for the control of this fund. The Montreal merchants who had bought experience in building the St Lawrence and Atlantic, John Young, Luther Holton, and D. L. Macpherson, with A. T. Galt of Sherbrooke, were first in the field, and pressed for a charter to build from Montreal to Kingston, intending later to extend this road to Toronto. Then the most noted firm of contractors in railway history, Peto, Brassey, Betts and Jackson (the forms of the firm name varied), who had built one-third of the railways of Britain, and also roads in France and Spain and Italy and Prussia and India, were attracted to this fresh field by Howe's campaign in England. They sent an agent to Toronto in 1851 to offer to construct all the roads needed, and to find all the capital required, with partial government guarantees.

Hincks, with whom the decision lay, was eminently an opportunist. In 1849 he had argued against government ownership; now he argued for it. Yet he did not close the door against retreat. The new Act, passed in April 1852, marked the second or Grand Trunk phase of his gradually shaping policy. Besides providing for the Canadian share of the Halifax to Quebec road, the Act contemplated three alternative methods of continuing this Trunk line westward. The province was to build it if the guaranteed loan could be stretched far enough; failing this, the province, together with such municipalities as wished, could undertake the extension; should both modes fail, private companies might be given the privilege, with a provincial guarantee of half the cost, covering both principal and interest. No roads except those forming part of the Trunk line and the three already under way were to be aided. The Montreal and Kingston Railway, in which Holton, Galt, and Macpherson were prime movers, was chartered, and also the Kingston and Toronto, but in both charters a suspending clause was included preventing the charters from taking effect until special proclamation was made—after the other plans had failed.

The next move was to arrange terms with the other provinces and secure the promised Imperial guarantee. How Hincks and Chandler's mission failed has already been told. Hincks then made another sharp curve and decided for company control. Before leaving Canada he had made up his mind that the construction should be entrusted to British contractors, and was authorized to negotiate with the Brassey firm. Now that the Imperial guarantee had faded away, capital was needed more than contractors. The Brasseys promised both, offering, if given the contract, to organize a company in England which would provide all the capital not guaranteed by the province.

This seductive offer was to prove the main cause of the financial embarrassment of the Grand Trunk. It involved at the outset a dubious connection between company and contractor, and also for two generations an attempt to manage a great railway at a range of three thousand miles. So fatal did it prove that in later years each party to it endeavoured to throw the responsibility for the initiative on the other, and enemies of Hincks declared that he, as well as Lord Elgin, the governor-general, had been bribed to wreck the negotiations with the British government in order to take up with Brassey. Whether or not Hincks was first to resume negotiations in London, it was the contractors who had already taken the initiative in America, sending a representative to Toronto, and taking part in the elections of 1851 in Nova Scotia against Howe. It is clear also that the British government was unwilling to consider anything but the unacceptable Major Robinson line. Hincks was justified in looking elsewhere for capital, but he was not justified in binding himself to one firm of contractors, however eminent.

Hincks returned to Canada with a tentative contract in his pocket. To Canada, too, came Henry Jackson, a partner in the Brassey firm for this enterprise, and one of the most skillful and domineering of the railway lobbyists in Canada's annals, rich in such methods. At once a battle royal began in parliament. On August 7, 1852, the Montreal and Kingston and the Kingston and Toronto charters were proclaimed in force; apparently the supposition of the government was that the English contractors would simply subscribe for the bulk of the stock in these companies. But the Canadian promoters were not willing to give up their rights so easily: a week after the books were opened, Galt, Holton, and Macpherson subscribed between them £596,500 and seven of their associates took up the nominal balance of the capital of £600,000 which was authorized. Hincks met this move by bringing down a bill to incorporate a new company, the Grand Trunk Railway Company of Canada, and the rights of the rival claimants came before parliament for decision.

On behalf of the English promoters it was urged that the Canadian promoters could not raise the necessary capital, that the Galt-Holton-Macpherson subscription was a fake, that the English contractors could induce capitalists to invest freely at low rates, and that their superior methods would result in a road of more solid construction and lower working expenses than the ordinary American railway. Holton and Galt, on the other hand, contended that their subscription was in good faith, that tenders were in, and that with provincial guarantee and municipal aid, and by paying the contractors partly in stock, they could finance the road. It would be better, they urged, to have the control in the hands of men who knew the province rather than in the hands of outsiders. The Grand Trunk Company, seeking incorporation, was only a sham company, under the thumb of the contractors, formed to ratify a foregone contract with them. If the Montreal and Kingston Company was given control, it would invite the Brassey firm to tender on the same basis as other contractors: no more could honestly be asked.

Galt and Holton had the best of the argument, but Hincks had the votes, and rumours which Jackson spread of the Brassey millions and the firm's open door to all the money markets of Europe brought conviction or afforded excuse. The railway committee reported in favour of the English promoters, though the competition had compelled them to reduce their price by a thousand pounds a mile, and to accept a guarantee of £3000 per mile instead of half the cost. At the same time the Brassey firm secured a charter for the Grand Trunk of Canada East, to run from Quebec to Trois Pistoles—Canada's first section of the Halifax to Quebec route. The same aggressive firm had already secured a contract for the Quebec and Richmond, which was to join the St Lawrence and Atlantic at Richmond, and, as has been seen, for New Brunswick and Nova Scotia roads. With these contracts seemingly secure, Jackson sailed for home. But Canadian promoters were quick to learn. Galt had another card to play. As president of the St Lawrence and Atlantic he proposed to amalgamate this road with the Montreal and Kingston, and to build a bridge at Montreal, thus securing an essential part of the trunk line. Hincks became alarmed at the Montreal interests thus arrayed against him, and proposed as a compromise that the Grand Trunk should absorb the St Lawrence road and build the bridge at Montreal on the condition that the opposition to its westward plans should be abandoned. Upon this all parties agreed, and the English and Canadian promoters joined forces.

Negotiations were completed in England early in 1853. As yet the Grand Trunk Company was but a name. The real parties to the bargain were many. First came John Ross, a member of the Canadian Cabinet, but representing the future Grand Trunk, of which he was elected president. The Barings and Glyns, eminent banking houses, had a twofold part to play, as they were closely connected with the contractors and were also the London agents of the Canadian government. The contractors themselves, Peto, Brassey, Betts and Jackson, of whom Jackson, accompanied by the company's engineer, A. M. Ross, had spent a year studying the Canadian situation, put in anxious weeks hammering out the details of the agreement and the prospectus to follow it. Galt represented the St Lawrence and Atlantic and the Atlantic and St Lawrence, while Rhodes and Forsythe of Quebec had charge of the interests of the Quebec and Richmond. An agreement was reached to amalgamate all the Canadian roads and to lease the Maine road for 999 years. This left Toronto the western terminus. An attempt to absorb the Great Western and thus secure an extension to Windsor came to nothing. This failure gave Galt an opening for another brilliant stroke of railway strategy. A company had recently been chartered to build a road from Toronto to Guelph and Sarnia, and the firm of Gzowski and Co., of which Galt was a member, had secured the contract. Galt, acting with Alexander Gillespie, a prominent London financier who was the agent of the Toronto, Guelph and Sarnia

Railway, now proposed to substitute this line as the westward extension. Everybody was in an amalgamating mood, and the bargain went through. All contracts previously made were taken over by the amalgamated company, and the investing public was told that all uncertainty as to the total amount was thus removed—as it emphatically was, for the time.

A glowing prospectus was drawn up. The amalgamated road would be the most comprehensive railway system in the world, comprising 1112 miles, stretching from Portland and eventually from Halifax (by both the northern and the southern route) to Lake Huron. The whole future traffic between west and east must therefore pass over the Grand Trunk, as both geographical conditions and legislative enactment prevented it from injurious competition. 'Commencing at the debouchere [sic] of the three longest lakes in the world,' the prospectus continued,'it pours the accumulating traffic in one unbroken line throughout the entire length of Canada into the St Lawrence at Montreal and Quebec, on which it rests on the north, while on the south it reaches the magnificent harbours of Portland and St John on the ocean.' It was backed by government guarantee and Canadian investment, and its execution was in the hands of the most eminent contractors. The total capital was fixed at £9,500,000 sterling. The revenue was estimated at nearly £1,500,000 a year, which, with working expenses at *forty* per cent of revenue, and debenture interest and £60,000 for lease of the Atlantic and St Lawrence Railway deducted, would leave £550,000 or 11 1/2 per cent on the share capital.

On the advice of Baring and Glyn only half the capital was issued at first. This decision proved a serious mistake. In 1853, when the company was floated, money was abundant and cheap; the shares and bonds issued were over-subscribed twenty times, and were quoted at a premium before allotment. Scarcely was the issue made when war with Russia loomed up, and money rose from three to seven or eight per cent. Never again was it possible for the Grand Trunk to secure capital in such abundance.

But this was for the future to disclose. At once construction began in Canada. A. M. Ross was appointed chief engineer, and S. P. Bidder general manager, both on the nomination of the English bankers and contractors. Plant was assembled in Canada, orders for rails and equipment were placed in England, and navvies came out by the thousand. At one time 14,000 men were directly employed upon the railways in Upper Canada alone. In July 1853 the last gaps in the St Lawrence and Atlantic had been filled up, though not in permanent fashion. In 1854 the Quebec and Richmond section was opened; in 1855, the road from Montreal to Brockville and from Lévis to St Thomas, Quebec; in 1856, the Brockville to Toronto and Toronto to Stratford sections. Not until 1858 was the western road completed as far as London. The year 1859 saw the completion of the Victoria Bridge, the extension from St Mary's to Sarnia, and a new road in Michigan, running from Port Huron to Detroit. By 1860 the eastern section extended to Rivière du Loup, where a halt was made.

From the outset difficulties undreamed of had developed. Money was hard to get and early traffic returns were disappointing, so that the company found it almost impossible to secure the balance of the capital required. The road from Montreal to Portland was found to require heavy expenditure to bring it up to the standard. The contractors, for their part, were embarrassed by the company's shortage of funds and by the great rise in the prices of land, materials, and labour. Their own activities, the Reciprocity Treaty of 1854 with the United States, the Crimean War, had combined to bring on a period of inflated prices such as Canada was not to experience again for half a century. With wheat at two dollars a bushel, and 'land selling by the inch,' even liberal margins of profit on contracts vanished.[1]

In these straits the company turned to the government for aid. It had many supporters in the House. No one could deny the benefits which its operations had conferred upon the province. The government guarantee of interest and the government nomination of a part of the board of directors were plausibly held to involve responsibility for the solvency of the company. It was not surprising, therefore, that for a decade after 1855 scarcely a year passed without a bill to amend the terms of the Grand Trunk agreement. One year it was an additional guarantee, another a temporary loan, again a postponement, and again a still further postponement of the government's lien. It soon came to be recognized that the money which had been advanced under the guarantee provisions must be considered a gift, not a loan, though to this day the amount nominally due still figures as an asset on the Dominion government's books. Incidentally, the embarrassing government directors were dispensed with in 1857.

The Grand Trunk was complete from Lake Huron to the Atlantic in 1860. In the ten years that followed, working expenses varied from fifty-eight to eighty-five per cent of the gross receipts, instead of the forty per cent which the prospectus had foreshadowed; not a cent of dividend was paid on ordinary shares—nor has been to this day.

What were the reasons for this disappointing result? The root of the

---

[1] The Brassey firm were paid about £9000 sterling a mile for the line from Toronto to Montreal, £8000 for the section from Quebec to Rivière du Loup, £6500 for the Quebec and Richmond road, and £1,400,000 for the Victoria Bridge. Gzowski and Co., consisting of Messrs Gzowski, Holton, Macpherson, and Galt, secured the Toronto to Sarnia contract at £8000 a mile. In both cases these prices included equipment. The English contractors were required to take a large portion of their pay in depreciated bonds and stock, whereas the Canadian contractors were given cash; on the other hand, Brassey had a higher price and less difficult country to work in. The English firm, with all their experience, were not familiar with building roads in countries where labour was dear, and the plant they sent out was antiquated compared with the labour-saving equipment familiar to American and Canadian contractors. They claimed to have lost a million pounds on their enterprise, while Galt, Holton, Macpherson, and Gzowski all made fortunes. - R.B.

trouble was that the road was not built solely or even mainly with a view to operating efficiency and earning power. It was the politicians' road, the promoters' road, the contractors' road, at least as much as the shareholders' road. The government had encouraged the building of unprofitable sections, such as that east of Quebec, for local or patriotic reasons. Promoters had unloaded the Portland road and later the Detroit and Port Huron road at excessive prices. The contractors, east of Toronto, had had an eye mainly to construction profits in planning the route, and heavy grades, bad rails, and poor ballast increased maintenance charges beyond all expectations. The prophecy that operating expenses would not exceed forty per cent of earnings, based on English experience, failed partly because earnings were lower, but more because operating expenses were higher than anticipated. The company had more than its share of hard luck from commercial depression, and from loss on American paper money in the Civil War. Water competition proved serious in the east, while other railways waged traffic wars in Upper Canada. The trade of the far west, which had been the most attractive lure, did not come in any great amount for the first twenty years. Differences of gauge, lack of permanent connections at Chicago, lack of return freight, rate wars with the American roads which had been built west at the same time or later, the inferiority of Montreal to New York as of old in harbour facilities and ocean service, the failure of Portland to become a great commercial centre—all meant hope and dividends deferred. Finally, the management was working at long range: the road did not enjoy the vigilant inspection or the public support that would have attended control by Canadian interests.

The Grand Trunk did Canada good service, well worth all the public aid that was given. It would probably have given better service, and its shareholders could not have fared worse, had the plans of Galt and his associates not been interfered with, and the line been built gradually under local control.

While the building of the Grand Trunk was the main achievement of the period, it was by no means the only one. The fifties were the busiest years in the railway annals of older Canada. In 1850 there were only 66 miles of road in all the provinces. In 1860 there were 2065, of which over 1700 had been added in the Canadas alone. The Great Western and the Northern were pushed forward under the provisions of the earlier Guarantee Act; roads of more local interest were fostered by municipal rivalry. Their building brought unwonted activity in every branch of commerce. A speculative fever ran through the whole community; fortunes were made and lost in the provision trade, and land prices soared to heights undreamed of. This mood was the promoter's happy chance, and still more charters were sought. The pace quickened till exhaustion, contagious American panics, poor harvests, and the Crimean War—which first raised the price of the wheat Canada had to sell, but later raised the price of the money she had to borrow—brought collapse in 1857.

In this boom period jobbery and lobbying reigned to an extent which we rarely realize in our memory of 'the good old times.' Railway contractors were all-powerful in the legislature, and levied toll at will. The most notable 'contractor-boss' of the day was able, dealing with the Great Western, to hold up a bill for double-tracking until assured of the contract himself; dealing with the Grand Trunk, to force from the English contractors a share in the enterprise before consenting to help their schemes through; with the Northern, to collect $100,000 as a condition of securing from the government the guarantee bonds before they had been rightly earned. Municipal officials were bribed to help bonuses through. Existing roads were blackmailed by pedlars of rival charters. Glaringly fraudulent prospectuses were issued. On a smaller scale, the excitement and the rascality which had marked the beginning of the great railway eras in the United Kingdom and the United States were reproduced in Canada.

Of the other roads completed in this period, the two which had been aided by Hincks' first Guarantee Act were most important.

The Great Western had a promising outlook. It ran through a rich country and had assured prospects of through western traffic. The road was completed from Suspension Bridge to Windsor in January 1854. An extension from Hamilton to Toronto was built in 1856, and a semi-independent line from Galt to Guelph absorbed in 1860. The Great Western came nearest of any early road to being a financial success; alone of the guaranteed roads it repaid the government loan, nearly in full. But after a brief burst of prosperity, from 1854 to 1856, it, too, was continually in difficulties. In 1856 it paid a dividend of 8 1/2 per cent, but three years later it paid nothing, and in the next decade averaged less than three per cent.

The troubles of the Great Western came chiefly from competition, actual and threatened, and uncertain traffic connections. To the north, the chartering of the Toronto, Guelph and Sarnia, amalgamated later with the Grand Trunk, cut into its best territory. An endeavour was made in 1854 to divide the remaining area, but two years later the battle was renewed, the Great Western building to Sarnia and the Grand Trunk tapping London and Detroit. Between the Great Western and Lake Erie a rival road direct from Buffalo to Detroit was threatened time and again, but was not built until after Confederation. South of Lake Erie, the Lake Shore and Michigan Southern was built shortly afterwards by interests connected with the New York Central, thus threatening the traffic connections of the Great Western both east and west. To avert loss of its western trade, the Great Western sunk large sums in aiding the construction of a road from Detroit to Grand Haven, with ferry connections to Milwaukee; but this experiment did not prove a success and caused serious embarrassment.

The Northern Railway, whose promoters, as we have seen, naively recognized that railways and lotteries were close akin, was opened as far as Allandale in 1853, and to Collingwood in 1855. It was scamped by the contractors, poorly built, and overloaded with debt. The sanguine policy of building up a through traffic from the American West, by water to Collingwood and rail to Toronto, proved a will-o'-the-wisp. In turn the company relied on independent steamers, and set up a fleet of its own, but equally in vain so far as profit went. By 1859 the road was bankrupt. A new general manager, Frederick Cumberland, brought in a change of policy. Local traffic was sedulously cultivated, and a fair degree of prosperity followed.

Most of the lesser roads constructed looked to the municipalities rather than to the provinces for aid. The Municipal Loan Fund of 1854 was the third and last phase of Hincks' railway policy. This was an ingenious attempt to give the municipalities the prestige of provincial connection without accepting any legal responsibility. Municipalities had previously been permitted to bonus or take stock in railways and toll roads, but their securities were unknown in the world's markets. Hincks now provided that municipalities which wished money to aid railways or other local improvements might practically pool their credit and share in the credit of the province. Provincial debentures were issued against the municipal obligations pooled in the Fund, and the proceeds of their sale given to the municipalities. A sinking fund was to be maintained, and, if need be, the province could levy through the sheriff on any defaulting town.

The municipalities made full use of their privileges. It was believed that railway investments would yield high dividends, and the more optimistic expected to see all taxes made unnecessary by the profits earned. Town vied with town in extravagant enterprises.[1] Not a cent brought a dividend; instead, the municipalities found themselves saddled with heavy interest payments. One after another declined to pay; Port Hope was $312,000 in arrears by 1861 and Cobourg $313,000.

The provincial government had not the political courage to send in the sheriff, and accordingly it was forced at last to assume the whole burden. Prudent municipalities which had declined to borrow at eight per cent found themselves compelled to share the burdens of their reckless neighbours. Demoralization was widespread.

The railways constructed by such aid may be briefly noted. The Buffalo and Lake Huron, extending from Fort Erie to Goderich, was com-

[1] Port Hope borrowed for railway investment $740,000, Cobourg and Brantford $500,000 each, and Brockville $400,000 —all towns of less than 5000 people. The counties of Lanark and Renfrew borrowed $800,000, and villages borrowed in proportion. In all some $6,500,000 was borrowed through the Loan Fund for railway purposes alone, the bulk of it in Upper Canada, while another three million was invested by towns that borrowed on their own responsibility. To aid the Brockville and Ottawa Railway, for example, Lanark and Renfrew advanced $800,000, Brockville $415,000, and the township of Elizabethtown $150,000, or over half the cost of the road. Huron and Bruce invested $300,000 in the Buffalo and Lake Huron, and other municipalities $578,000, and so on throughout the province.

pleted in 1858. It had its origin in the ambition of Buffalo to have more immediate connection with the rich western peninsula of Upper Canada and the Lake trade beyond than was afforded by the Great Western. The London and Port Stanley, built in 1854-56, mainly by the city of London, with smaller contributions from Middlesex and Elgin counties and the city of St Thomas, failed to realize the expectations that it would become the main artery of trade between Canada and the states across the lake, but it developed a fair excursion trade and coal traffic, and indirectly justified its construction. The Erie and Ontario portage road, rebuilt in 1854, has already been noted. Another portage road round Niagara Falls was the Welland Railway, planned by W. Hamilton Merritt, the projector of the Welland Canal. It ran from Port Colborne on Lake Erie to Port Dalhousie on Lake Ontario, twenty-five miles, and was completed in 1859, only to add one more to the list of unprofitable roads, and eventually to be absorbed by the Great Western.

Farther east the rivalry of Port Hope and Cobourg led to the construction of two roads, the Cobourg and Peterborough and the Port Hope, Lindsay and Beaverton. Both relied chiefly on timber traffic and aimed to develop the farming country in the rear. The Cobourg line, begun in 1853, suffered disaster from the start: the contractor's extras absorbed all the cash available; the three-mile bridge built on piles across Rice Lake gave way, and after $1,000,000 had been expended the road was sold for $100,000. The Port Hope line, which absorbed a branch from Millbrook to Peterborough in 1867, fared somewhat better. The Brockville and Ottawa was a lumber road, carrying supplies up and timber down. It was chartered to run from Brockville to Pembroke, with a branch from Smith's Falls on the Rideau Canal to Perth. By 1859 it had reached Almonte, and six years later struggled as far as Sand Point on the Ottawa, when it halted, till the Canadian Pacific project gave it new life. After failing to make ends meet for some years the company went through repeated reorganizations in the early sixties. The Bytown and Prescott, later the St Lawrence and Ottawa, built in 1854, was also a lumber road, promoted by interests connected with the Ogdensburg Railway, whose terminus was opposite Prescott. It suffered the same financial fate, and was sold to the English company which had supplied the rails, at a total sacrifice of municipal and other creditors' interests. Around the Long Sault rapids in the Ottawa there was built in 1854 the thirteen-mile Carillon and Grenville, a summer portage road, an early enterprise which retained its independence and its old five-foot-six-inch gauge until 1912, when it was absorbed by the Canadian Northern. In Lower Canada the only minor road built which has not been referred to was the Stanstead, Shefford and Chambly, opened in 1859 from St Johns to Granby, and forming practically an extension of the Champlain and St Lawrence from the former point.

CHAPTER SIX
THE INTERCOLONIAL

The first 'age of iron—and of brass' came to an end before 1860. Between 1850 and i860, it has been seen, the mileage of all the provinces grew from 66 to 2065. By 1867 it had increased only 213 miles. In two of the intervening years not a mile was built. A halt had come, for stock-taking and heart-searching.

This first era of activity had given as its most obvious result over two thousand miles of railway. In Nova Scotia, Halifax was linked with the Bay of Fundy and the Gulf of St Lawrence; in New Brunswick, St John was connected with the Gulf, and a road was struggling Canada-ward from St Andrews. In the Canadas a 'Grant Trunk,' so nicknamed, ran from Rivière du Loup the whole length of the province to Sarnia, while lesser roads opened up new districts to the north or gave connection with the grain-fields and the ocean ports of the United States. The western province, at all events, was well served for a pioneer country, and the shipper and consumer had no great cause for complaint.

To the taxpayer it seemed otherwise. He had been induced to embark on a lavish policy of financial aid on the assurance that the roads would at worst be no burden, and at best might yield large profits to the state. As a matter of fact, nine out of every ten dollars advanced might be written off as lost. The Grand Trunk, Great Western, and Northern roads were indebted to the old province of Canada on July 1, 1867, in over twenty million dollars for principal advanced and in over thirteen millions for interest. Other roads were indebted to Canadian municipalities in nearly ten millions for principal alone. Yet the taxpayer was not wholly justified in his grumbling. There had been waste and mismanagement, it is true, but the railways had brought indirect gain that more than offset the direct loss. Farming districts were opened up rapidly, freights were reduced in many sections, intercourse was facilitated, and land values were raised. The contribution to the railways was bread well cast upon the waters. It would have been better, if foresight had equaled hindsight, to have given the money out and out.

For the shareholder, English or Canadian, there was little but disappointment. Grand Trunk ordinary stock in 1865 was selling at 22, and even Great Western at 65. The securities of several of the minor roads had been almost entirely wiped out by reorganizations. In 1866 some $4,180,000 was paid in dividends and leases, representing only 2.7 per cent on the $158,000,000 which the roads had cost or were alleged to have cost. Premature extension into un-remunerative territory, for political or contracting reasons, excessive competition in the fertile areas, heavy fixed charges on inflated capital or leased roads, water competition, absentee proprietorship, all played their part. Whatever the causes, the results were clear, and capitalists long fought shy of Canadian railway projects.

In the first thirty years of Canadian railway development no question aroused more interest than that of the gauge to be adopted. The cows of the good Dutch burghers of New Amsterdam fixed the windings of Broadway as they remain to this day. The width of the carts used in English coal-mines centuries ago still determines the gauge of railway track and railway cars over nearly all the world. 'Before every engine,' declares Mr H. G. Wells, 'trots the ghost of a superseded horse.' When the steam locomotive was invented, and used upon the coal-mine tramways, it was made of the same four-foot-eight-and-a-half-inch gauge. In England, in spite of the preferences of Brunel, Stephenson's great rival, for a seven-foot gauge, the narrower width soon triumphed, though the Great Western did not entirely abandon its wider track until 1892. In Canada the struggle was longer and more complicated.

It was a question on which engineers differed. Speed, steadiness, cost of track construction, and cost of maintenance were all to be considered, and were all diversely estimated. In early years, before the need of standardizing equipment was felt, many experiments were made, especially in the United States. In the southern states five feet was the usual width, and the Erie was built on a gauge of six feet, to fit an engine bought at a bargain. But in the United States, as in England, the four-foot-eight-and-a-half-inch width was dominant, and would have been adopted in Canada without question, had not local interests, appealing, as often, to patriotic prejudice, succeeded in clouding the issue.

When the road from Portland to Montreal was being planned, the astute Portland promoters insisted upon a gauge of five feet six inches, to prevent the switching of traffic to Boston. Montreal, in its turn, insisted on the same gauge for the Grand Trunk line, to ensure that all east-bound traffic should be brought through Canada to Montreal. It carried its point, and the wider or ' provincial' gauge became the standard in the Canadas, and later in the Maritime Provinces.

Experience proved that it was impossible to maintain different gauges in countries so closely connected as Canada and the United States. As roads became consolidated into larger systems, the inconvenience of tran-shipping at break of gauge became more intolerable. The expedients of lifting cars bodily to other trucks, of making axles adjustable, and even of laying a third rail, proved unsatisfactory. Late in the sixties and early in the seventies the Great Western and the Grand Trunk had to adopt the four-foot-eight-and-a-half-inch gauge solely, and other lines gradually followed.

Meanwhile, the cry was going up for a still narrower gauge. In pioneer districts, at least, it was contended, a road three feet six inches wide, such as had recently been adopted in Norway, would suffice, and would be much cheaper both to build and to operate. Between 1868 and 1873 two experimental narrow-gauge lines were built running north from Toronto—the Toronto and Nipissing, and the Toronto, Grey and Bruce. This proved only a temporary diversion, however, and the decision of the Dominion government in 1874 to change the gauge of the Intercolonial to four feet eight and a half inches, and the adoption of the same standard by the Ontario government, ended the controversy.

Memory is short and hope eternal. Soon after Confederation another burst of activity began in all the provinces of the new Dominion. It was distinctly the period of local development.

In Ontario the opportunity which the fertile western peninsula, jutting down between New York and Michigan, offered for both local and through traffic, led to many projects, much parliamentary jockeying, and at last construction. The Canada Southern was built in 1873, running between Fort Erie, opposite Buffalo, and Amherstburg on the Detroit river. It was controlled by the Vanderbilt interests and operated in close co-operation with their other roads, the Michigan Southern, Michigan Central, and New York Central. The Great Western met this attack upon its preserves by building in the same year the Canada Air Line, from Glencoe near St Thomas, to Fort Erie, giving more direct connection with Buffalo. Both roads made use of the magnificent International Bridge, built across the Niagara in 1873, under Grand Trunk control.

The marked feature of this period, so far as Ontario was concerned, was the rivalry of the cities along the lake and river front in building new roads to tap the north country. From London there was built in 1875 the London, Huron and Bruce, halting at Wingham. From Hamilton, or rather from Guelph, with connections to Hamilton, the Wellington, Grey and Bruce reached Southampton on Lake Huron in 1873 and Kincardine in 1874. Both roads were virtually branches of the Great Western, and were expected to bring to London and to Hamilton respectively the trade of the rich northwestern counties. The Ambitious City, as Hamilton came to be called at this period, a few years later invaded the Northern Railway's territory by a line from Hamilton to Collingwood, also extended southerly to Port Dover, but control of this road was immediately acquired by the Northern interests. From still more ambitious Toronto two narrow-gauge routes were built between 1869 and 1874—the Toronto, Grey and Bruce running northwest to Owen Sound and Teeswater, and the Toronto and Nipissing northeast to Coboconk and Sutton. Whitby also had its visions of terminal greatness, when the Whitby and Port Perry was built in the later seventies. The Port Hope, Beaverton and Lindsay, renamed the Midland, was pushed northeast to Orillia in 1872 and to Midland in 1875. Cobourg's unfortunate northern line was continued to the iron mines of Marmora. Belleville was linked with Peterborough in 1878-79 by the Grand Junction. Kingston, with the co-operation of interests in New York state, planned the Kingston and Pembroke, which reached Mississippi in 1878, and five years later compromised on Renfrew as a terminus. The bankruptcy of the Brockville and Ottawa did not prevent its extension through an allied company, the Canada Central, to Pembroke in 1869 and to Ottawa, by a branch from Carleton Place, in 1876.

In Quebec the chief developments were the building of a line connecting Quebec, Montreal, and Ottawa along the north shore of the St Lawrence, and of further connections between Montreal and Quebec and United States roads. The North Shore route had been projected early in the fifties, but, in spite of lavish cash and land bonuses, it was not until the Quebec government took it up as a provincial road, in the seventies, that it was pushed to completion. On the south shore the Eastern Townships triangle was interlaced by a series of smaller roads. From Lévis, opposite Quebec, the Lévis and Kennebec ran south to the Maine border, and the Quebec Central to Sherbrooke. From Sherbrooke and Lennoxville the Massawappi Valley gave connection with the Connecticut and Passumpsic, to which it was leased for 999 years, while branches of the Central Vermont and minor roads opened up new sections and gave further connection with Montreal.

An interesting experiment, motived by the same desire for cheap pioneer construction which in Ontario brought in the narrow gauge, was the wooden railway built in 1870 from Quebec to Gosford. The rails were simply strips of seasoned maple, 14' x 7" x 4", notched into the sleepers and wedged in without the use of a single iron spike. The engine and car wheels were made wide to fit the rail. In spite of its cheap construction the road did not pay, and the hope of extending it as far as Lake St John was deferred for a generation. A similar wooden railway was built from Drummondville to L'Avenir.

In Nova Scotia the chief local development was the opening in 1869 of a road through the Annapolis Valley, the Windsor and Annapolis. This formed an extension of the government road from Halifax to Windsor, but the province preferred to entrust it to a private company, giving a liberal bonus. In New Brunswick there was much activity, all by private companies. The western section of the European and North American, from St John to the Maine boundary, was completed in 1869, though it was not until 1871 that the road was opened through to Portland—by a more circuitous route than Poor had originally planned. From Fredericton a branch was built to meet this road, and a line to Woodstock, which in turn was connected with the old New Brunswick and Canada, still pushing slowly north. In the meantime Prince Edward Island was building a narrow-gauge railway nearly two hundred miles long; in 1873 she was forced into Confederation to find aid in paying for it.

All this varied activity was made possible by a revival of the policy of provincial and municipal assistance. Whether from reasoned conviction as to the indirect benefits of more roads, or because of the log-rolling activities of rival towns and wily promoters, a systematic and generous policy of aid was adopted. This aid came chiefly from the provinces and municipalities, the Dominion as yet confining itself to works of interprovincial concern. Outright gifts for the most part took the place of loans, since experience had proved that direct returns upon the money invested were not to be looked for. Curiously meandering were the routes which promoters mapped out in the endeavour to follow the shortest line between two bonuses.[1]

Governments could help to build roads, but could not ensure for them traffic. It took very few years to show that the interests of the public were not best served by scores of petty isolated roads, and that the interests of shareholders were not secured by the cut-throat competition which prevailed in certain areas. This competition was keenest between the roads which were intimately connected with the lines in the United States and dependent upon through traffic. The Grand Trunk had cut into the territory of the Great Western by acquiring the Buffalo and Lake Huron line, and the Canada Southern and the Great Western were disputing for every ton of freight between the Niagara and the Detroit. All were involved in the rate wars which marked this period in the United States. In 1867 the Grand Trunk and the Great Western agreed to maintain rates, pool certain traffic receipts, refrain from competitive building, and co-operate in service. The agreement broke down; another was made in 1876, only to fail in turn. More effective measures had to be adopted.

The outstanding achievement of the period, however, was the build-

---

[1] Ontario in 1871 offered subsidies ranging from two to four thousand dollars a mile for colonization roads to the north; Quebec in 1869 offered money and later land; New Brunswick in 1864 gave $10,000 a mile to various roads, besides taking $300,000 in stock in the European; while Nova Scotia aided the Annapolis extension. Municipal aid was even more lavish in proportion: Toronto gave $350,000 to the Toronto, Grey and Bruce, $150,000 to the Nipissing road, $100,000 to the Northern, and $350,000 to the Credit Valley. Hamilton backed the Hamilton and North-Western by $200,000, London gave the London, Huron and Bruce $150,000, and generous Kingston gave to the Kingston and Pembroke over $300,000. Counties like Elgin and Simcoe, Grey, and Frontenac offered from $150,000 to $300,000, while from townships alone the Wellington, Grey and Bruce received $680,000. Montreal and Quebec each helped the North Shore by a gift of a million dollars; Ottawa county's $200,000 and the parish of Canrobert's $1000 were equally sought; while to a lesser degree the Maritime Provinces showed the same tendency.

ing of the Intercolonial. It had been projected largely in order to make closer union between the provinces possible, but, as it turned out, it was Confederation that brought the Intercolonial, not the Intercolonial that brought Confederation.

After the breakdown of the negotiations in London in 1852, each province had turned to its own tasks. But each in building its own roads had provided possible links in the future Intercolonial chain. In Canada the Grand Trunk ran to a point 120 miles east of Quebec; in New Brunswick, St John was connected with both the east and west boundaries of the province; in Nova Scotia, a road ran north from Halifax as far as Truro. A gap of nearly five hundred miles between Rivière du Loup and Truro remained. To bridge this wilderness seemed beyond the private or public resources of the divided provinces. Unanimous on one point only, they once more turned to the British government. In 1857 and 1858 dispatches and deputations sought aid, but sought it in vain. When the Civil War broke out in the United States, official British sympathy was given to the South, and the *Trent* affair showed how near Britain and the North were to war, a war which would at once have exposed the isolated colonies to American attack. The military argument for closer connection then took on new weight with the British government, and it proposed, to a joint delegation in 1861, to revert to its offer of ten years earlier—to guarantee a colonial loan for a railway by an approved route. The colonies opposed the demand for a sinking fund, and again agreement was postponed. In 1863 Canada suggested that, as the British government had made an approved route an essential condition, a definite survey and selection should be undertaken forthwith. It was agreed that a commission of three engineers should be selected, one nominated by Canada, one by New Brunswick and Nova Scotia, and one by Great Britain. Canada nominated Sandford Fleming, a distinguished Scottish-Canadian engineer, who had been connected with the Northern and other Upper Canada enterprises. The other authorities paid him the compliment of naming him as their representative also, to facilitate the work. During the progress of the survey negotiations for the union of the provinces had begun, and when Confederation came about in 1867, the building of the Intercolonial at the common expense of the Dominion, with an imperial guarantee to the extent of £3,000,000, was one of the conditions of union. The old difficulty as to the route through New Brunswick was still to be settled. Again western and southern New Brunswick struggled against the north and against far east Quebec; again Halifax and St John found plausible arguments to uphold their respective interests. Finally, the views of Sir George Cartier and Peter Mitchell triumphed in the Cabinet councils, and in March 1868 the engineer-in-chief advised the selection of the roundabout Bay of Chaleurs route—roughly 'Major Robinson's line'—ostensibly because safer from American attack, nearer possible steamship connection with Europe, and no worse, if no better, than the other routes in potentialities of local traffic.

The construction was entrusted in December 1868 to a commission of four; six years later the minister of Public Works took over direct control. Sandford Fleming remained engineer-in-chief for the building as well as for the survey. Tenders were submitted for the construction of the whole road, but the government decided to award the contract in small sections. The road was not completed as speedily as had been expected. Difficulties arose, expected and unexpected—cuttings in heavy rock, sliding clay banks, extensive swamps, lack of rock bottom for heavy bridges. Contractor after contractor found that he had underestimated the task, and went bankrupt or threw up the contract. Sometimes the contract was re-let, sometimes the government completed it by day work. At last, on July 1, 1876, nine years after Confederation, the five hundred miles between Truro and Rivière du Loup were opened for traffic throughout. In the meantime the Dominion had taken over the Nova Scotia, New Brunswick, and Prince Edward Island government roads. In 1876 there were in all 950 miles of railway under the control of the Dominion government, as against 4268 miles of private lines.

CHAPTER SEVEN
THE CANADIAN PACIFIC—BEGINNINGS

On March 3, 1841, Sir George Simpson, governor-in-chief of the Hudson's Bay Company's domains, left London on a journey round the world. All the resources of a powerful and well-organized corporation were at his disposal, and his own reputation for rapid travelling gave assurance that on the actual journey not an hour would be lost. A fortnight's sail brought him from Liverpool to Halifax, and thence he journeyed by steamer to Boston, by rail to Nashua, by coach to Concord, and by sleigh to Montreal. The portage railway from St John to Laprairie was on his route, but it was not open in winter.

From Montreal Sir George and his party set out on May 4 in two light thirty-foot canoes, each carrying a crew of twelve or fourteen men. At top speed they worked their way up the Ottawa and the Mattawa out to Lake Nipissing, and down the French River into Georgian Bay. They camped every night at sunset, and rose each morning at one. Their tireless Canadian and Iroquois voyageurs worked eighteen hours a day, paddling swiftly through smooth water, wading through shallows, or towing the canoes through the lesser rapids, or portaging once to a dozen times a day round the more difficult ones. Each voyageur was ready to shoulder his 180 pounds, strapped to his forehead, or to ferry passengers ashore on his back. They reached Sault Ste Marie on May 16, only to find Lake Superior still frozen. They picked their way very slowly through the opening rifts along the shore, made the Company's post at Fort William in eleven days, exchanged their large canoes for smaller craft, and paddled and portaged through the endless network of river and lake to Fort Garry, which they reached on June 10, thirty-eight days out from Montreal.

From Fort Garry a fresh start was made on July 3, on horseback, with baggage sent ahead in lumbering Red River carts. Past Fort Ellice and Fort Carlton, they pushed on with fresh supplies of horses at the topmost speed that the limitations of their convoy of carts would permit. Band after band of Plains Indians, adorned with war-paint and scalp-locks, crossed their trail, but mosquito and sand-fly proved more troublesome. The travellers passed a band of emigrants making slowly for the Columbia, and everywhere found countless herds of buffalo. In three weeks from Fort Garry they reached Fort Edmonton. Here forty-five fresh horses were in readiness for riding, pack-horses took the place of carts, and the journey was continued to the southwest. The Rockies were crossed through Kootenay Pass, and at last—after many a halt to find straying horses, and after continuous annoyance from mosquitoes and venomous insects 'which in size and appearance might have been mistaken for a cross between the bulldog and the house-fly'—Fort Colville on the Columbia was reached on August 18. Their long horseback ride was over. Favoured by wonderfully fine weather, in the saddle eleven to twelve hours a day, they had made their way through open prairie and rolling plain, tangled thicket and burning forest and rushing river, and had covered the two thousand miles from Fort Garry in six weeks and five days. From Fort Colville they reached the waters of the Pacific at Fort Vancouver (Washington) in another six days. The continent had been crossed in twelve weeks of actual travelling.

Sir George Simpson's journey stood as the record for many a year. For a generation after his day the scattered travellers from Red River westward were compelled to rely on saddle-horse and plains cart and canoe. From Montreal and Toronto the railway could be utilized as far as Collingwood, and thence the steamer to Port Arthur. Then for a time the government opened up a summer route to the Red River, beginning it in 1869 and maintaining it until 1876. The Dawson route, as it was called, included forty-five miles of wagon-road from Port Arthur to Lake Shebandowan, then over three hundred miles of water travel, with a dozen portages, and again ninety-five miles of wagon-road from the Lake of the Woods to Fort Garry.[1] In 1870 it took ninety-five days to transport troops from Toronto to Fort Garry over this route. Such makeshifts could not serve for long. South of the border the railway was rapidly pushing westward, and in the new nation of the north, as well, its time had come.

---

[1] "Lord Strathcona may still remember the man who came into his office at Winnipeg and said: "Look at me; ain't I a healthy sight? I've come by the government water route from Thunder Bay, and it's taken me twenty-five days to do it. During that time I've been half-starved on victuals I wouldn't give a swampy Indian. The water used to pour into my bunk at nights, and the boat was so leaky that every bit of baggage I've got is water-logged and ruined. I've broke my arm and sprained my ankle helping to carry half a dozen trunks over a dozen portages, and when I refused to take a paddle on one of the boats, an Ottawa Irishman told me to go to hell, and said that if I gave him any more of my damned chat he'd let me get off and walk to Winnipeg.'"—W. L. Grant in *Geographical Journal*, October 1911, p. 36s. - R.B.

Ever after the coming of the locomotive, it needed only imagination and a map to see all British North America clamped by an iron band. Engineers like Bonnycastle and Synge and Carmichael-Smyth wrote of the possibility in the forties. Politicians found in the theme matter for admirable after-dinner perorations—colonial governors like Harvey in 1847, colonial secretaries like Lytton and Carnarvon in the fifties, and colonial premiers like Joseph Howe, who declared in Halifax in 1851: 'I believe that many in this room will live to hear the whistle of the steam-engine in the passes of the Rocky Mountains, and to make the journey from Halifax to the Pacific in five or six days.' Promoters were not lacking. In 1851 Allan Macdonnell of Toronto sought a charter and a subsidy for a road to the Pacific, and the Canadian authorities, in declining, expressed their opinion that the scheme was not visionary and their hope that some day Great Britain and the United States might undertake it jointly. Seven years later the same promoter secured a charter for the Northwest Transportation, Navigation, and Railway Company, to operate between Lake Superior and the Fraser river, but could get no backing; four years previously John Young, A. N. Morin, A. T. Galt, and John A. Poor had petitioned in vain for a similar charter. Then in 1862, on behalf of the Red River Settlement, Sandford Fleming prepared an elaborate memorial on the subject. Edwin Watkin, of the Grand Trunk, negotiated with the Hudson's Bay Company for right of way and other facilities, but the project proved too vast for his resources.

Two things were needed before dreams on paper could become facts in steel—national unity and international rivalry. Years before Confederation, such far-seeing Canadians as William M'Dougall and George Brown had pressed for the annexation of the British territories beyond the Lakes. After Confederation, all speed was made to buy out the sovereign rights of the Hudson's Bay Company. Then came the first Riel Rebellion, to bring home the need of a western road, as the *Trent* affair had brought home the need of the Intercolonial. The decisive political factor came into play in 1870, when British Columbia entered the federation. Its less than ten thousand white inhabitants—deeming themselves citizens of no mean country, and kept to their demands by the urging of an indefatigable Englishman, Alfred Waddington— made the construction of an overland railway an indispensable condition of union, and Sir John Macdonald courageously accepted their terms.

The other factor, international rivalry, exercised its influence about the same time. In the United States the railway had rapidly pushed westward, but had halted before the deserts and the mountains lying between the Mississippi and the Pacific. The rivalry of pro-slavery and anti-slavery parties in Congress long brought to deadlock all plans of public aid to either southern or northern route. Then the Civil War broke the deadlock: the need of binding the West to the side of the North created a strong public demand for a Pacific road, and Congress, so stimulated, and further lubricated by the payment, as is proven, of at least $476,000 in bribes, gave lavish loans and grants of land. The Central Pacific, working from Sacramento, and the Union Pacific, starting from Omaha, met near Ogden in Utah in 1869—or rather here the rails met, for the rival companies, eager to earn the high subsidy given for mountain construction, had actually graded two hundred superfluous miles in parallel lines. In 1871 the Southern Pacific and the Texas Pacific were fighting for subsidies, and Jay Cooke was promoting the Northern Pacific. The young Dominion was stirred by ambition to emulate its powerful neighbour.

These factors, then, brought the question of a railway to the Pacific on Canadian soil within the range of practical politics. Important questions remained to be settled. During the parliamentary session of 1871 the government of Sir John Macdonald decided that the road should be built by a company, not by the state, that it should be aided by liberal subsidies in cash and in land, and, to meet British Columbia's insistent terms, that it should be begun within two, and completed within ten, years. The Opposition protested that this latter provision was uncalled for and would bankrupt the Dominion, but the government carried its point, though it was forced to hedge later by a stipulation—not included in the formal resolutions—that the annual expenditure should be such as not to press unduly upon the Dominion's resources.

The first task was to survey the vast wilderness between the Ottawa valley and the Pacific, and to find, if possible, a feasible route. So able an explorer and engineer as Captain Palliser, appointed by the British government to report upon the country west of the Lakes, had declared in 1863, after four years of careful labour in the field, that, thanks to the choice of the 49th parallel as Canada's boundary, there was no possibility of ever building a transcontinental railway exclusively through British territory. The man chosen for the task of achieving this impossibility was Sandford Fleming. Appointed engineer-in-chief in 1871, he was for nine years in charge of the surveys, though for half that time his duties on the Intercolonial absorbed much of his energy. Mr Fleming possessed an unusual gift of literary style, and his reports upon the work of his staff gave the people of Canada a very clear idea of the difficulties to be encountered. His friend, the Rev. George M. Grant, who accompanied him in a rapid reconnaissance in 1872, gave, in his book *Ocean to Ocean*, a vivid and heartening record of the realities and the promise that he saw.

It had been decided, in order to hold the balance even between Montreal and Toronto, to make the proposed Pacific road begin at some angle of Lake Nipissing. From that point nearly to the Red River there stretched a thousand miles of woodland, rugged and rock-strewn, covered by a network of countless lakes and rivers, interspersed with seemingly bottomless swamps or muskegs—a wilderness which no white man had ever passed through from end to end. Then came the level prairie and a great rolling plain rising to the southwest in three successive steppes, and cut by deep watercourses. But it was the third or mountain section which presented the most serious engineering difficulties. Four hundred miles from the Pacific coast, and roughly parallel, ran the towering Rocky Mountains, some of whose peaks rose fifteen thousand feet. Beyond stretched a vast plateau, three or four thousand feet above sea-level, intersected by rivers which had cut deep chasms or, to the northward, wide sheltered valleys. Between this plateau and the coast the Cascades interposed, rivalling the Rockies in height and rising sheer from the ocean, which thrust in deep fiord channels. At the head of some one of these fiords must be found the western terminus.

Early in the survey a practicable route was found throughout. Striking across the wilderness from Lake Nipissing to Lake Superior at the river Pic, the line might skirt the shore of the lake to Fort William, or it might run northerly through what is now known as the clay belt, with Fort William and the lake made accessible by a branch. Continuing westward to the Red River at Selkirk, with Winnipeg on a branch line to the south, the projected line crossed Lake Manitoba at the Narrows, and then struck out northwesterly, through what was then termed the 'Fertile Belt,' till the Yellowhead Pass was reached. Here the Rockies could be easily pierced; but once through the engineer was faced by the huge flanking range of the Cariboo Mountains, in which repeated explorations failed to find a gap. But at the foot of the towering barrier lay a remarkable deep-set valley four hundred miles in length, in which northwestward ran the Fraser river and southeastward the Canoe and the Columbia waterways. By following the Fraser to its great southward bend, and then striking west, a terminus on Bute or Dean Inlet might be reached, while the valley of the Canoe and the Albreda would give access to the North Thompson as far as Kamloops, whence the road might run down the Thompson and the lower Fraser to Burrard Inlet. The latter route, on the whole, was preferred.

While this route was feasible, the mountain portion promised to be extremely expensive. This factor, together with the uncertainty of government policy and the desire of Victoria to have the road built to Bute Inlet and thence, by a bridge across Valdes Strait, carried down to Esquimalt, made it necessary to seek untiringly, year after year, for alternative routes. The only important change made, however, until after 1880, was the deflection of the line south of Lake Manitoba to serve existing settlements.

Who was to build the road? It would be a tremendous task for either the government or the private capitalists of a nation of four million people. The United States had not begun its Pacific roads till it had over thirty millions of people, and wealth and experience to correspond. It was estimated that the Canadian road would cost $100,000,000, and it was certain that the engineering difficulties would be staggering. In Canada few roads had paid the shareholders, and though some had profited the contractors, the new enterprise meant such a plunge in the dark that contractors and promoters alike hesitated. In the United States, however, the Pacific roads had proved gold-mines for their promoters. The land-grants were valuable, and the privilege of granting contracts to dummy construction companies controlled by themselves and thus reaping larger profits was still greater.

It was not to be wondered at, therefore, that the first offer came from American capitalists. Alfred Waddington, enthusiast rather than practical promoter, sought at Ottawa a charter for the road he had done so much to secure, but his bill went no further than a first reading. At Ottawa he was met by G. W. M'Mullen, a Canadian residing in Chicago, who was visiting the Dominion on a canal deputation. M'Mullen became interested, and with his Chicago partners endeavoured to enlist the aid of the men behind the Northern Pacific—Jay Cooke, General Cass, W. B. Ogden, T. A. Scott, and others.[1] M'Mullen soon found that Waddington had exaggerated his influence, and that the government was not yet prepared to discuss terms. Sir Francis Hincks, stormy petrel of railway building, whom Sir John Macdonald had just made his finance minister, suggested to Sir Hugh Allan of Montreal that he should get into touch with these Americans and provide the substantial Canadian interest which was essential.

Sir Hugh Allan was then the foremost business man in Canada. He was head of the great Allan steamship line, and had become interested in railways shortly before, when rumours of the intention of the Grand Trunk to establish a rival steamship line to Great Britain had led him to assist in promoting the North Shore from Quebec westward, to compete with the Grand Trunk and ensure traffic for his steamers. He now opened negotiations with the American capitalists through M'Mullen, came to terms, and then sought associates in Canada. Here difficulties arose: Ontario objected that Allan's control would mean a Quebec rather than an Ontario terminus, and that the Northern Pacific directors with whom he was associated were simply conspiring to get control of the Canadian road, in order to delay its construction and prevent it becoming a rival to their own northerly route. Sir George Cartier, too, powerful in the Cabinet and salaried solicitor of the Grand Trunk, was a stumbling-block; he declared himself emphatically opposed to control by any '*sacrée compagnie americaine*' [bloody American company]. But Sir Hugh, believing much in money and little in men, resolved to buy his way through. He soon started a backfire in Quebec which brought Cartier to terms. Ontario rivalry was harder to control: D. L. Macpherson and other Toronto men organized the Interoceanic Railway Company to oppose Allan's

---

[1] The Northern Pacific was at many stages in its history closely connected with Canadian affairs. It had originally been projected in New England: the first proposal was to use the Central Vermont and a Canadian road to be built or acquired as the eastern links, then, crossing- into Michigan, the railway was to strike northwestward to the Pacific. When control fell into the hands of New York and Philadelphia interests, these plans were dropped, but later the new management negotiated with Governor Archibald of Manitoba, as well as with Sir John Macdonald, to endeavour to put through an international road, the first section running through Canada to Sault Ste Marie, the second through Michigan and Minnesota, the third through the Canadian plains, and the fourth through the Rockies to the sea on American territory. Nothing came of the negotiations, though it may be noted that the Canadian Pacific today has carried out precisely this plan, in addition to its all-Canadian line.

Canada Pacific Company. Both companies sought charters and aid. Allan pretended to drop his American associates; Macpherson charged that the connection still existed. The government endeavoured to bring about an amalgamation, with Allan as president, and, failing this, to organize a new company. In the meantime Allan was spending money so freely that even his New York associates were astounded. The Dominion elections were held in August 1872, and Macdonald, Cartier, and Langevin drew heavily on Allan's funds, $162,500 in all, with a promise from Cartier that 'any amount which you or your Company shall advance for that purpose shall be recouped to you.' After the election a new company, the Canadian Pacific, was organized, with representative men from each province as directors; and the new board, of its own motion, it was declared, elected Allan president. To this company the government granted a charter, promised a subsidy of thirty million dollars and fifty million acres of land, but insisted upon excluding the American interests. Allan acquiesced, and, repaying the advances made, informed New York that negotiations were ended. M'Mullen and his associates, angry at this treatment, conveyed rumours to Opposition leaders, and finally Allan's confdential correspondence, stolen by a clerk in the office of J. J. C. Abbott, Allan's solicitor, was made public.[1] The fat was in the fire.

With the political controversy which followed we are not here concerned. In Sir John Macdonald's defence it could be said, that though Allan's money was taken no special favours were shown in the contract made ; and that all that Allan secured by the government's victory was the certainty that the railway project would not be postponed or dropped altogether, and that he would be given control. Sir Hugh Allan had said with much force : 'The plans I propose are in themselves the best for the interests of the Dominion, and in urging them on the public I am really doing a most patriotic action.' Undoubtedly Sir John Macdonald sincerely held a similar opinion.

The Allan Company gave up its charter, unable to raise capital in face of financial depression and political upheaval. The Liberal party, led by

---

[1] This correspondence will be found in the Journals of the House of Commons, vol. vii, 1873. In no other documents available to the public has the connection between politics and railway promoting in Canada been made so evident. The following are a few brief extracts from letters addressed by Sir Hugh Allan to various American associates during 1872:

> Thinking; that as I had taken up the project there must be something very good in it, a very formidable opposition was organized in Toronto, which for want of a better took as their cry 'No foreign influence; no Yankee dictation; no Northern Pacific to choke off our Canadian Pacific,' and others equally sensible. ... I was forced to drop ostensibly from our organization every American name, and put in reliable people on this side in place of them. . . . Mr M'Mullen was desirous of securing the inferior members of the Government, and entered into engagements of which I did not approve, as I thought it was only a waste of powder and shot. On a calm view of the situation I satisfied myself that the decision of the question must ultimately be in the hands of one man, and that

Alexander Mackenzie, and swept into power by a wave of popular indignation, first endeavoured to induce other capitalists to take up the work. But the government's offers of $10,000 in cash and of 20,000 acres of land for each mile, plus an undetermined guarantee, had no takers in the years of depression that followed. Mackenzie then decided that the government should itself build the road. He planned to build at first only the indispensable sections, using the waterways wherever possible, and hoped, but in vain, to secure British Columbia's consent to an extension of the time set for completion. His first step was to subsidize the Canada Central, which ran from Ottawa via Carleton Place to Pembroke, to extend its line as far as Lake Nipissing, in order to connect with the proposed eastern terminus of the Pacific road, and to award a contract (it was afterwards cancelled) for a branch from this junction point to Georgian Bay. Passing by for the time the country north of Lake Superior, he next let contracts for the greater part of the distance between Fort William and Selkirk and for a road from Selkirk to Emerson, on the Manitoba border. Here connection was to be made with an American line, the St Paul and Pacific, of which more will be heard presently.

When Mackenzie left office in 1878 the work of location or construction was well advanced in all three sections. For two years the new administration of Sir John Macdonald carried on the same policy of government construction at a moderate pace. The work in hand was continued and the gaps in the road between Port Arthur and Selkirk were put under contract. The line was made to pass through Winnipeg—instead of striking west from Selkirk, as the engineers had previously advised, and thus side-tracking the ambitious city growing up around old Fort Garry. Contracts were let for two hundred miles of the extension westward from Winnipeg. Two seasons passed before the new government could make up its mind as to the British Columbia section. Late in 1879 it decided to adhere to the route chosen under the Mackenzie administration, through

---

(cont.) man was Sir George E. Cartier, the leader of the French party, which held the balance of power between the other factions... It was evident that some means must be adopted to bring the influence of this compact body of men to bear in our favour, and as soon as I made up my mind what to do, I did not lose a moment in following it up. A railroad from Montreal to Ottawa, through the French country, north of the Ottawa river, has long been desired by the French inhabitants; but Cartier, who is a salaried solicitor of the Grand Trunk road, to which this would be an opposition, has interposed difficulties, and by his influence prevented it being built... The plans I propose are in themselves the best for the interests of the Dominion, and in urging them on the public I am really doing a most patriotic action. But even in that view, means must be used to influence the public, and I employed several young French lawyers to write it up in their own newspapers. I subscribed a controlling influence in the stock, and proceeded to subsidize the newspapers themselves, both editors and proprietors. I went to the country through which the road would pass, and called on many of the inhabitants. I visited the priests and made friends of them, and I employed agents to go among

the Yellowhead Pass, down the Thompson and the Fraser to Port Moody on Burrard Inlet. The difficult section from Yale, the head of navigation on the Fraser, to Savona's Ferry, near Kamloops, was shortly afterwards placed under contract. The ten years' time allotted for the construction of the Canadian Pacific was nearly gone and there was little completed work to show. Hard times, depression in the railway world, changes of government and political upheavals, disputes as to route and terminus, had delayed construction. The building of the link north of Lake Superior, necessary for all-rail connection between East and West on Canadian territory, had been indefinitely postponed.

Something had been done, it is true. Manitoba was being linked up with the East by a road south to Minnesota and by another line to the head of Lake Superior, and a start had been made in British Columbia. Some day, under some administration, the gaps would be filled up and the promise to British Columbia would be redeemed.

Suddenly, in June 1880, Sir John Macdonald, speaking at Bath, made the announcement that a group of capitalists had offered to build the road, on terms which would ensure that in the end it would not cost Canada a single farthing. Four months later a contract was signed in Ottawa by which the Canadian Pacific Syndicate undertook to build and operate the whole road. An entirely new turn had been given to the situation, and the most important chapter in Canada's railway annals, if not in her national life, had been begun.

(cont.) the principal people and talk it up. I then began to hold public meetings, and attended to them myself, making frequent speeches in French to them, showing them where their true interests lay . . . and I formed a committee to influence the members of the Legislature. This succeeded so well that in a short time it had 27 out of 45 on whom I could rely, and the electors of the ward in this city, which Cartier himself represents, notified him that unless the contract for the Pacific Railway was given in the interests of Lower Canada he need not present himself for re-election. . . .

The policy adopted has been quite successful, the strong French influence I succeeded in obtaining has proved sufficient to control the elections, and as soon as the Government realized this fact, which they were unwilling to admit and slow to see, they opened negotiations with me. . . . Yesterday we entered into an agreement, by which the Government bound itself to form a Company of Canadians, only according to my wishes. That this Company will make me President, and that I and my friends will get a majority of the stock, and that the contract for building the railroad will be given to this Company, in terms of the Act of Parliament. Americans are to be carefully excluded in the fear that they will sell it to the Union [sic] Pacific, but I fancy we can get over that some way or other. This position has not been attained without large payments of money. I have already paid over $200,000, and will have at least $100,000 more to pay.

CHAPTER EIGHT
BUILDING THE CANADIAN PACIFIC

In the months and years that followed, no men were so much in the mind and speech of the Canadian public as the members of the new syndicate. The leading members were a remarkable group of men. Probably never in the history of railway building, not even in the case of the 'Big Four' who built the Central Pacific—Huntingdon, Stanford, Crocker, and Hopkins—had the call of the railway brought together in a single enterprise men of such outstanding individuality, of such ability and persistence, and destined for success so notable. The Canadian Pacific was not their first joint enterprise. It was the direct outcome of a daring venture in connection with a bankrupt Minnesota railway, which had brought them wealth beyond their wildest dreams, and had definitely turned their thoughts to railway work.

Early in the settlement of the northwestern states the need of railways, and of state aid to railways, was widely realized. In 1857 Congress gave the territory of Minnesota a large grant of public lands to use in bonusing railway building, and in the same year the legislature of the territory incorporated a company, the Minnesota and Pacific, to build from Stillwater through St Paul and St Anthony's Falls (Minneapolis) to Red River points. The state gave the new company millions of acres of land and a cash subsidy, municipalities offered bonuses, and a small amount of stock was subscribed locally. Five years passed, and not a mile had been completed. The company, looted into insolvency by fraudulent construction company contracts, was reorganized as the St Paul and Pacific, heir to the old company's assets but not to its liabilities, and a beginning was made once more. Trusting Dutch bondholders lent over twenty millions, and by 1871 the road reached Breckenridge on the Red River, two hundred and seventeen miles from St Paul. Again a halt came. Russell Sage and his associates in control had once more looted the treasury. The Dutch bondholders, through their agent, John S. Kennedy, a New York banker, applied for a receiver, and in 1873 one Jesse P. Farley was appointed by the court. It seemed that the angry settlers might whistle in vain for their road.

In St Paul at that time there lived two Canadians who saw the opportunity. The elder, Norman W. Kittson, had been Hudson Bay agent and head of a transportation company on the Red River. The younger, James J. Hill, an Ontario farm-boy who had gone west while still in his teens, owned a coal and wood yard in St Paul, and had a share in the transportation company. Neither had the capital or the financial connection required to take hold of the bankrupt company, but they kept on thinking of it day and night. Soon a third man joined their ranks, Donald A. Smith. A Highland lad who had come to Canada at eighteen, Donald Smith had spent a generation in the service of the Hudson's Bay Company, mainly in the dreary wilds of Labrador and on the shores of Hudson Bay. When in 1871 he became chief commissioner of the organization he had served so long and so well, it seemed to most men that he was definitely settled in his life work and probably near the height of his career. But Fate knew, and Donald Smith knew, that his career was only beginning. Coming down from the north each year by the Red River to St Paul, on his way east, he talked over the railway situation with Hill and Kittson. The more they talked the greater grew their faith in the country and the railroad. It was a faith, however, that few in the moneyed East shared with them. It had been the smashing of the rival road, the Northern Pacific, in 1873, that had given the signal for the brief panic and the long depression of the seventies. The Minnesota road itself had twice become bankrupt. The legislature would undoubtedly soon declare the land-grant forfeited, unless the construction promised was completed. To fill the cup, in the middle seventies Minnesota and the neighbouring lands were visited by unprecedented swarms of grasshoppers or Rocky Mountain locusts. Swarming down from the plateau lands of the Rockies in columns miles high, covering the ground from horizon to horizon, they swept resistlessly forward, devouring every green thing in their way. When they had passed, hundreds of deserted shacks stood silent witnesses to the settlers' despair. It was in 1876 that the further allies needed came from the East. Thirty years earlier George Stephen, a younger cousin of Donald Smith, had left his Highland hills to seek his fortune in London, and after a short apprenticeship there had gone still farther afield, joining an uncle in Montreal. He rose rapidly to a foremost place in the wholesale trade of Montreal; selling led him into manufacturing, and manufacturing into financial activities. In 1876 he became president of the Bank of Montreal. Associated with him in the same bank was still another shrewd, forth-faring Scot, Richard B. Angus, who had risen steadily in its service until appointed to succeed E. H. King as general manager in 1869.

A lawsuit in connection with the bank's affairs took both Stephen and Angus to Chicago in 1876. A week's adjournment left them with unwonted leisure. A toss of a coin sent them to St Paul rather than to St Louis to spend the week. Smith had already spoken of the project while in Montreal, but at that distance caution had prevailed. Now Stephen, who had never before seen the prairie, was immensely taken with the rich, deep soil he saw before him. He knew from reading and experience that grasshopper plagues did not last for ever. He decided, therefore, to join in the attempt to get control of the Minnesota road and its land-grant, and the famous group was complete.

Once George Stephen had made up his mind, little time was ever lost. He sailed for Europe and interviewed the Amsterdam committee in charge of the Dutch bondholders' interests, Messrs Chouet, Weetjin and Kirkhoven. They despaired of ever seeing their money back, and were weary of being assessed by the receiver for funds to keep the road together. Stephen left Amsterdam with an option in his pocket, given for the sum of one guilder, agreeing to sell him the Dutch bonds for something like the amount of the unpaid interest, and agreeing, further, to wait until six months after reorganization for part of the payment. The next step was to provide the cash required for immediate necessities. About $300,000 was put up by the members of the group.[1] Money was borrowed from the Bank of Montreal, $280,000 in the first advance, and something under $700,000 in all, as Stephen stated to inquiring shareholders at the bank's annual meeting in 1880. Money was advanced to the receiver to complete the most necessary extensions, those required to save the land-grant and that necessary to reach the Canadian border to join the government road being built south from Winnipeg. The threatened forfeiture of the land-grant was thus averted for a time. Then the bonds were purchased for $6,780,000, the floating obligations and part of the stock were bought up, and the mortgage which secured the bonds was foreclosed. The assets were bought by the new company organized for the purpose, the St Paul, Minneapolis and Manitoba, of which George Stephen was president, R. B. Angus vice-president, and James J. Hill general manager. Thus in June 1879 the whole system, comprising six hundred and sixty-seven miles of railway, of which five hundred and sixty-five were completed, and the land-grant of two and a half million acres, came into the possession of the little group.[2]

The after fortunes of the road, which ten years later expanded into the Great Northern of today, do not concern us here. It is only necessary

---

[1] Stephen, Smith, Hill, and Kennedy each took one shire, and Kittson half a share; and later Angus, after leaving the service of the bank to go with the railway, took the remaining half-share.

[2] Not all were willing to attribute to courage and luck alone the full success of this stroke. Some Dutch bondholders, independently of the committee, asserted that Kennedy had not played fair, and Farley, the receiver of the road, sued Hill for a share of the profits which he alleged had been promised for his collusion. In repeated trials Farley was unable to produce evidence satisfactory to the courts, which held that in any case his claim must be rejected because 'based on inherent turpitude.'

to recount that the harvest reaped by the adventurers[1] put the tales of El Dorado to shame. A few days after control of the railway had been assured, the grasshoppers had risen in flight, and Minnesota knew them no more. Settlers swarmed in, the railroad platforms were jammed with land-seekers, and between the land-buyers of today and the wheat-shippers of to-morrow the owners of the once discredited railway saw their coffers fill to overflowing. In 1879 they divided among themselves the whole fifteen millions of stock issued, floating sixteen millions of bonds for extension and equipment. For three years they took no dividends, letting the profits go to further building. Then in 1882 another $2,000,000 stock was issued, and in 1883 a deferred dividend came in the shape of a $9,000,000 issue of bonds, or, rather, the stockholders sold to themselves a $10,000,000 issue for ten cents on the dollar. Aside entirely from interest and dividends, the stockholders of the Great Northern in the seventeen years following 1889 were presented with over $300,000,000 of interest-bearing securities.

All the railway annals of the United States cannot present a duplicate of the startling success attained by these four or five Canadians and their associates.[2]

These were the men to whom the Canadian government turned when the minister of Railways, Sir Charles Tupper, urged them to unload upon a private company the burden of completing the road to the Pacific. 'Catch them before they invest their profits,' was the advice of Sir John's most intimate adviser, that shrewd Eastern Townships politician, John Henry Pope. Probably they came halfway. They knew the West as well as any men, and with their road built to the Canadian boundary and with a traffic arrangement beyond to Winnipeg, they were already in the field. Of all the group Stephen was most reluctant to undertake the new enterprise, but he was assured by his associates that the burdens of management would be shared by all. The government had also approached Duncan M'Intyre, a Montreal capitalist who controlled the Canada Central, running from Brockville by way of Ottawa to Pembroke, and under construction from that point to Callender, the eastern end of the Canadian Pacific main line. He was more than willing to link up this railway with the larger project, and the group was formed.

They debated the question with the government early in 1880. It was felt, however, that negotiations could not be concluded in Canada. More capital would be needed than even these new-fledged millionaires could or would furnish, and nowhere was capital so abundant as in London. In July, therefore, Sir John Macdonald, Sir Charles Tupper, and John Henry

---

[1] 'Most men who have really lived have had, in some shape, their great adventure. This railway is mine' (James J. Hill, in *Valedictory to the Shareholders of the Great Northern*, July I, 1912).

[2] It was from their St Paul investment that the leading men in the group secured the basis and the bulk of their great fortunes; the Canadian Pacific added little to their coffers.

Pope sailed for London, accompanied by George Stephen and Duncan M'Intyre. London capitalists did not bite as freely as anticipated. Barings and Rothschilds alike were chary about the enterprise. Sir Henry Tyler, president of the Grand Trunk, was approached, and agreed to build if the link north of Lake Superior were omitted in favour of a line through the United States, south of the lake, a condition which Sir John, strongly urged on by Tupper, would not accept. An arrangement might have been made with a London group, but only on condition of a four per cent guarantee for twelve years, another condition which, less wisely, was also rejected. In the end the quest proved unavailing. It is true that the Paris firm of Cohen, Reinach and Co. entered the syndicate, and that the London house of Morton, Rose and Co. also joined. It was really, however, the New York end of that firm, Morton, Bliss and Co., which was interested. Contrary to the general impression, the fact is, that though most of the shares when issued eventually drifted into English hands, no English financiers shared in the building of the Canadian Pacific until it was within one hundred days of completion. Perhaps, in view of the Grand Trunk's record, it was as well that the men on this side of the Atlantic were to be thrown on their own resources from the start, and given the chance for bigness which responsibility brings. Back to Ottawa the pilgrims came, and there on October 21, 1880, the contract was signed by Charles Tupper for the government and by George Stephen, Duncan M'Intyre, James J. Hill, John S. Kennedy, Morton, Rose and Co. of London, and Cohen, Reinach and Co. of Paris. Donald A. Smith's name was not there. It was only two years since he and Sir John, on the floor of the House of Commons, had called each other liar' and 'coward' and any other sufficiently strong epithet they could put their tongues to, and it was to be a few years more before the two Highlanders could cover their private feud with a coating of elaborate cordiality. So, to preserve appearances, Smith's interest was kept a secret—but a very open one.

When parliament met in December 1880 the contract was laid before it. The terms were princely. For constructing some nineteen hundred miles the syndicate were to be given free and complete the seven hundred and ten miles under construction by the government,[1] $25,000,000 in cash, and 25,000,000 acres of selected land in the Fertile Belt. They were promised exemptions from import duties on construction materials, from taxes on land for twenty years after the patents were issued and on stock and other property for ever, and exemption from regulation of rates until ten per cent per annum was earned on the capital. Assurance was given that for twenty years no competitive roads connecting with the western states would be chartered : 'no line of railway south of the Canadian Pacific, except such line as shall run southwest or to the westward of southwest, nor to be within fifteen miles of latitude 49o.' Ten years were given to complete the task, and a million dollars were deposited as security.

[1] Including the Yale-Port Moody section, not yet formally under contract.

The contract was received by Blake, then leader of the Opposition, and his followers with a unanimous shout of disapproval. During the Christmas recess Blake endeavoured to raise the country against it. A rival syndicate was hastily organized, with Sir William Howland, A. R. M'Master, William Hendrie, A. T. Wood, Allan Gilmour, George A. Cox, P. Larkin, James M'Laren, Alexander Gibson, and other well-known capitalists at its head. After depositing $1,400,000 in chartered banks as evidence of good faith, they offered to build the road for $3,000,000 and 3,000,000 acres less, to pay duty on all supplies imported, and to abandon the monopoly clause, the exemptions from taxation, and the exemption from rate regulation. With this weapon to brandish Blake gave the government proposal no respite, but on a straight party vote the contract was ratified by parliament and received the formal royal assent in: February 1881.

It was in many ways unfortunate that from the outset the Canadian Pacific project was made the football of party politics, but it was perhaps inevitable. The first duty of an Opposition is to oppose, and even if some good measures are factitiously resisted, many a 'job' is prevented by this relentless criticism. The government proposal, it would now seem, was on the whole in the country's interest, but it had weak points. In attacking these the Opposition was led on to take up a position of hostility to the whole project, while the government was equally indiscriminate in defending every jot and tittle of the bargain. In any event, with the bitter rivalry of the Grand Trunk and the Canadian Pacific looming up, it is doubtful if it could have been possible to prevent this antagonism being reflected in the politics of a country where the issues are so largely economic issues.

That the government was right in deciding for private construction and operation, there has since been little question. To build and operate a pioneer road, to make the inevitable United States connections or extensions, to undertake the subsidiary enterprises and to enter into the flexible, intimate relations with producers and shippers necessary for success, were tasks for which government departments were not well fitted. With the traditions which has unfortunately become established in Canadian politics, there would probably be campaign contributions in the one case and graft in the other, but in the one case, also, there would probably be efficiency, and in the other red tape and stagnation.

As to what private company should be given the contract, there seemed more room for discussion. The members of the Howland syndicate were successful and substantial business men, and their offer appeared to be much better than the offer accepted. It was, however, denounced as a sham by the government forces, on the ground that its signers knew that there was not the faintest likelihood of the ministry failing to carry through the contract it had signed. How successful the Howland group would have proved we can only conjecture; it is certainly not likely that they would have developed more courage, persistence, or enterprise than the men who actually carried out the project; nor could they have fulfilled their obligations more fully and more honourably.

The parties differed, again, on the question of the Lake Superior link. The government urged the necessity of building at once an all-Canadian route, regardless of the added expense. The Opposition favoured such a route eventually, but urged that it was better for the present to make use of a road running from the Sault through Northern Michigan and Minnesota. Such a road would bring to Montreal the traffic of the American as well as the Canadian West. Then, when our West had been settled and traffic warranted, the task of cutting a road through the wilderness north of the lake could be faced, and meantime it would not be necessary to offer any company the extravagant terms necessary to induce it to assume this burden from the start. There was much weight in this argument, which Sir Charles Tupper himself had strongly urged only a few months before, and in the light of the later Canadian Pacific extension through precisely this American territory as well as through Maine, there was much buncombe in the flag-waving answer made. Yet, on the whole, so necessary to national unity was an unbroken road, so hard a country was this to make into one, that it was best to err on the side of safety. The political interests at stake warranted some risk of money loss.

It was, however, on the question of the form and amount of the aid offered that most controversy arose. Sir John Macdonald had lightly prophesied that in the end the road would not cost Canada a single farthing. He doubtless meant that land sales would repay the expenditure; even this did not prove true, and the statement awoke unreasonable expectations as to the bargain to be made. When the contract was made public it was denounced as meaning nothing more or less than that the country was to build the road and present it gratis to the company. To anticipate a few years, we may note the actual results at the end of 1885, when the last rail had been laid, the cost of the main line only, including the government sections, and of equipment, to that date, was approximately $150,000,000. From private sources some $50,000,000 net had been secured: the $65,000,000 stock had been sold at varying prices, realizing slightly over $30,000,000 for the treasury, and first mortgage bonds, land-grant bonds less amount redeemed, and outstanding accounts made up the balance. The government, on its part, had given, by the final arrangements, $35,000,000 cash, and completed road costing another $35,000,000; three and a half million acres of the land-grant had been sold for about $11,000,000, and at only two dollars per acre the fourteen odd million acres left were worth over $29,000,000.

On the other hand, it was urged that the aid given was not so great as it seemed. The value of the government sections was particularly questioned.[1] Whatever its value, it was not more than enough to induce capitalists to run the great risks involved. The road had to be operated as well as built, and few believed that for years to come there would be sufficient traffic to make ends meet. Its future depended on the future of the West, and it needed a robust optimism at times to believe that the West would overcome frost and drought and other plagues. The fact that in 1885 Canadian Pacific stock sold as low as 33 3/4 in London, and a shade lower on this side of the water, shows the estimate the world of finance put upon the bargain it had made. Nor was the road completed in 1886. It was then only begun. Grades had to be bettered, trestle-work filled up, extensions flung out, terminals secured, and a new road built every few years.

Looking back now, after the lapse of thirty years, it would seem that the government would have done better if it had given less of the land which was to prove so valuable, and had, instead, guaranteed the dividend on the stock for a term of years. In the eighties, however, western acres were held in little esteem and money guarantees, with Grand Trunk memories fresh, looked dangerous—and it was in the eighties that the decision had to be made.

More valid was the criticism of the remaining terms. The exemption from duties was wise, if inconsistent in a protectionist government, and the exemption from regulation of rates until ten per cent was earned had a precedent in a clause in the General Railway Act, not repealed until 1888, exempting all roads from such regulation until fifteen per cent on the capital invested had been earned. The exemption from taxation, however, was an unwarranted privilege, throwing undue burdens on homesteading settlers; and the interpretation afterwards given that the exemption on lands extended until twenty years after the patent had been issued still further increased the difficulty. Objectionable, also, was the monopoly clause, barring United States connections for ten years. It was claimed that this exemption was essential if traffic was to be secured for the Lake Superior link, and essential also if capital was to be secured from England. The Englishman, one of the heads of the road declared, hated a monopoly at home as he hated the devil, but he looked with favour on monopolies abroad. The monopoly clause, as will be seen later, for a time did more to split East and West than the Lake Superior link did to bind them together in spirit.

But enough of discussion. Action came quick. Not a day was lost in organizing and beginning work.

---

[1] Giving evidence before the Senate Committee on Interstate Commerce in New York in 1889, President Van Horne stated that the company was obliged to abandon part of the surveys on which the government had spent millions, and make new ones; that the government sections were unwisely located, especially in British Columbia ; that the cost of the remainder was increased by having to join it to the unwisely located sections, and that, allowing for the saving which could have been made in location, he could have duplicated the latter for twelve or fifteen millions.

George Stephen was chosen president, and held the post until 1888. To him more than to any other man the ultimate success of the Canadian Pacific was due. Indomitable persistence, unquenchable faith, unyielding honour stamped his character. He was one of the greatest of Empire builders. He never despaired in the tightest corner, and never rested while a single expedient remained untried. Duncan M'Intyre became one of the two vice-presidents, and took an active part in the company's affairs until he dropped out in 1884. Richard B. Angus came back from St Paul to become vice-president and a member of the executive committee. His long banking experience and his shrewd, straightforward judgment proved a tower of strength in days of trial.

Donald A. Smith, while after 1883 a director and a member of the executive committee, took little part in the railway's affairs, though at Stephen's urging he more than once joined in going security when help was most needed. James J. Hill left the directorate and unloaded his stock at the close of 1882, because the company refused to accept his advice to omit the Lake Superior section, and because of the growing divergence of interests between the St Paul, Minneapolis and Manitoba and the Canadian Pacific. With him retired John S. Kennedy. The Baron de Reinach also withdrew at an early stage. The English directors, representing Morton, Rose and Co. of London, retired as soon as the road was completed, being replaced by representatives of Morton, Bliss and Co. of New York. E. B. Osier came in with the Ontario and Quebec in 1884. The board became more and more distinctively Canadian.

One of the first steps taken by the directors was to open offices in Winnipeg, and put two men with United States experience in charge —A. B. Stickney, later president of the Chicago Great Western, as general superintendent, and General Rosser as chief engineer. The rate of progress was not satisfactory, and early in 1882 a fortunate change was made. William C. Van Horne, at that time general superintendent of the Chicago, Milwaukee and St Paul, and still under forty, was appointed general manager with wide powers. Some years earlier, when he was president of the Southern Minnesota, the leading members of the St Paul syndicate had had an opportunity of learning his skill. He had been in railroading since fourteen, beginning as a telegraph operator on the Illinois Central, and had risen rapidly in the service of one Middle West road after another. His tireless driving force was precisely the asset the company now most needed.

The first task was to find the money necessary to build the nineteen hundred miles remaining of the main line, to build or acquire necessary branches and extensions, and to provide equipment.

The government subsidies were the first resource. The $25,000,000 cash and the 25,000,000-acre land-grant were to be paid as construction advanced. If the land-grant were put on the market at once, for sale to settlers, it would bring relatively little, in face of the competition of the free homestead land in adjoining sections. Three expedients were devised to make it available as soon as possible. An extensive campaign was begun to advertise the government free land and thus exhaust the supply along the railway line, and at the same time provide producers of freight. Bonds based on the security of the land-grant were issued to the amount of $25,000,000; $10,000,000 of this issue was sold in 1881 at 92, and varying proportions of the remainder were used as pledge for the government loans or execution of the contract. These bonds were redeemed and cancelled as the lands on which they were based were sold. Further, the Canada North-West Land Company was organized to buy five million acres for a long hold. The company included several members of the syndicate as well as some English investors to whom land appealed more than railway stocks. It found itself unable to handle this amount and the purchase was reduced to 2,200,000 acres. Sales to other companies and to individuals brought the total amount received or due from land by the end of 1885 up to $11,000,000.

Next came the contributions of the members of the syndicate and other private investors. The capital stock authorized was $100,000,000. In 1881 the members of the syndicate subscribed $5,000,000 at par. In May 1882 they allotted themselves $10,000,000 at 25. In December of the same year $30,000,000 was issued at 52 1/2 to a syndicate of New York bankers organized by W. L. Scott; this stock was eventually sold largely in Holland and in England. A final ten millions were pledged in New York and Montreal for a loan of half that sum, and later sold for about the amount of the loan. All told, sixty-five millions of stock had been issued and some thirty-one million dollars had been brought into the treasury.

Then the flow ceased. The brief gleam of prosperity which had shone over North America after the gloom of the later seventies vanished. Never had railway building been carried on so vigorously in the United States as in the years 1881-83, and the reaction was correspondingly severe. The collapse of the boom which had accompanied the first operations in Manitoba, the failure of harvest after harvest, the fading away of settlers and speculators alike, robbed all but a persistent few of faith in the Canadian North-West and in the railway whose fortunes rose or fell with it. The way of the Canadian Pacific was made particularly hard by the manoeuvres of rival companies. Some of the United States Pacific roads, awake to the seriousness of the competition threatened, attacked it in the New York market. The Grand Trunk, naturally alarmed by the incursion of the new road into its best paying territory in the East, used all the power of its influential directors and its army of shareholders in England to bar the London market.

The financial policy adopted by the Canadian Pacific was unique in the records of great railway enterprises on this continent. It was simply to rely entirely on stock issues, to endeavour to build the road without incurring any bonded debt. Not until the last year of construction, 1885, were bonds based upon the security of the road itself issued for sale. It was doubtless desirable, if possible, to avoid the reckless methods by which so many American roads had been hopelessly waterlogged by excessive bond issues. The memory of the St Paul and Pacific's six-million share capital as against its twenty-eight-million bonded indebtedness was fresh in the minds of the members of the syndicate. By keeping fixed charges low, while earning power was still uncertain, they lessened the risk of having the road pass out of the stockholders' control into a receiver's hands. Yet as bonds could have been sold more easily than stock, it increased the difficulty of finding the necessary capital. Even so, it came within an ace of succeeding.

In pursuance of this policy the management, faced with a hesitating market, decided upon a bold step. Late in 1883, acting in accordance with the advice of New York and London financiers, they decided to endeavour to make a market for the unissued stock by giving assurance of a dividend for a term of years. They offered to deposit with the government as trustees a sum sufficient to provide for ten years a dividend of three per cent on the $65,000,000 stock already issued, to be supplemented, if possible, by a further dividend out of current revenues, and they arranged to make similar provision for the remaining $35,000,000 as it was sold. Over half the $16,000,000 necessary to purchase this annuity was deposited with the government at once and security given for the early payment of the balance. Only success could have justified such a locking up of the funds urgently needed for construction, and success did not come, though for a time it seemed probable. The sudden smash of the Northern Pacific, just completed by Villard, brought the stock down lower than before the fillip had been given. With sixteen millions locked up or pledged the company was in a worse state than before.[1]

In this emergency Stephen and Smith and M'Intyre pledged their St Paul or other stock for loans in New York and Montreal, but still the gap was unfilled. They turned to the government, requesting a loan of $22,500,000, to be secured by a first charge on the main line. In return, they agreed to complete the road by May 1886, five years earlier than the contract required. The request at first was scouted by Sir John Macdonald. Parliament would not consent, and if parliament consented the country would revolt. Bankruptcy stared the company in the face when John Henry Pope came to the rescue. He soon convinced Sir John that if

---

[1] The payment to the government of $8,710,240, in advance, of secured dividends, has deprived the company for the moment of the means for continuous, vigorous exertion in construction, without enabling it to recoup itself by the sale of its stock, as was confidently and reasonably expected' (Letter of George Stephen to the government, January 15, 1884).

Speaking in parliament in 1885, Edward Blake declared that, omitting the last ten millions issued, the company had raised on stock $24,500,000, and, counting the next two dividend payments, they would have paid or provided for dividends $24,875,000. Already $7,000,000 had been paid out in dividends, members of the syndicate receiving $3,610,000 on their $10,000,000 investment. In other words, before the road was opened for traffic, every cent paid in by the shareholders would have been paid back or set aside for dividends, leaving not a dollar for building the road

the Canadian Pacific smashed, the Conservative party would smash the day after, and the aid was promised. The Cabinet was won over, and Sir Charles Tupper, hastily summoned by cable from London, stormed it through caucus, and the loan was made.

The funds thus secured were soon exhausted in rapid and costly construction in the mountain and Lake Superior sections. The government's blanket mortgage on the road made it impossible to borrow elsewhere. So, after the Riel episode, to be noted later, a new arrangement was made with the government by which the $35,000,000 stock unsold was cancelled and an equal amount of first mortgage bonds issued. Twenty millions of this issue and the unsold lands were substituted for the government's security, and the remainder of the bonds sold at 95. This put the company once more in funds. The relief came none too soon. In one fateful day in July, when the final passing of the bill was being tensely awaited, the Canadian Pacific, which now borrows fifty millions any day before breakfast, was within three hours of bankruptcy for lack of a few hundred thousand dollars. But by March 1886 every cent of the company's obligations to the government was paid off, twenty millions in cash and the remainder in land at $1.50 an acre.

The men behind the Canadian Pacific proved themselves possessed of courage and determination such as will always win them honour. At more than one critical stage they staked their all to keep the work going. But the fact remains that the bulk of the resources utilized in the original building of the road were provided or advanced by the people of Canada. The Canadian Pacific is as truly a monument of public as of private faith.

Meanwhile, the work of construction had been going ahead. Under William Van Horne's masterful methods the leisurely pace of government construction quickened into the most rapid achievement on record. A time-schedule, carefully made out in advance, was adhered to with remarkably little variation.

Work was begun at the east end of the line, from the point of junction with the Canada Central, but at first energy was devoted chiefly to the portion crossing the plains. Important changes in route were made. The main line had already been deflected to pass through Winnipeg. Now a much more southerly line across the plains was adopted, making for Calgary rather than Edmonton. The new route was shorter by a hundred miles, and more likely to prevent the construction of a rival road south of it later. For many years after the Palliser-Dawson-Hinds reports of the late fifties, it had been assumed that the tillable lands of the West lay in a 'Fertile Belt' or rainbow, following roughly the Saskatchewan valley and curving round a big wedge of the American desert projecting north. Certainly the short, withered, russet-coloured grasslands of the border country looked forbidding beside the green herbage of the North Saskatchewan. But in 1879 Professor Macoun's investigations had shown that the southern lands had been belied by rumour, and that only a very small section was hopelessly arid. With this objection removed, the only drawback to the southern route was the difficulty of finding as good a route through the mountains as the northerly Yellowhead Pass route afforded, but on this the company decided to take its chances.

Work on the plains was begun in May 18 81, and by the end of the year 161 miles had been completed. This progress was counted too slow, and under Van Horne's management a contract was made in 1882, with Langdon and Shepard of St Paul, to complete the line to Calgary. Later in the year a construction company was organized, the North American Railway Contracting Company, to build all the uncompleted sections of the main line for $32,000,000 cash and $45,000,000 common stock. This was really a financing rather than a construction expedient, and was abandoned within a year.

In this section the engineering difficulties were not serious, but the pace of construction which was demanded, and the fact that every stick of timber and every pound of food, as well as every rail and spike, had to be brought a great distance, required remarkable organization. Three hundred sub-contractors were employed on the portion of the line crossing the plains. Bridge-gangs and track-layers followed close on the graders' heels. In 1882 over two and a half miles of track a day were laid. In the following year, for weeks in succession, the average ran three and a half miles a day, and in one record-smashing three days twenty miles were covered. By the end of this year the track was within four miles of the summit of the Rockies.

The change of route across the plains had made it essential to pierce the Rockies by a more southerly pass than the Yellowhead. The Kicking Horse or Hector Pass, short but steep, was finally chosen, but here, as at the Yellow-head, to cross the first range did not mean victory. The towering Selkirk range faced the pass, as the Cariboo Mountains flanked the Rockies farther north. Until the rails reached the hills the engineers had found no way through them, and had contemplated a long detour to the north, following the winding Columbia. Then Major Rogers, the engineer whom James J. Hill had suggested to take charge of the location of the mountain section, following up a hint of Moberly, an earlier explorer, found a route, steep but practicable, across the Selkirks, following the Beaver river valley and Bear Creek, and then through Rogers Pass into the valley of the Illecillewaet, and so through Eagle Pass to the settled location at Kamloops. Both in the Kicking Horse and in the Rogers Pass gradients of 116 feet to the mile were found necessary, but these difficult stretches were concentrated within one operating section of a hundred and twenty miles, and could easily be overcome by the use of additional engines. Unique provision was made against the mountain avalanches by erecting diverting timbers near the summits and building mile upon mile of snow-sheds, over which the avalanches passed harmless. As a result of these expedients and of raising the road-bed across the prairies unusually high, the Canadian Pacific lost less time through snow blockades than the great railways of the eastern United States.

It was not until 1884 that the wilderness north of Lake Superior was attacked in strong force. Nine thousand men were employed here alone.

Rock and muskeg, hill and hollow, made this section more difficult to face than even the Fraser Canyon. In one muskeg area today seven layers of Canadian Pacific rails are buried, one below the other. The stretch along the shore of the lake was particularly difficult. The Laurentian rocks were the oldest known to geologists, and, what was more to the purpose, the toughest known to engineers. A dynamite factory was built on the spot and a road blasted through. One mile cost $700,000 to build and several cost half a million. The time required and the total expenditure would have been prohibitive had not the management decided to make extensive use of trestle-work. It would have cost over two dollars a cubic yard to cut through the hills and fill up the hollows by team-haul; it cost only one-tenth of that to build timber trestles, carrying the line high, and to fill up later by train-haul.

An unexpected test of the need of this section came before it was completed. Early in 1885 the government realized too late that serious trouble was brewing among the half-breeds and Indians of the North-West. Unless troops could be sent in before the grass grew, Riel would have thousands of Indians on the war-path, and a long and bloody contest and a serious setback to the West would be inevitable. The railway was far from complete, with a hundred and twenty miles of gaps unfilled, and the government considered it impossible to get the troops transported in time. But Van Horne, who had had much experience in handling troops in the Civil War, did not have that word in his vocabulary, and astonished the authorities by offering to take men from Kingston or Quebec to Qu'Appelle in ten days. Part of the gaps were bridged by temporary rails laid on ice and snow, only ninety miles being uncompleted by spring. In one stretch the men were marched across the ice to save a long detour. Through the rest they were carried, covered with furs and straw, in contractors' sleighs along the tote-roads from one camp to the next. In four days from leaving Kingston the first troops landed at Winnipeg; and though the revolt was not prevented, it was speedily crushed. There was no longer any question about the value of the north shore link, and the opposition to the Canadian Pacific fell from that hour. It was even suggested that the company should build a statue to Louis Riel. As for the government, it could well claim that its persistence in pushing through this part of the road nearly offset its red-tape carelessness in permitting the rebellion to come to a head.

Meanwhile, the government section between Port Arthur, or rather Fort William, and Winnipeg had been taken over by the company in 1883, though not entirely completed. Two years later the thousands of Chinese navvies working on the difficult Kamloops-Port Moody section finished their task, and the government work was done. The only gap remaining lay in the Gold Range, and here in the Eagle Pass, at Craigellachie, on November 7, 1885, the eastward and westward track-layers met. Only a year or so before the Northern Pacific had celebrated the driving of the last golden spike by an excursion which cost the company a third of a million, and heralded the bankruptcy of the road. So there was no banquet and no golden spike for the last rail in the Canadian Pacific. William

Van Horne had announced that 'the last spike would be just as good an iron spike as any on the road,' and had it not been that Donald A. Smith happened along in time to drive the spike home, it would have been hammered in by the navvy on the job. Six months later the first passenger train went through from Montreal to Vancouver. The longest railway in the world was open from coast to coast, five years before the end of the time required by the original contract.

To realize how great a work had been accomplished requires today some effort of the imagination. The Canada the present generation knows is a united Canada, an optimistic, self-confident Canada, with rapidly rounding-out industries and occupations which give scope for the most ambitious of her sons as well as for tens of thousands from overseas. It is a Canada whose nine provinces stretch almost unbroken from ocean to ocean. But the Canada of a generation earlier was far other. On the map it covered half a continent, but in reality it stopped at the Great Lakes. There was little national spirit, little diversity of commercial enterprise. Hundreds of thousands of our best-born had been drawn by the greater attraction of United States cities and farms, until one-fourth of the whole Canadian people were living in the Republic. It was the opening up of the West that changed the whole face of Canadian life, that gave a basis for industrial expansion, that quickened national sentiment and created business optimism. And it was the building of the Canadian Pacific that opened up the West and bound it fast to the distant East. Certainly not least among the makers of Canada were the men who undertook that doubtful enterprise and carried it through every obstacle to success; and not least among the generations whose toil and faith have made possible the nation of today were the four millons of the Canada of the eighties who flung a great railway across the vast unpeopled spaces of a continent to the far Pacific.

CHAPTER NINE
THE ERA OF AMALGAMATION

With the building of the Intercolonial, the Grand Trunk, and the Canadian Pacific, the main lines of communication from ocean to ocean were completed. In the decade which followed, the marked features were the adoption by the Dominion government of a policy of aid to purely local roads, and the expansion of the two great private companies, partly by new construction and partly by acquisition of the smaller lines.

It has been seen that the policy of Canada after 1851 and of the Dominion after Confederation was to give assistance only to lines of more than local and usually more than provincial importance. During the first ten or fifteen years after Confederation promoters looked to province and municipality for aid, and did not look in vain. Soon the provinces outran their resources, and began to clamour for increased federal subsidies to meet the pressing charges. But the Dominion government concluded that, if it had to provide the money needed, it might as well give it direct, and secure whatever political credit the grants would entail. In 1882 it decided to embark on a new subsidy policy.

In that year Sir Charles Tupper, minister of Railways, introduced a resolution to grant a subsidy of $3200 per mile—sufficient to provide the hundred tons of steel rails required for each mile at the existing price of $32 a ton—to each of four carefully selected roads, one in each of the four original provinces. During the next year eleven subsidies were voted, chiefly to Quebec and New Brunswick roads; in 1885 twenty-five were voted, and fresh votes were made every year thereafter. Many of the subsidies lapsed through failure to begin construction, but usually they were revoted. The payments made averaged a million dollars a year. The practice did not make for pure politics, and it often led to the construction of lines for which there was no economic justification whatever. Trusting shareholders were induced to invest on the unfortunately wrong assumption that the government had assured itself of the need and the potential profit of the line before endorsing it by a subsidy.[1] In the western provinces a parallel policy of aiding local lines was adopted in 1884, except that land instead of cash was offered, a policy maintained until 1894.

He who paid the piper then stood on his rights to call the tune. Acting upon the wide power conferred by the British North America Act, the Dominion government in 1883 sweepingly designated as 'works for the general advantage of Canada,' and therefore subject to federal control, not only the main lines of railways, but the branch lines then or thereafter connecting with or crossing these lines or any of them. The power thus claimed was not effectively exercised for some time. D'Alton M'Carthy repeatedly urged in parliament from 1880 onward the creation of a Dominion Railway Commission, but the opposition of the railways proved too strong for him. When in 1886 the United States set up its Interstate Commerce Commission, the government moved and appointed a royal commission, with Sir A. T. Galt as chairman, to consider the general question. Their report noted the existence of many grievances and suggested specific remedies, but considered that until further experience of the workings of the English and American commissions was available, Canada's needs could best be met by an extension of the powers of the Railway Committee of the Cabinet.

It may be noted that in 1882 the selling of railway tickets by private persons, a practice known as 'ticket scalping,' was prohibited in Canada, though the railways were forced to buy the exclusive privilege of selling their own tickets by agreeing to redeem unused portions.

The original contract with the Canadian Pacific had provided for an eastern terminus near Lake Nipissing, in order to show preference neither to Montreal nor Toronto, either of which could make connections by independent roads. Similarly, we shall see, thirty years later, Moncton was chosen as a terminus of the National Transcontinental, to hold the balance even between Halifax and St John. It was, however, impossible for the Canadian Pacific to accept as permanent an arrangement which left it halting in the wilderness, and depending upon possibly rival railways for outlet to the great cities and ports of the east. It had, in fact, been empowered in its charter to acquire the Canada Central and 'to obtain, hold, and operate a line or lines of railway from Ottawa to any point at navigable water on the Atlantic seaboard, or to any intermediate point'—terms sufficiently sweeping. Few were surprised, therefore, when the directors began a policy of eastward expansion, though many were

[1] One such company, the Caraquet, which was given $400,000 in subsidies, declared, in floating $500,000 in bonds in England, that the capacity of the road was taxed to its utmost, and that an immense traffic was in sight. At that time its entire rolling-stock consisted of two locomotives, one passenger car, two box and fifteen flat cars, and a snow-plough.

surprised at the boldness and extent of the plans and the speed and masterful strategy of the execution.

The first and most obvious move was to buy out the Canada Central, extending from Ottawa through Carleton Place to Pembroke, and under construction westward to Callender on Lake Nipissing. This was done in 1881, and the road was completed two years later. Again, in 1881, the parent line of the Canada Central, the Brockville and Ottawa, was acquired, and three years later a controlling interest was secured in the stock of the St Lawrence and Ottawa, thus giving connection with the St Lawrence both at Brockville and at Prescott. Still pressing eastward, the Canadian Pacific next sought entrance to Montreal and to Quebec. The North Shore road, built by the province of Quebec, would most easily give the connection sought. The province was induced, in 1882, to sell to the Canadian Pacific the western section, from Montreal to Ottawa. At the same time the eastern section, from St Martin to Montreal, was sold to the North Shore Syndicate. The Grand Trunk, alarmed at this advance, attempted to block further expansion by securing, jointly with the Central Vermont, control of the latter section. But the Canadian Pacific had the ear of both the Dominion and the provincial governments, and threats of aid in building a parallel line forced the Grand Trunk to relinquish control to its great rival. Not yet content, the Canadian Pacific sought winter ports at St John and Halifax. It secured control of the Southeastern Counties in Quebec, built a short line through Maine to Mattawamkeag with the aid of a large Dominion subsidy, acquired running rights or control by lease over part of the old European and North American, and thus entered St John. In 1890 its eastern development was completed for a time by the lease of the New Brunswick Railway, which had recently absorbed nearly all the small lines in western New Brunswick.[1]

Meanwhile the management had been equally aggressive in obtaining feeders in central and western Ontario, the very heart of the Grand Trunk's territory. In 1881 the Ontario and Quebec was chartered, by interests friendly to the Canadian Pacific, to build a line from Ottawa to Toronto, by way of Smith's Falls. Two years later this company acquired leases for 999 years of three important lines, and transferred them, along with its own road, to the Canadian Pacific. The first of these lines was the Toronto, Grey and Bruce, the narrow-gauge railway which ran north to Georgian Bay; the second was the Credit Valley, extending from Toronto to St Thomas; the third, the Atlantic and North-West, a road with little mileage but most useful charter powers, used for the seaward extension. Later, a railway was built from St Thomas to Windsor. Thus the Canadian Pacific secured access to Lake Ontario, Georgian Bay, and the Detroit river. Not yet content, it built a branch to Sault Ste Marie. Here connection was made with the 'Soo' lines, giving outlet to St Paul and Minneapo-

---

[1] The earliest intercolonial project, a railroad from St Andrews north, was brought to completion in 1889 when a short road, the Temiscouata, was built, linking the Intercolonial at Rivière du Loup with the New Brunswick Railway at Edmundston.

lis, and with the several roads later combined to form the Duluth, South Shore and Atlantic. Both of these lines shortly afterwards came definitely under its control.

In the prairie West the Canadian Pacific had been promised in 1880 a monopoly of through traffic for twenty years. The Dominion government, it will be remembered, had agreed not to charter, nor to permit the territories to charter, any lines between the Canadian Pacific and the United States border, running south or southeast. Going beyond these terms, the Dominion endeavoured also to prevent Manitoba from authorizing the construction of any such road, and disallowed one chartering act after another.

From the outset this provision proved a source of bitter and dangerous strife. On the one side it was contended that without this clause the necessary capital could not have been secured and that faith must be kept; that the traffic of the West should go to build up the eastern provinces, which had made a vast outlay on the road, rather than a foreign country; that the rates of the Canadian Pacific were as reasonable as those of American roads; and that other causes than railroad monopoly were responsible for the slow growth of the West. But the West protested that the rates were exorbitant—otherwise American competition would not have been feared—pointed to the exodus of settlers and the discontent of those who stayed, and refused to be sacrificed in the interests of foreign shareholders or even of sister provinces. Undoubtedly immigration was deterred, and relations between East and West were seriously strained. Finally, in 1888, the Dominion government was forced to yield. The company's consent was secured by a bond guarantee for some necessary extensions, and the provision was repealed. The Northern Pacific was brought in by the Manitoba government, and competitive local roads were chartered, but in this period the control of the Canadian Pacific over the western field was not seriously called in question.

The task before the management to secure traffic for the great system thus built up was a difficult one. It was a greater achievement to operate the Canadian Pacific successfully than to build it. When it is realized that when the company began operation the number of white settlers between Portage la Prairie and Kamloops, within twenty miles of the line, could be counted virtually on the fingers of one hand, the difficulty of finding traffic may be appreciated. Sandford Fleming had estimated that the road could not pay until there were two million people in the West. Yet pay it did from the start. The company capitalized its scenery, and built up a paying tourist trade. When wheat was lacking, ends were made to meet by carrying train-load upon trainload of buffalo bones to eastern factories. United States traffic was carefully cultivated at both ends of the line. An active immigration campaign was carried on. Various industries along the line, from coal companies to flour mills, were helped forward for years. A loyal staff was built up, and by grace of efficiency the company pulled through until the lean days of the early nineties were over.

During this decade of extraordinary activity the Grand Trunk had been neither content nor passive. Offended by the incursions into its best paying territory, it fought its younger rival in parliament and on the stock exchange, but with no lasting success in either quarter. It was more successful in its own constructive policy of expansion. In 1879 it had made a good bargain by selling to the Intercolonial the branch from Lévis to Rivière du Loup, which did not earn operating expenses, and by expending the proceeds in buying an extension to Chicago, which enabled it at last to secure the through traffic from the West for which it had been in large part originally designed. Its great coup came, however, in 1882, when the onward march of the Canadian Pacific and the bitter experience of fruitless rate wars led it to purchase its old rival, the Great Western, with its Michigan extensions. The construction of the St Clair tunnel between Port Huron and Sarnia, completed in 1890, marked another forward step in its western territory. Meanwhile it had acquired, in 1884, the Midland Railway, itself a recent amalgamation of the Midland, running from Port Hope to Midland, with the Toronto and Nipissing, the Grand Junction, from Belleville to Peterborough, and the Whitby and Port Perry, effected by two enterprising financiers, George A. Cox and Robert Jaffray. Four years later it absorbed the Northern and Northwestern roads, which had acquired jointly a branch from Gravenhurst to North Bay, so that here at least the older road checkmated its rival, securing the very paying link between Toronto and the western lines of the Canadian Pacific.

CHAPTER TEN
THE CANADIAN NORTHERN

The first quarter-century of Confederation failed to redeem the glowing promises and high hopes of the founders of the new nation. Much had been done: the half-continent from ocean to ocean had been brought into the fold of one union; national consciousness was slowly growing; great efforts had been spent in linking the scattered parts by railways and waterways. But still political unity and economic prosperity both lagged. The country was torn by racial and religious bickering. In the East, the exodus to the United States bled the country white; in the West, drought, frost, and the low prices of grain kept settlers away. Canadian Pacific stock, selling in the middle nineties at 35, registered the market's estimate of the future of the Canadian West.

Then, slowly at first, and soon with cumulative momentum, came a transformation. World-wide causes worked with local factors to change the whole face of affairs. New discoveries of gold and rising prices gave everywhere a fillip to trade. In the United States the disappearance of free land set its farmers looking elsewhere. In Canada change of methods, or the favourable turn of a climatic cycle, enabled the lands of the North-West to prove their abounding fertility. The discovery of gold in the Klondike afforded good advertising for Canada if little more of permanence. In the government and in the financial, the railway and the industrial worlds, there were men who rose to the opportunity: no longer was Canada's light hid under a bushel. The most was made of the alluring gifts she had to offer to men the world over who strove to better themselves, and the flood of immigration began.

The first result of the swarming of thousands to the West was a demand for new railways, to open up plain and prairie and mineral range, and to make connection with East and West. The building of the railways in its turn gave a stimulus to every industry. As in the early fifties and early eighties, this period of rapid railway expansion—much longer, however, than previous periods—was an era of optimistic planning and feverish speculation.

First to seize the golden opportunities were the group of men who built the Canadian Northern. Railway history offers no more remarkable record than the achievement of these few men, who, beginning in 1895 with a charter for a railway one hundred miles long in Manitoba, leading nowhere in particular, succeeded in building in twenty years a road from ocean to ocean, and in keeping it in their own hands through all difficulties and vicissitudes.

Yet it is not exactly correct to say that they began in 1895. A long apprenticeship had been served before that time. William Mackenzie and Donald Mann, the leaders in this group, had both been trained in railway construction. Both were Canadian-born; and had fared forth as youths to make their way in the world. William Mackenzie, born at Kirkfield, Ontario, in 1849, had been in turn school-teacher, country-store keeper, and lumberman before a contract on the Victoria Railway—part of the Midland—revealed his destiny. Donald Mann, born four years later at Acton, Ontario, near James J. Hill's old home, had been brought up for the Christian ministry, but by twenty-one he was foreman in a lumber camp. At twenty-five he joined in the first rush to Winnipeg, and next year he undertook the first of many contracts on the Canadian Pacific. William Mackenzie had also carried through much work for this company. In 1886 the notable partnership of Mackenzie and Mann was formed. The firm built the Calgary and Edmonton, the Qu'Appelle, Long Lake and Saskatchewan, the Canadian Pacific short line through Maine, and many minor railways. They developed capacities which made each the complement of the other—Mackenzie a master of finance, and Mann as successful in extracting a subsidy from a politician as in driving ahead the work of construction. Later Z. A. Lash, a shrewd and experienced corporation lawyer, joined them, and the three, with able lieutenants, carried through their ambitious plans without more than momentary pause, until within sight of the goal.

It was in 1895 that William Mackenzie and Donald Mann, along with two fellow-contractors, James Ross and H. S. Holt—it is noteworthy how many Canadians eminent in finance and industry found their start in the building of the Canadian Pacific—decided to buy some of the charters of projected western roads then going a-begging, and to build on their own account. They secured the charter of the Lake Manitoba Railroad and Canal Company, carrying a Dominion subsidy of 6000 acres a mile for a line from Portage la Prairie to Lake Manitoba and Lake Winnipegosis, and induced the Manitoba government to add a valuable guarantee of bonds and exemption from taxes. In 1896 running rights were secured over the track of the Manitoba and Northwestern from Portage to Gladstone, and construction was pushed a hundred miles northwest from

Gladstone to Dauphin. Next year Lake Winnipegosis was reached. Then the partners looked eastward. The coming need of the West was an outlet from Winnipeg to Lake Superior, to supplement the Canadian Pacific. Accordingly in 1898, under powers given by Dominion, Ontario, and Minnesota charters, construction was begun both at Winnipeg and near Port Arthur. Three years later the line was completed. Meantime the earlier road had branched westerly at Sifton, and by 1900 had crossed the border into Saskatchewan at Erwood; while in 1899, in amalgamation with the Winnipeg Great Northern, chartered and subsidized to Hudson Bay, the name of the combined roads was changed to the Canadian Northern.

Then came the coup which first made the public and rival railways realize the ambitious reach of the plans of the new railway. It will be recalled that when, in 1888, the ban upon competition southward with the Canadian Pacific had been lifted, the Northern Pacific had entered Manitoba. It had gradually built up a system of three hundred and twenty miles, but had not given the competition looked for, dividing traffic with the Canadian Pacific rather than cutting rates. Now the parent line was in the receiver's hands, and its straits gave the Manitoba government its opportunity. It leased for 999 years all the Manitoba lines of the Northern Pacific, but decided it could not profitably operate them itself without connection with the lakes. The only question was whether to re-lease them to the Canadian Pacific or to the Canadian Northern. After a lively contest the younger road secured the prize. At a stroke it thus obtained extensive terminals in Winnipeg, a line south to the American border, branches westward through fertile territory, and a link which practically closed the gap between its eastern and its western roads.

The Canadian Northern had now become the third largest system in the Dominion, stretching from Lake Superior to Saskatchewan, with nearly thirteen hundred miles in operation in 1902. The feeders were extending through the rich farming lands of the West; the line to Port Arthur supplemented the Canadian Pacific, providing a second spout to the funnel. But this merely local success did not long content its promoters. They announced their intention to build from sea to sea. Transcontinental railways were then much in the air: the Grand Trunk, the Trans-Canada, the Great Northern all planned extensive projects. Reviving prosperity and new-found confidence were making a dollar look as small to government and public alike as a dime had seemed some years before. Aid might confidently be looked for—but by which aspirant?

In 1902 and 1903 a junction of forces between the Grand Trunk and the Canadian Northern was proposed, and would have had much in its favour. The negotiators could not come to terms, however, and each road continued on its independent plan. Nothing daunted by the Dominion government's decision to recognize and aid the Grand Trunk, the Canadian Northern turned to a policy of piecemeal construction, seeking aid from the provinces as well as from the Dominion.

Making hay while the subsidy sun shone and the prosperity of the Laurier regime was at its height, the Canadian Northern pressed forward extensions, flung out branches, filled in gaps on every side. The main line was pushed westward to Edmonton in 1905. Branch lines were thrown out freely in all the prairie provinces. In Ontario the gap north of Lake Superior was bridged by a line from Port Arthur to Sudbury, not completed until 1914. Toronto and Ottawa were linked with the western lines, and several feeders were acquired which gave connection with Kingston and Brockville. In Quebec the Great Northern, running from Hawkesbury on the Ottawa to Quebec City, was absorbed in 1902, and the Quebec and Lake St John five years later. By building a tunnel three miles long under Mount Royal, an entrance was secured into the heart of Montreal. Nova Scotia did its part by lending money to another Mackenzie and Mann enterprise, the Halifax and Southwestern. The Inverness Railway in Cape Breton and the Nova Scotia Central with minor lines were built or acquired, giving the Canadian Northern first place in mileage in the province.

The most difficult task still remained—building a third railway through the mountains to the Pacific. Surveys for a road from Yellowhead Pass to Vancouver by Sandford Fleming's old route were begun in 1908. By the aid of lavish guarantees and subsidies this last link in the transcontinental system was pushed to completion in 1915.

The financial and political aspects of this great enterprise were as striking as was the construction. Governments have many a time given lavish aid, promoters have often built roads entirely out of the proceeds of bond issues, financiers have dominated great railway systems by a majority or controlling interest in the stock. But never before did a group of men plan to unite, on such a scale, all three arrangements—to build ten thousand miles of railway without themselves investing a dollar and still retain control. The men behind the Canadian Northern not only planned such a project, but carried it through, displaying in the process, and at every stage of the undertaking, a mastery of political diplomacy, an untiring persistence, and great financial resourcefulness. They are, therefore, entitled to a special place among the world's railway builders.

Their plan was simple in principle, if wondrously complicated in working out. It was to build the road by government subsidies and the proceeds of the bonds guaranteed by government, and to control the road by issuing to themselves, for their services of promotion and management, practically all the common stock. To carry out this audacious plan, political influence, public enthusiasm, and the confidence of outside investors in Canada's future were all required and were all forthcoming.

Dominion and province vied in aid. This aid took many forms. The Dominion had abandoned in 1894 its policy of giving land-grants, but the original companies which combined to form the Canadian Northern had previously been promised and later received over four million acres: up to 1914 about eighteen million dollars had been realized from the sale of parts of this land, and the grants unsold were worth at least ten millions more. In addition, Ontario gave two million acres and Quebec one-third as much. Cash subsidies were not wanting. The Liberal government of Sir Wilfrid Laurier voted something less than two millions in cash to aid in building the link between Winnipeg and Lake Superior. It declined to recognize or aid the extension to the Pacific coast; but in 1912 the Conservative government of Sir Robert Borden gave over six millions for this work, and in the following year fifteen millions more for the Ontario and western Alberta sections of the main line. The provinces were less lavish, Quebec, Ontario, and Manitoba offering all told six millions.

But it was neither to land-grants nor to cash subsidies that the Canadian Northern looked for its chief aid, but to government guarantees. This device, the main form of state aid given in our first railway era, had long been discredited by the unlucky fate of the Grand Trunk and the Northern guarantees, and had been sparingly used since. To the Canadian Northern its revival was chiefly due. It was a seductive form of aid: provided that the railway thus helped had good traffic prospects, the government stood little chance of loss and the railway greatly gained by the certainty of the sale of its bonds and the higher price secured. But, like other forms of the extension of public credit, such as the issue of paper money, state guarantees are difficult to keep within bounds, and compel ever-fresh extensions to save the old liability. So Dominion and province alike found. From 1903 to 1911, under Sir Wilfrid Laurier, the Dominion guaranteed bonds of the Canadian Northern system to the extent of fifty-six millions; from 1912 to 1914, under Sir Robert Borden, it endorsed the Canadian Northern's notes for forty-nine millions more. Nor were the provinces behind hand. Mainly in the seven years from 1908, the five westernmost provinces pledged their credit on behalf of the same system to the astounding amount of over one hundred and thirty millions, British Columbia leading; Nova Scotia made a loan of another five millions. Thus endorsed, usually as to both principal and interest, the bonds of the Canadian Northern were floated with little difficulty, so long as money was to be had at all by any seeker.

In the meantime, while the road was being built by state gifts and bondholders' lendings, the great bulk of the stock of the parent road and of the chief subsidiaries was conveyed to Messrs Mackenzie and Mann for their services in promoting and managing the system. This method of financing had its dangers. It meant that there was no large commitment of shareholders' capital, to secure support in difficulty and compel responsibility in management. It meant that the control of the vast enterprise was in the hands of a few men, unchecked by public inquiry or the criticism of independent shareholders—whatever that might be worth. It meant that with all the cash capital taking the form of bonds, any failure to make ends meet, any lengthened depression, would bring risk of the mortgage-holders' foreclosure and receivership—not merely the shareholders' waiting for a turn of the tide—except in so far as the burden could be shifted to the governments that had endorsed the notes.

In the early years, thanks to general prosperity and to the strategic location and careful management of the system, ends always met, and a little over, and funds were always forthcoming for fresh expansion. But early in 1914 a crisis arrived in the company's affairs. The mountain section particularly, what with the higher cost of labour and the unexpected engineering difficulties, was calling for tens of millions more; the stringency in the world's money markets, following the Balkan Wars, made investors chary of even gilt-edged offerings. There were many millions of subsidies and guarantees still to come from the state, but they would come only as the road was completed, and meantime construction had to be financed. The partner-owners could not provide the ready cash needed for completing the gigantic task. The bondholders had no inducement to do so unless further guaranteed by the state. The western provinces were at last becoming frightened of the load they had already assumed. There was only one resource, the Dominion government. True, it had only in 1913 made a gift of $15,000,000 on solemn assurances that not a cent more would be needed. But, it was urged, the emergency was real. The road could not be left hanging half finished, after all the millions already spent. Canada's credit must be protected, and so the government, after a lively struggle, put through a positively last guarantee of forty-five millions. In return it was given forty out of the hundred millions stock to which the capital was reduced, and took the right to appoint one government director. Whether this step meant that the government was now going to share the control and the profits of the company, or whether it meant that it was henceforth to be saddled with the responsibility for any deficits, was a point much in dispute. Later, the outbreak of war in Europe delayed, but did not altogether halt, the floating of the loan and the completion of the remaining links.

Meanwhile, the many subsidiary enterprises, which the example of the Canadian Pacific has caused us to think appropriate to the transcontinental railway, had been undertaken by its youngest rival. Fast steamers between Montreal and Bristol, grain elevators, hotels, express and telegraph companies, all brought grist to the mill. Hardly to be distinguished were the allied interests of the partner-owners—iron mines in the Lake Superior district, coal mines in Alberta and Vancouver Island, whaling and halibut fisheries on the Pacific, and lumber mills on the British Columbia coast—all bearing some relation to the development of the railway system.

In 1896: a railway a hundred miles long, beginning and ending nowhere, operated by thirteen men and a boy! In 1914: a great transcontinental system practically completed, over ten thousand miles in length, and covering seven of Canada's nine provinces! The impossible had been achieved.

CHAPTER ELEVEN
THE EXPANSION OF THE GRAND TRUNK

In the eighties, it will be recalled, the activity of the Canadian Pacific in the eastern province had stirred the Grand Trunk to an aggressive counter-campaign. Line after line had been absorbed, extension after extension had been built. New life seemed to have been injected into the old system. Holders of even ordinary shares began to dream of dividends.

The activity was brief and prosperity briefer. Only in the golden days from 1881 to 1883, when the West was enjoying its first 'boom' and railway construction was at its height, did the policy of expansion justify itself from the shareholder's point of view. The year 1883 saw the high-water mark of prosperity for the Grand Trunk; for in that year dividends were paid not only on guaranteed but on first, second, and third preference stock. Not again until 1902 was even a partial payment made on the third preference; not until 1900, save for a fraction in 1887, was anything paid on second preference; first preference dividends were fractional and occasional, and even the guaranteed stock dividends were passed time and again. The financial position of this great system in the middle nineties may be briefly summed up in the statement that securities of the par value of £16,000,000, which in 1883 had a market value of £12,000,000, were worth in 1894 only £3,500,000. The junior securities had become only gambling counters on the stock exchange.

Where did the cause lie? There was not one; there were several. The first was in capitalization. The line had been hopelessly over-capitalized to begin with, and the new acquisitions doubled fixed charges, while net receipts increased only ten per cent; feeders had proved suckers.[1] Secondly, in the general commercial situation. The whole continent was undergoing a trying test of panic and depression, of low prices and industrial stagnation.

For a quarter of a century after 1873 the gloom had been broken only at brief intervals—from 1880 to 1883, and from 1887 to 1889. In 1893 the price of wheat fell to the lowest point in a century. The great Mississippi valley had been flooded with settlers, railway and steamship threw their millions of bushels on the world's markets, while the gold basis of prices failed to expand in proportion. Western farms were, it was said, 'plastered with mortgages'; one-sixth of the railways in the United States went into receivers' hands in 1893 alone. Free-silver agitators denounced the 'gold bugs' of the east; Coxey armies marched to Washington. Another cause was in excessive competition. The St Lawrence was more accessible to shippers than ever, while the Canadian Pacific had cut into the best paying territory in Ontario. In the Chicago traffic absolute demoralization ruled—reckless rate wars were waged, agreement after agreement was broken, line was played against line by grain-shipper or by dressed-beef magnate. A final cause was in management. The attempt was still being made to manage a great railway from London, three thousand miles away. The Canadian officials had little independent discretion; interminable delays, lack of initiative, red tape, nepotism, followed inevitably. Here and there officials strove strenuously to better conditions, but the odds were against them. Practically no Grand Trunk stock was held in Canada; it was not even quoted on Canadian exchanges; Canadians regarded the road entirely from the user's point of view.

The traveller and shipper had less to complain of than the shareholder. The service of the road had been greatly increased. The mileage was large in proportion to population. Rates were low. True, it was a rare event for a Grand Trunk train to arrive on time, but it usually arrived.

For these various ills corresponding remedies were sought in turn. Drastic capital reorganization was discussed, but nothing was done. Commercial prosperity could not be revived by the efforts of a single railway. Competition was met by agreement after agreement, 'gentleman's' and otherwise, but in vain. The most hopeful resource lay in the only remaining direction: change of management.

In 1895 Sir Henry Tyler resigned from the presidency after twenty-three years of faithful service. His place was taken by Sir Charles Rivers-Wilson, who had a record of efficient service on the borders of politics and finance. The new president and a committee of directors made a thorough investigation of the Grand Trunk, and recommended some immediate improvements. Their chief contribution to its success, however, was the discovery of Charles M. Hays.

---

[1] One recent acquisition, the Toronto Belt Railway, to meet a rental of $19,000 and working expenses of $22,500, had gross receipts of less than $5000 a year.

The great rival of the Grand Trunk had pressed forward to prosperity under the driving power of an American general manager. The new administration decided that it, too, would look to the United States for a chief executive of the ruthless efficiency and modern methods which the crisis demanded. They found him in the man who had pulled the Wabash out of a similar slough of despond. Mr Hays was not quite forty when, in 1895, he was appointed general manager of the Grand Trunk. He had risen rapidly since the days when, a boy of seventeen, he had entered the office of the Atlantic and Pacific. At twenty-nine he had been secretary to the general manager, and three years later manager himself, of the Wabash.

His presence was soon felt. The staff realized, some with relief, some with consternation, that the good old leisurely days, the days of vested interests, were gone. Many were pensioned, some were dismissed. In some cases American officials were imported to fill the vacant posts, to the patriotic discontent of the old guard. Equipment was overhauled, larger freight cars were ordered, and new terminals acquired. The main bridges on the road—the Suspension at Niagara Falls, the International at Fort Erie, and the Victoria at Montreal—were all rebuilt on a larger scale between 1896 and 1901. The double tracking of the main line from Montreal westward was continued, and many of the sharp curves and heavy grades of the original construction were revised. Elevators at Portland, Montreal, Midland, Tiffin, Goderich, Point Edward, and Fort William were built or acquired. Trains came in on time. The whole system was 'speeded up.'

Later changes in the administration may be briefly summarized here. In 1900 Mr Hays' five-year contract as general manager expired. At the same juncture a vacancy occurred in the presidency of the Southern Pacific, which had fallen on evil days, and Hays was offered and accepted the post at four times his salary with the Grand Trunk of $25,000 a year. A year later he was back again in Canada. There was not room in the Southern Pacific for both Hays and Harriman, then in financial control, and the Grand Trunk directors seized the opportunity which the breach afforded. In 1909 the wide recognition of Mr Hays' great services led to long overdue increase of the authority of the Canadian officials of the road by his appointment as president, on the retirement of Sir Charles Rivers-Wilson. Three years later, with his projects for expansion still incomplete, he met a tragic death in the sinking of the *Titanic*. Mr Edson J. Chamberlin, who had increased his reputation for efficiency by his management for four years of the Grand Trunk Pacific, was chosen as successor in the presidency.

Fortune favoured the new administration from the start. The tide in the continent's business affairs turned soon after the new men took the helm. The long depression ended, prices rose, farmers met mortgage payments, factory chimneys smoked once more, traffic multiplied.

The first result of the improved conditions was the easing of the tension in railway relations. There was no longer a life-and-death necessity for rate-cutting and traffic-stealing. Rate wars between the trunk lines in the United States came to an end. On the Canadian side peace was longer in coming. The rush to the Klondike in 1897 started a rate war between the Canadian Pacific and the Grand Trunk, with its American connections, which lasted nearly a year. In its course rates were cut in the east as well as in the west, and the Canadian Pacific sent its west-bound freight from Toronto by Smith's Falls rather than use any longer the direct line of the Grand Trunk to North Bay. Peace was patched up, but the Canadian Pacific shortly afterwards set about building a road of its own from Toronto north to its main line, thus threatening the Grand Trunk with permanent loss of western business, and providing it with one incentive toward the great westward expansion it was soon to undertake. Along with prudent retrenchments went increasingly aggressive expansion, both east and west. It was one of the main objects of Mr Hays' policy to secure a hold on the rich traffic possibilities of New York and the New England states. Portland, the original New England terminus of the Grand Trunk, had not become the great commercial centre it once expected to be. The first further step was taken in 1899, when the Grand Trunk secured control of the five hundred miles of the Central Vermont, with which relations had been close for some years past. With running rights over a gap controlled by the Boston and Maine, this gave a line from St Johns, Quebec, to the port of New London, Connecticut; from this point connection was made by boat to New York, where valuable terminal docks were owned.

New London was not the final goal, however—Providence and Boston offered greater possibilities. But to seize them it was first necessary to break through the monopoly of New England land and water transport, which the New York and New Haven line had acquired, or to come to terms with the interests in control. At first the word was to fight. The Grand Trunk was received with open arms by the business men of Massachusetts and Connecticut, eager for competition in railways, and in spite of all the political influence of the New Haven, Hays secured a charter for his Southern New England Railroad, to run from Palmer, on the Central Vermont system, to Providence; a branch from Bellows Falls to Boston was also planned. Construction was begun on the Providence line in May 1912, but suddenly halted. The Grand Trunk management declared the halt due to financial conditions, but New England suspected a compromise with the New Haven. Probably the change in policy was mainly due to the change in management, the new administration setting less store on the extension than the Hays-Fitzhugh executive had done.

All these eastern activities, however, were overshadowed by the Grand Trunk Pacific scheme. It was not the first plan the Grand Trunk had formed for westward expansion. In the embryo days of the Canadian Pacific, it may be recalled, the government had offered to the old line the opportunity of carrying through the new one. Later, a connection with the Northern Pacific through Sault Ste Marie had been discussed, but Van Horne had forestalled this move. Still later an extension of the Grand Trunk from Chicago northwesterly, possibly through control of the Wisconsin Central, had been under consideration. Nothing came of these plans until the proved fertility and rapid settlement of the Canadian North-West, the improved position of the Grand Trunk in the money markets, and the threatened loss of traffic between Toronto and North Bay, lured and urged the new administration forward.

In 1902 Mr Hays announced that the directors were considering building a line from North Bay, through New Ontario westward, to a terminus on the Pacific at Port Simpson or Bute Inlet. It would be a line of the highest standards. Government aid, the announcement continued, would certainly be sought and expected.

Once more railways became Canadian politics. There was little doubt that the government would aid either this or some rival transcontinental scheme. Opposition to the lavish subsidy policy of the past had developed, indeed, but it was overwhelmed by the demands from every quarter for a vigorous forward policy. It was Canada's growing time, and new-born confidence spurred country and government on. But if the line was to be not merely a private enterprise, but in part a policy of state, then considerations of high politics and low politics alike came in, and compelled material changes in the Grand Trunk's scheme before it could secure government acceptance.

A road from North Bay west would satisfy the local demands of the western provinces, but would not satisfy the local demands of the East, or meet certain common national aspirations. Eastern, and particularly Quebec interests, demanded that any new transcontinental should be built far to the north, opening up the wilderness between Hudson Bay and the Laurentian highlands bordering the St Lawrence. A Quebec company, the Trans-Canada, was in fact urgently seeking support for such a line, endeavouring, since patriotism is in Canada the last refuge of the promoter, to stimulate investors by stressing the military advantages of the remote route. Again, the Maritime Provinces protested against aid to a company to carry the traffic of the West to Boston and Portland instead of to St John and Halifax.

Sir Wilfrid Laurier, the prime minister, endeavoured to combine all these ends. His plan provided for a road 3550 miles in length, beginning at Moncton—a neutral point between the politically inconvenient rivalries of St John and Halifax—crossing New Brunswick northwesterly, skirting the Maine border, and on to Quebec City, where the St Lawrence was to be crossed by a great bridge. Thence it would strike westerly far to the north of existing settlements. From Winnipeg the previously proposed route was followed. The West would have the development and competition demanded, the hinterland of Quebec and Ontario would be opened, and the ports of the Maritime Provinces put on an equality with their American rivals. And since this vast project was much beyond the power of the Grand Trunk to finance, it was arranged that the road should be divided into two sections. The eastern, from Moncton to Winnipeg, was to be built and owned by the government and leased to the Grand Trunk Pacific, free for seven years and at a rental of three per cent of the cost for forty-three years following. The western, from Winnipeg to the coast, was to be built and operated by the company, aided by a government guarantee of principal and interest on the greater part of the bond issue.

The announcement of this plan in July 1903 led to a storm of controversy as fierce as that which followed the launching of the Canadian Pacific. The Opposition brought forward various policies, looking to a greater measure of government ownership; the minister of Railways, Andrew G. Blair, resigned in protest; rival railways opposed openly and sometimes by secret plot; two general elections were fought on the issue. But rarely is a government in Canada defeated on a proposal, sound or unsound, to spend untold millions, if the money is to be had at all. The agreement went through, with modifications, in the following year, and the building of the great northern road began.

The railway policy of the past twenty years is still on its trial, but some tentative conclusions may be ventured.

In the first place, it seems clear that a new transcontinental was needed, not only to open the West, but to develop the hinterland of eastern Canada. The rediscovery of a vast clay belt north of the height-of-land between Hudson Bay and the Great Lakes, its known resources in timber and pulp and its probable mineral wealth, as well as the farming areas of the western plains, and the forest, mine, and fishery wealth of northern British Columbia, all gave some economic justification for the adventure. Perhaps even stronger were the political considerations. Here, again, if railways were Canada's politics, it was not only because Canadians were materialists, but because they were idealists. They were determined that, in spite of geography and diplomacy, in spite of Rocky Mountains and Lake Superior wildernesses, Laurentian plateaus and Maine intrusions, Canada should be made one and independent. Often this national spirit has been manipulated to serve sordid ends in railway as in tariff matters; the flag has covered a multitude of sinners. Yet whether it was the Grand Trunk or the Intercolonial, the Canadian Pacific or the Grand Trunk Pacific, the national purpose has been strong, and must fairly be set on the assets side of the sheet. Sir Wilfrid Lauder and Sir John Macdonald both worked with high courage and enduring faith for a greater and more united Canada. Any one who looked at a map of the Dominion and realized how incredibly narrow a fringe of population was strung out on the southern border, could not but feel that some attempt to add a second storey to the structure, to give breadth as well as length, was a national necessity. Perhaps least defensible was the Quebec-Moncton section; true, it was essential, if freight was to reach the Maritime ports, that a shorter line with better grades than those of the Intercolonial should be secured if possible. Grades were bettered in the lines secured, but the saving in distance was not as great as old and incorrect surveys had led the government to anticipate.

How should the road be built, granted its need ? Government ownership had its advocates, but experience of political 'machines' and a recognition of the difficulties of a government line in carrying on steamship or irrigation or other subsidiary activities, or in making international extensions, told heavily against such a policy. The real choice lay between the two private companies, the Grand Trunk and the Canadian Northern, which were seeking to rival the Canadian Pacific. Undoubtedly the best solution would have been to amalgamate these companies, and thus to save the eventual outlay on a line north of Lake Superior, on closely parallel lines in the prairies, and on the enormously costly rival lines to be built through the Rockies. True, competition even in railway matters has still its merits, but one strong competitor of the Canadian Pacific would have better served the country than two in financial straits. This solution appeared for a time possible. As has been seen, negotiations were carried on in 1902 and 1903 looking to such a union, but unfortunately without result. Forced to choose, the government had no alternative but to give its aid to the older and better known system.

What standards were to be set for the new road? The continent's pioneer traditions were plain : build the road in the cheapest way it could be made to hold together, with sharp curves and steep grades if need be, with scanty ballast, wooden bridges, and light rails, since traffic would be light and capital hard to get. Then, if the country developed, and perhaps after a reorganization or two, rebuild the road on a permanent basis. But 1903 was not 1873, and Mr Hays had learned on the Wabash and on the Grand Trunk how difficult it was for a second-class road to compete, and how costly was the process of rebuilding with the line in operation. He knew that with high and rising wages for trainmen, and with frequency of service a minor matter on the long stretches, it was essential to concentrate loads in as few trains as possible, and that a locomotive could haul almost twice as great a load on a four-tenths grade as on a one per cent grade. So he determined to build from the outset up to the highest standard, securing a lower ruling grade than any other transcontinental enjoyed. The policy meant high fixed charges and low operating costs.

What outlay would be involved and what state aid was needed? Given the route and the standard set, the outlay could not but be vast. It proved, in fact, much greater than the estimates, as is the way with most big enterprises. The government section cost about a hundred and sixty instead of sixty millions, and the Grand Trunk Pacific section about a hundred and forty, or three hundred millions in all—twice the estimate for the Panama Canal and nearly its actual cost.[1] The standard set was high, and proved difficult to attain; labour was scarce and expensive, and prices of all materials were soaring constantly. The large expenditure lent colour to charges of corruption in the construction of the government section. Investigation after investigation was held, however, without revealing any gross betrayal of trust. One contractor had been handled too tenderly

[1] The Chicago, Milwaukee and Puget Sound, a high-grade road built to the Pacific coast at nearly the same time, was capitalized, it may be noted, at $157,000 a mile, or nearly $70,000 a mile more than the cost of the Grand Trunk Pacific and National Transcontinental.

for repeated delays, possibly engineers sometimes stretched classification on a losing contract, and doubtless contractors were as usual given the privilege of contributing to party campaign funds. But, fortunately for the good name of Canada, the serious charges of corruption were not sustained.

Of this great outlay the country bore the lion's share. The Grand Trunk Pacific was organized as a subsidiary company of the old Grand Trunk, which secured control of ownership of all but a nominal share of the $25,000,000 common stock, given it in return for guaranteeing part of the Pacific bonds. Only $20,000,000 preference capital stock was provided for, and this was not issued. The interest of the independent shareholder was thus negligible. The money required was secured by the issue of bonds and debenture loans guaranteed by the government or the Grand Trunk. Up to 1914, in connection with the western section, the government had guaranteed the company's bonds to the amount of over eighty millions, had lent twenty-five millions for ten years at four per cent, and had made or promised a cash gift of twenty-three millions. On the eastern section, the company was subsidized by the use for seven years of the road, rent free, equivalent to thirty-four millions. It was a vast outlay, though not as difficult for the country to bear as one-third the amount would have been a generation earlier. The unique and consoling feature, so far as posterity was concerned, was that the bulk of the government expenditure was provided out of surplus current revenue, so that for the future the net income to be received from rental would much more than balance interest on borrowings.

Once the contract was ratified by parliament and by the Grand Trunk, and the new company had been formally organized with Mr Hays as president and Mr Frank Morse, and later Mr Chamberlin, formerly of the Canada Atlantic, as general manager, the work of surveying and determining the route began. On the government section political difficulties were met in New Brunswick, from the advocates of a route down the St John to the city at its mouth, and engineering difficulties of many forms in the long trail through the northern wilderness. The bridge which was being constructed by an independent company across the St Lawrence at Quebec collapsed in 1907, with great loss of life, and the delay in completing the second bridge made it necessary to depend upon car-ferries for some time. On the western section a good route through the prairies was decided upon, not without vigorous protest from the Canadian Pacific because of the close paralleling of its line. After repeated surveys of the Peace, Pine, Wapiti, and Yellowhead Passes, the last was chosen, and a line was settled upon down the Fraser and Skeena valleys, passing through two million acres of fertile land. Remarkably low grades were secured; in fact, as favourable as on the prairie section. Kaien Island, 550 miles north of Vancouver, was chosen as the terminus, rather than Port Simpson as originally designed, and soon on its magnificent harbour and most unpromising site of rock and muskeg the new and scientifically planned city of Prince Rupert began to rise.

As the main line ran far to the north of the St Lawrence lake and river system, the original plan provided for the construction of branch lines to Fort William, to North Bay, and to Montreal. Of these only the first, aided by the Dominion and also by the Ontario government, was built. For the connection with North Bay running rights over the provincial road, the Timiskaming and Northern Ontario, sufficed. Later, in 1914, the Dominion government itself decided to build the Montreal branch. In Alberta and Saskatchewan over 1200 miles of branch lines were begun, under guarantees of bonds by the provincial governments. In British Columbia an independent road, projected by the contracting firm of Foley, Welch and Stewart—the Vancouver, Pacific and Great Eastern—promised when completed to give the Grand Trunk Pacific, by a traffic agreement, entrance into Vancouver.

The first contracts on the main line were let in 1905. For ten years construction went on, at the rate of a mile a day, with occasional slackening from scarcity of labour or financial stringency, but with no complete halt. Last to be completed were the section to be built by the company in the Central plateau of British Columbia and the section built by the government west of Cochrane. Meanwhile, the prairie lines had been in operation through to Edmonton since 1910, and grain reached Fort William over the Lake Superior branch in the same year.

From the beginning it had been questioned whether the Grand Trunk Pacific would carry out its bargain to operate the government section. The management professed its intention to perform every promise, but fulfillment was delayed. In 1915 the company demurred to assuming the lease, on the double ground that the road was not definitely completed, and that, since the change of government in 1911, the standard of construction agreed upon had not been maintained. Accordingly the government took power to operate the road from Winnipeg to Moncton, and to expropriate the company's branch from Superior to Fort William, pending further negotiations.

The great Canadian railway companies are much more than railways. The Grand Trunk system, in its new expansion, branched into every neighbouring field which could be made to increase the traffic. Fleets of steamers, on the Pacific coast, on the Great Lakes, and on the New England route, filled in gaps in its lines. Modern car-ferries crossed Lake Ontario and Lake Michigan, as well as the river Detroit. Elevators, it has been noted, were built at strategic points on the way from the wheat-field to the sea. Magnificent hotels were opened at Ottawa, Winnipeg, and Edmonton, with more rustic resorts in the parks along the route. Tourist traffic was stimulated by lowered fares and alluring advertising.

The Grand Trunk of 1914 was a much greater factor in the life of Canada than the Grand Trunk of 1894; it had become nationwide in its interests, and had shaken off the unfortunate traditions of its earlier stagnant days. Difficult tasks still faced it: the building up of the traffic of the far north would demand ceaseless effort, and when the wheel of time should bring round slackened business once more, it would call for all its powers to make ends meet in face of rising wages, taxes, outlays of every kind. The record of the recent past gave assurance that the need would be met with courage and alert endeavour.

CHAPTER TWELVE
SUNDRY DEVELOPMENTS

All the restless activity upon the part of its older and its younger rival did not rob the Canadian Pacific of the place it had held in the life and interest of the Canadian people. With a confident assurance based on the extent and the strategic location of its lines, the imperial richness of its endowment, and the proved efficiency of its management, it pressed steadily forward until it became the world's foremost transportation system.

The unbroken success and the magnitude of the operations of the Canadian Pacific in this period are almost without precedent in railway annals. By 1914 it had under its control more than eighteen thousand miles of railway, or more than six times the length of the original transcontinental line. It gave employment directly to ninety thousand men, whose monthly pay-roll reached five million dollars, and indirectly maintained many more, justifying the boast of its president in 1907 that directly or indirectly one-twelfth of the people of Canada received their income from the Canadian Pacific. In 1913 alone, the supreme year of Canadian railway expansion, the Canadian Pacific appropriated for new construction and betterments, equipment, terminal facilities, steamships and hotels, shops and elevators, nearly one hundred million dollars, or more than the original cost of the road. It touched the life of the nation at every conceivable point. From Atlantic to Pacific there was scarcely a town of any importance that was not reached by its lines. But its position was not merely national. It controlled over five thousand miles of railways in the United States, taking rank amongst the foremost systems of the Republic. Its steamship lines stretched more than half-way round the world, and in Liverpool and Trieste, Hong-Kong and Yokohama and

Sydney, the red-and-white house flag of the Canadian Pacific made the company and the country known.

The management of the Canadian Pacific showed stability and continuity. It trained up in its own ranks the men for its highest posts. Sir George Stephen, later Lord Mount Stephen, on resigning the presidency in 1888, had been succeeded by Mr, afterwards Sir, William C. Van Horne. As general manager, and then for eleven years as president, Van Horne carried the road through its most difficult period. In spite of failure of crops, low prices, and the slow trickling in of settlers, he kept aglow his own faith in the West and communicated it to others. Indomitable courage, tenacity of purpose, breadth of vision, mastery of organization and detail marked him as one of the great railroad builders of the century. Even when he retired from the presidency, becoming for another twelve years chairman of the board of directors, it was only to find new outlets for his energy in building pulp and paper mills in Quebec and railways in Cuba; for though, unlike many millionaires, he had not narrowed into his own business groove, and could paint a picture as well as buy one, the call to action never failed to stir him.

When Van Horne came to the Canadian Pacific in 1882, he brought with him the man destined to be his successor, Thomas G. Shaughnessy, a young Irish-American still under thirty, who had been engaged in railway work since he was sixteen. Appointed general purchasing agent, he rose rapidly, becoming president in 1899 and chairman of the board in 1911. Sir Thomas Shaughnessy maintained the progressive policy and the honourable record of straightforward management which has distinguished the Canadian Pacific—a railway singularly free from the questionable manipulations which have brought so many great American systems to bankruptcy. Other men left their impress on the road: men like Sir William Whyte, for over twenty years in charge of the western lines, David M'Nicoll, George M. Bosworth, and many others gave most effective service.

After the first hurried staking out of the claim was over, by 1890, the Canadian Pacific refrained from further expansion until about 1898: between these years only three hundred miles were added to the system. Then reviving prosperity and the activity of rival roads led to a new period of expansion. The additions made in this time can best be realized by a glance at the map. The most important may be noted briefly, beginning at the Pacific coast.

On Vancouver Island, the Esquimalt and Nanaimo Railway, which had been projected originally when it was hoped that Canada's first transcontinental would find its terminus at Victoria by crossing the straits from Bute Inlet, was acquired from the Dunsmuir interests. On the mainland of British Columbia activity was concentrated in the southern section. The rich mineral discoveries in the Boundary country led to the extension of the Canadian Pacific westward from Lethbridge, through the Crow's Nest Pass. The company was given a Dominion subsidy, and in return a general reduction of rates was secured. After years of contention with the Hill roads which were crowding into the same territory, and in face of immense engineering difficulties, a continuation of this line by way of Penticton gave promise of a second through route. Meanwhile, entrance was secured to Spokane and Portland in the United States. In the plains and prairie section a close network of lines developed. The narrow-gauge line of the Alberta Railway and Irrigation Company, which had done good pioneer service, under the guidance of Elliott Galt, in developing Alberta's possibilities in coal and irrigated land, was absorbed in 1911. The northern country was traversed by two new east and west lines. The Qu'Appelle, Long Lake and Saskatchewan, extending from Regina to Prince Albert, lost to the Canadian Northern in 1906, was replaced by a new line and 'cutoffs' and extensions built in every quarter. South of the border equal activity was displayed in throwing out feeders for the Soo and Duluth lines. The acquisition of the Wisconsin Central in 1909 gave the Canadian Pacific entrance into Chicago, while an agreement with the Wabash made it possible to link up its western United States lines with its southern Ontario road at Detroit. In Ontario, a branch from Toronto to Sudbury made the Canadian Pacific independent of the Grand Trunk's North Bay link, an extension from Guelph to Goderich tapped a fertile country, a line from Port M'Nicoll on Georgian Bay to Bethany near Peterborough gave a short through route for grain, a lake shore route eastward from Toronto provided access to the towns which the Grand Trunk, in its promoters' concern for through traffic or in its contractors' desire for low land charges, had side-tracked, while stock purchase and later a lease of the Kingston and Pembroke gave entrance into Kingston. In Quebec, short tentacles were pushed up into the Laurentian hills north of Ottawa; south of the St Lawrence the chief step taken was the 999-year lease of the Quebec Central, sanctioned in 1912. In the Maritime Provinces the New Brunswick Southern or Shore line and the Dominion Atlantic, successor to the Windsor and Annapolis, were leased in 1911, and running rights secured over the Intercolonial into Halifax.

A marked feature of the Canadian Pacific policy from the beginning was the endeavour to control subsidiary or allied activities, and thus gain well-rounded independence. Its steamship lines came to girdle half the world. On the Pacific, service to Hong-Kong and Yokohama had begun in 1892 and to Australia in 1893, while a service on the coast from Seattle to the far north, and on the lakes of central British Columbia, followed. The Great Lakes fleet was still earlier in being. In 1903 the purchase of fourteen Elder-Dempster vessels ranging from five to eight thousand tons gave a whole North Atlantic fleet for seven millions, or the cost of a single Lusitania. It was soon increased by larger and faster boats. A line to Trieste, to secure a share of the immigration traffic from Eastern Europe, led to prolonged complications with the Austrian government early in 1914, on account of the hostility of German rivals.

Hotels followed steamships, some eight or ten being erected at strategic points from St Andrews to Victoria. Departing from the usual American practice, the company owned and operated its own sleeping-cars, and maintained its own express and telegraph companies. Its car-shops provided much of its rolling stock. Grain elevators were built at terminal points. In the later years a systematic policy of developing its western lands was adopted. A special department of Natural Resources was established, irrigation works were begun on a huge scale in the tract of three million acres between Calgary and Medicine Hat, and ready-made farms were provided or loans made to selected settlers.

The method of financing these countless enterprises was equally striking. Instead of increasing the proportion of bonded indebtedness, as was customary, the company sought additional capital chiefly by the sale of common stock. This procedure was possible because of the speculative value of the stock, based primarily on the growth of traffic, and of the value of the western lands still unsold: the dividend rose steadily to ten per cent in 1912, and the practice which prevailed until 1909 of issuing the stock at par gave holders valuable rights. In the latter year 125 was charged for the shares allotted, in 1912 150, and in 1913 175. As a result of the earlier policy an unnecessarily high price was paid for new capital, but fixed charges were kept low, and no great system was as safe from foreclosure. In 1914 the total assets of the company were valued at over $800,000,000.

Fifth in mileage among the railway systems of Canada is the group of fragments connected with the Great Northern Railway of the United States. James J. Hill had not been least among the members of the original Canadian Pacific Syndicate, but differences with his colleagues led to his retirement in 1883. Thenceforward he devoted himself entirely to the building up of the St Paul, Minneapolis and Manitoba, the railway acquired from the Dutch bondholders. Under the name of the Great Northern it had been extended by 1893 from Lake Superior to Puget Sound, and continued to grow steadily until, twenty years later, it controlled nearly eight thousand miles. The Great Northern was remarkable in at least three respects. Except for the original grants for the Minnesota lines, it was built through to the coast without a dollar or an acre of subsidy from the state. Its capitalization was kept close to the actual cost of the road and its fixed charges were low. It took the lead among American roads in an aggressive and enlightened endeavour to build up the country through which it ran, not only by flexible rate charges, but by a direct campaign of education among the farmers and other shippers on its route.

The mineral wealth of southern British Columbia and the farming wealth of the western plains turned Hill's attention toward Canada once more about the beginning of the twentieth century. In British Columbia the progress of the Great Northern invasion was slow. The character of the country made construction difficult, and the Canadian Pacific, appealing to national prejudices, fought every inch of the way. But Mr Hill pressed on. The coal-fields of the Crow's Nest Pass, in which he acquired a controlling interest, were made accessible by a road from the south, and a series of lines branching from Spokane entered the Boundary mining region. Winding in and out across the border the road continued westward to Vancouver. Fortunately duplication was in large part avoided; by arrangements with the Canadian Pacific, the Canadian Northern, and the Northern Pacific, the difficult country south of the Fraser was pierced by common lines, and common terminal facilities were secured. Meanwhile, in 1906 and 1907, more ambitious schemes were announced—the building of north and south lines through Brandon and Regina, and the construction of an east and west line from Winnipeg to the Pacific. In ten years, it was officially forecasted, the Great Northern would have as extensive a system in Canada as in the United States. What was more startling, Mr Hill denounced 'spoon-feeding' and did not ask for a cent of subsidy. The building of the Grand Trunk Pacific and the Canadian Northern postponed indefinitely these larger plans. Actual operations were confined to the construction of branches running northward in Manitoba, to Brandon, Morden, and Portage la Prairie, and the acquisition, jointly with the Northern Pacific, of a lease of the Canadian Northern line from Pembina to Winnipeg, under the name of the Midland, and of terminals in Winnipeg. Meanwhile, branches from the main Great Northern line nosed up to the border at nearly a dozen other places.

The activities, real and projected, of the Great Northern in Canada brought up acutely the question of the interrelations of Canadian and American roads. To some these activities appeared evidences of an infamous plot to drain Canadian traffic southward to United States ports and roads : to others they seemed to be philanthropic endeavours to rescue Western Canada from the clutches of monopoly. They were not, however, due to either political intrigue or knight-errantry, but to the same desire for profit which had led the Canadian Pacific to build up its great system in the western states. Other things being at all equal, it was of course desirable that Canadian traffic should follow Canadian territory to Canadian ports; it was to this end that uncounted millions had been spent. Yet patriotism had a seamy reverse side of political buncombe. Every hint of outside competition in the preserves of railway or industrial corporations in Canada was denounced in interested quarters as dangerous and empire-smashing, while the counter-incursions into the territory of the United States were ignored or regarded as merely normal business enterprise.

As a matter of fact, in 1914 Canadian railways controlled four miles in the United States for every mile in Canada controlled by railways of the United States. The Canadian Pacific alone owned or leased over five thousand miles in the United States, chiefly in the northwest, while it had close working agreements with the Wabash and the New York, New Haven and Hartford. The Grand Trunk controlled over seventeen hundred miles, two-thirds in the Michigan peninsula and the remainder in New England, while the Canadian Northern ran for some forty miles through the United States, south of the Lake of the Woods. The American interests in Canada were more scattered, but the Great Northern, the Michigan Central, the Pere Marquette, and the New York Central all developed important Canadian extensions.

In short, the interrelations were certainly no more extensive than would have been expected in the case of two friendly nations lying side by side for three thousand miles, connected by ties of speech and by common commercial and social customs. The only difficulty which arose out of the situation was the division of jurisdiction between the Railway Commission of Canada and the Interstate Commerce Commission of the United States. The heads of the two commissions, Mr Justice Mabee for Canada and Mr Knapp for the United States, endeavoured in 1910 to work out a plan for joint control, but without final success.

In the past half-century government ownership of railways has been much discussed in Canada, dividing attention with the allied question of railway ownership of the government. It cannot be said that any decisive public opinion or policy has resulted. Important steps toward government ownership have been taken in the last twenty years. The Intercolonial and Prince Edward Island Railways have been retained by the government and extended, a federal line has been built in Manitoba and a provincial one in Northern Ontario, and the National Transcontinental has been constructed by the government for lease to a private company. Yet, at the same time, the main railway projects continued to be entrusted to private companies, and the proportion of the whole mileage under private operation increased.

The most important incident in the Inter-colonial's later history was its extension from Quebec to Montreal in 1898, by the purchase of the Drummond County Railway and the lease of a stretch of forty miles in length from the Grand Trunk. Six years later the Canada Eastern, running from Gibson to Loggieville, was purchased. Many bankrupt lines in the Maritime Provinces and Quebec were offered to the Intercolonial as valuable feeders. In the later years of the government of Sir Wilfrid Laurier and in the first years of Sir Robert Borden's administration, authority was sought to acquire such of these roads as might be desired, but restrictions due to the action of the Canadian Senate or the political difficulty of discriminating between the railways prevented any rapid acquisition. Changes in administration were tried. As a half-concession to the demand that the Intercolonial should be operated by an independent commission, a board of management was established in 1909, consisting of the chief officials of the road. In 1913 this board was dissolved and the management vested in a single commissioner, F. P. Gutelius, formerly of the Canadian Pacific.

Financial returns showed little improvement. True, the record, unbroken since 1873, of annual failure to meet even operating expenses, was varied after 1898 by small surpluses in two years out of three, but the net deficits since Confederation rose to over eleven millions by 1913; and while there was no question that the administration had been improved, there was room for belief that the surpluses had been in part book-keeping ones, obtained by including in the large capital expenditure items properly chargeable to revenue.

At first sight this failure to meet operating expenses, much less to pay interest on the investment, together with constantly increasing capital outlay, seemed to warrant strong condemnation of government methods. And, in truth, a serious indictment could be framed. Efficient government ownership is more difficult in a democratic country where shippers, employees, would-be employees, supply dealers, all have influence over the administration, than it is in a bureaucratic state. Intercolonial employees were given their posts and kept in them by political influence, and their numbers were often as excessive as energy was lacking. Supplies of coal and new land as required were usually purchased from political friends, with an additional margin for campaign contributions;[1] at election times the road became a vast political machine. Under the administration of the governments of Laurier and Borden the grosser scandals ceased, but in one form or other political influence continued to be exerted.

Yet this was not the whole story. If the Intercolonial did not earn dividends, there were other reasons at work than government inefficiency. The road ran for long stretches through barren country where little local traffic originated. In competing for through traffic it was handicapped by the roundabout length of its route: it ran along two sides of a triangle, while the Canadian Pacific, subsidized by one political party, was built along the base, and the National Transcontinental, built by the other party, came in between; in summer it had to face the competition of the St Lawrence route as well. Nor was dividend-earning the sole standard of success to be applied. The Intercolonial was built originally for political and military ends, not merely for commercial gain. It had given shippers the lowest rates in the world: 'the surplus is in the pockets of the people,' one of the political heads declared. If, it was often urged, the canals of Ontario and Quebec were operated by the government at a dead loss, without a cent of tolls, why grudge the Maritime Provinces, to whom Confederation had been less kind, the benefit of operating at bare cost the government railways! The Intercolonial had undoubtedly done much to weld the eastern and central provinces together, and this was worth more than a million dollars or two in interest charges.

The desire for rates at cost, or lower, which has made the people in Eastern Canada oppose all suggestions to turn over the Intercolonial to the Canadian Pacific or Canadian Northern, led those of Western Canada to urge government ownership of the other federal venture, the Hudson Bay Railway. Owing to its far northern position, Manitoba possesses ocean ports, Nelson and Churchill, which are nearer Liverpool than New York is. Why, then, carry the grain of the prairie fifteen hundred or two thousand miles to an Atlantic port before loading it on the ocean freighter? Proposals to build a railway to a Hudson Bay port and to establish a steamship line to carry the traffic at sea seemed plausible and won

---

[1] The deputy-minister, Mr Collingwood Schreiber, instanced in 1882 an attempt of a farmer, whose claim was nursed by influential politicians, to collect $70,000 for a gravel-pit liberally estimated to be worth $5.

much western support. Investigation soon made the difficulties clear. Hudson Bay was fairly free from ice, but Hudson Straits were studded with icebergs far into the summer.

Ships of special construction would be needed for the dangerous passage, and, in any event, grain could not be shipped until the spring after it was harvested and would have to be stored in elevators during the winter. And in the meantime the three transcontinental railways were enlarging the eastern funnels, while the Panama Canal made an outlet by Vancouver feasible. Still, there was a gambling chance that something would come of a railway to Hudson Bay, and if the stroke succeeded, Canada would be given a new coast, and would front the sea at the north as well as at the east and the west. The territory between Le Pas, a terminus of the Canadian Northern, and Port Nelson, selected as the better port on Hudson Bay, had some mineral and agricultural promise. So, in the prosperous days of 1911, it was decided to attempt the work. As it was largely an experiment, the government's plan of state construction and possibly operation found wide support. The line was still under construction in 1914. Another exploration road which amply justified the faith of its promoters was the Timiskaming and Northern Ontario. This railway, striking up from North Bay into the mineral region and clay belt beyond the height-of-land was begun by the Ontario government in 1902 as a colonization road. It was fortunate enough to uncover the riches of Cobalt's silver-camp in its construction; later, mining development at Gowganda and Porcupine brought it traffic; and the building of the Grand Trunk Pacific made it an important connecting-link. It was able, then, from the outset to show favourable results, direct as well as indirect. It was built and controlled by a government commission, efficient and more or less free from politics.

CHAPTER THIRTEEN
SOME GENERAL QUESTIONS

When the pace of construction slackened in 1914, Canada had achieved a remarkable position in the railway world. Only five other countries—the United States, Russia, Germany, India, and, by a small margin, France— possessed a greater mileage; and, relatively to population, none came anywhere near her. Three great systems stretched from coast to coast. Need still existed for local extensions, but by a great effort the main trunk lines had been built. Not only in mileage were the railways of Canada notable. In the degree to which the minor roads had been swallowed up by a few dominating systems, in the wide sweep of their outside operations, in their extension beyond the borders of Canada itself, and in the degree to which they had been built by public aid, they challenged attention. While there were nearly ninety railway companies in Canada in 1914, the three transcontinental systems controlled more than eighty per cent of the total mileage. The variety of the subsidiary undertakings— steamships, hotels, express service, irrigation and land development, grain elevators—has already been indicated. The control by Canadian railways of seven or eight thousand miles of lines in the United States, with corresponding, if smaller, extensions into Canada by American lines, was an outcome of geographic conditions, intimate social and trade connections, and a civilized view of international relations which no other countries could match.

The aid given by the state had been remarkable in variety and in extent. In cash subsidies alone, up to 1913, municipalities, chiefly in Ontario, had given over $18,000,000; the provinces, in the order of Quebec, Ontario, Nova Scotia, New Brunswick, Manitoba, and British Columbia, double that sum; and the Dominion $163,000,000. Land-grants exceeded fifty million acres. Guarantees reached $275,000,000—the Dominion, British Columbia, Alberta, Saskatchewan, and Manitoba leading—with some sixty millions looming up in the year to follow. The privately owned railways of the Dominion were then capitalized at a billion and a half; allowing for the 'water' in this capitalization on the one hand, and for construction out of earnings on the other, it may fairly be computed that, omitting the guarantees, the state had contributed from one-third to one-half their cost. The objections to this policy were manifold. It had been one great source of rottenness in politics. It had pauperized some sections of the country, leading them to look to the government to take the initiative in every movement. The land subsidies had delayed settlement, and the exemption of grants from taxation had pressed heavily on the average settler. The wealth of Canada tended to concentrate in a few dominating groups. Roads were built that were a sheer waste of capital, useless for traffic or colonization, or recklessly cutting into territory sufficient only for existing lines. Yet the profits side of the account was large. Settlement had been hastened, transport facilities had been provided, values had increased, social intercourse had been ameliorated, national unity had been fostered, in ways impossible had private enterprise been left to struggle on unaided. In future, it might be hoped, private capital could build unaided, or the state act directly.

In the allied field of government regulation progress had been made. Until very recent years, Canada had been more anxious to get new railways than to control old ones, and, besides, the worse forms of discrimination which stirred indignation in the United States had not been widely practised in Canada. But with the growing complexity of the industrial organization, and the recognition that competition could not solve the difficulties, a demand rose for more efficient regulation. The Dominion government, acting upon an able and thorough report by Dr S. J. M'Lean, established in 1904 a Railway Commission, permanent, non-political, and large enough to make it possible for its members, singly or jointly, to hear complaints in all sections of the Dominion. Later, telegraph, telephone, and express rates and services were added to its jurisdiction. Hampered by few of the constitutional limitations which have lessened the usefulness of the Interstate Commerce Commission, and guided by efficient businesslike heads—Blair, Killam, Mabee, Drayton—it soon established a unique reputation for fairness, promptness, and common sense.

But it is not merely in mileage or in relationship to the state that change has come in the three-quarters of a century since the first locomotive whistle was heard in Canada. Let us glance at some of the more striking changes in equipment and methods of operation. In the road bed, new standards of solidity have been set, grades cut down and curves straightened at a cost of uncounted millions, busy stretches double-tracked, steel bridges built in place of wooden trestles. The greatest single advance was the substitution, in the eighties chiefly, of steel for iron rails, making construction cheaper and repair easier, and permitting the running of heavier and faster trains. Heavier trains in turn brought heavier rails, eighty to one hundred pounds to the yard being the usual weight on main tracks, instead of forty or fifty in early days. Locomotives grew steadily in size from the *Kitten* of 1837 to the huge *Mallet* of today. Freight engines were differentiated from passenger engines. Coal was substituted for wood as fuel, and in some cases oil for coal. Electricity replaced steam in tunnels and other places where smoke was troublesome. The crude little freight cars, carrying four or five tons, gave way to cars carrying thirty tons or more, specialized for all conceivable purposes, from cattle and coal cars and oil tanks to refrigerator cars for fruit or meats or milk. Passenger coaches, following, as in other matters, American rather than English models, underwent a similar change, and improved steadily in size, strength, and convenience. The formal division into classes which marks European railway travel has not taken root in Canada; but between Pullman and parlour cars, first and second classes, the actual variety is great. Train dispatching, at first by telegraph, and latterly by telephone, has become a fine art; safety devices such as the air-brake, and more slowly block signals, have been adopted. The old confusing diversity of local time has been remedied by the adoption of a zone system, in consequence largely of the persistent advocacy of Sir Sandford Fleming. Thus the increase in mileage by no means represents the increase in service rendered: every year the engines grow more powerful, the cars larger and the trains longer, and the freight service more speedy and trustworthy. True, the service is still far from perfect, and when a heavy snowstorm paralyses traffic, or the diversion to new competitive building of money which should have gone into equipment brings about congestion, vigorous denunciation follows these brief reversions to the traffic conditions of the good old days.

There is no work that man has wrought that would give nobler and more enduring title to fame than the great cathedrals which mediaeval Europe bequeathed to the world. Yet no man's name is linked with theirs. They were the work of generations, of an epoch, the expression of the genius and the labour and the worship of uncounted thousands. There is a whole world of difference between the mediaeval cathedral and the modern railway, but this they have in common, that they are the work not of a few hands but of many, not a sudden creation, but the product of labours continued year after year. Leaders were indispensable; we cannot forget the men who planned and the men who carried through and the men who organized the working of the great railway systems. Keefer and Fleming, Poor and Waddington, Galt and Hincks and Howe, Macdonald and Laurier, Mount Stephen and Strathcona, Van Horne and Hays, Shaughnessy and Mackenzie, these and many more, though often bearing feet of clay, we shall honour as builders of a mighty heritage.

But behind these loom up forgotten myriad who also were indispensable. The surveyor, often an explorer as well, striking out into the wilderness, braving sheer precipice and arctic blizzard in search of mountain pass or lower grade; the man with the pick and shovel, a mighty and ever-shifting army—English navvy, Irish canaller, Chinese coolie, Swede or Italian or Ruthenian—housed in noisome bunkhouses, often fleeced by employment agent or plundering sub-contractor, facing sudden death by reckless familiarity with dynamite or slower death by typhoid and dysentery; the men who carried on the humdrum work of every day, track-mending, ticket-punching, engine-stoking; the patient, unmurmuring payer of taxes for endless bonuses—these, too, were perhaps not least among the Railway Builders of Canada.

LaVergne, TN USA
25 August 2009

155819LV00004B/14/P

228-3